IN PRAISE OF FAILURE

IN PRAISE OF FAILURE

Four Lessons in Humility

COSTICA BRADATAN

HARVARD UNIVERSITY PRESS

Cambridge, Massachusetts

London, England

2023

Library of Congress Cataloging-in-Publication Data

Names: Brădățan, Costică, author.
Title: In praise of failure : four lessons in humility / Costica Bradatan.
Description: Cambridge, Massachusetts : Harvard University Press,
2023. | Includes bibliographical references and index.
Identifiers: LCCN 2022010828 | ISBN 9780674970472 (cloth)
Subjects: LCSH: Weil, Simone, 1909–1943. | Seneca, Lucius Annaeus,
approximately 4 B.C.–65 A.D. | Gandhi, Mahatma, 1869–1948. |
Cioran, E. M. (Emile M.), 1911–1995. | Mishima, Yukio, 1925–1970. |
Failure (Psychology) | Humility.
Classification: LCC BF575.F14 B73 2023 | DDC 158.1—dc23/
eng/20220616
LC record available at https://lccn.loc.gov/2022010828

Cristinei şi Anastasiei

Contents

IN PRAISE OF FAILURE

PROLOGUE

Picture yourself on a plane, at high altitude. One of the engines has just caught fire, the other doesn't look very promising, and the pilot has to make an emergency landing. Finding yourself in such a situation is no doubt shattering, but also illuminating. At first, amid the wailing and gnashing of teeth, you cannot think in any detached, rational fashion. You have to admit it, you are paralyzed by fear and scared to death, just like everyone else. Eventually, the plane lands safely, and everybody gets off unharmed. Once you've had a chance to pull yourself together, you can think a bit more clearly about what just happened. And you start learning from it.

You learn, for instance, that human existence is something that happens, briefly, between two instantiations of nothingness. Nothing first—dense, impenetrable nothingness. Then a flickering. Then nothing again, endlessly. "A brief crack of light between two eternities of darkness," as Vladimir Nabokov would have it.[1] These are the brutal facts of the human condition—the rest is embellishment. No matter how we choose to reframe or retell the facts, when we consider what precedes us and what follows us, we are not much to talk about. We are *next to nothing*, in fact. And much of what we do in life, whether we know it or not, is an effort to address the sickness that comes from the realization of this next-to-nothingness. Myths, religion, spirituality, philosophy, science, works of art and literature—they seek to make this unbearable fact a little more bearable.

One way to get around this is to deny the predicament altogether. It's the optimistic, closed-eye way. Our condition, this line goes, is not that precarious after all. In some mythical narratives, we live elsewhere before we are born here, and we will reincarnate again after we die. Some religions go one step further and promise us life eternal. It's good business, apparently, as takers have never been in short supply. More recently, something called transhumanism has entered this crowded market. The priests of the new cult swear that, with the right gadgets and technical adjustments (and the right bank accounts), human life will be prolonged indefinitely. Other immortality projects are likely to do just as well, for our mortality problem is unlikely to be resolved.

No matter how many of us buy into religion's promise of life eternal, however, there will always be some who remain unpersuaded. As for the transhumanists, they may know the future, but they seem largely ignorant of the past: "human enhancement" products have, under different labels, been on the market at least since the passing of Enkidu of *Gilgamesh* fame. Compared with what the medieval alchemists had to offer, the transhumanists' wares seem rather bland. Yet thousands of years of life prolongation efforts haven't put death out of business. We may live longer lives today, but we still die eventually.

Another way to deal with our next-to-nothingness is to confront it head-on, the bullfighting way: no escape routes, no safety nets, no sugarcoating. You just plow ahead, eyes wide open, always aware of what's there: *nothing*. Remember the naked facts of our condition: nothing ahead and nothing behind. If you happen to obsess over your next-to-nothingness and cannot buy into the life eternal promised by religion or afford a biotechnologically prolonged life, this may be right for you. Certainly, the bullfighting way is neither easy nor gentle—particularly for the bull. For that's what we are, after all: the bull, waiting to be done in, not the bullfighter, who does the crushing and then goes on his way.

"Human beings are so made," writes Simone Weil, that "the ones who do the crushing feel nothing; it is the person crushed who feels what is happening."[2] Pessimistic as this may sound, there is hardly a higher form of human knowledge than the one that allows us to understand *what is happening*—to see things as they are, as opposed to how we would like them to be. Besides, an uncompromising pessimism is superbly feasible. Given the first commandment of the pessimist ("Whenever in doubt, assume the worst!"), you will never be taken by surprise. Whatever happens on the way, however bad, will not put you off balance. For this reason, those who approach their next-to-nothingness with open eyes manage to live lives of composure and equanimity, and rarely complain. The worst thing that could befall them is exactly what they have expected.

Above all, the eyes-wide-open approach allows us to extricate ourselves, with some dignity, from the entanglement that is human existence. Life is a chronic, addictive sickness, and we are in bad need of a cure.

The failure-based therapy that I offer in this book may seem surprising. After so much worshipping of success, failure's reputation is in tatters. There seems to be nothing worse in our world than to fail—illness, misfortune, even congenital stupidity are nothing by comparison. But failure deserves better. There is, in fact, much to praise about it.

Failing is essential to what we are as human beings. How we relate to failure defines us, while success is auxiliary and fleeting and does not reveal much. We can live without success, but we would live for nothing if we didn't come to terms with our imperfection, precariousness, and mortality, which are all epiphanies of failure.

When it occurs, failure puts a distance between us and the world, and between ourselves and others. That distance gives us the distinct feeling that we don't fit in, that we are out of sync with the world and others, and that there is something amiss. All of this makes us seriously question our place under the sun. And that may be the best thing to happen to us: this existential *awakening* is exactly what we need if we are to realize who we are. No healing will come unless preceded by it.

Should you experience failure and be visited by such feelings of inadequacy and out-of-placeness, don't resist them—follow them. They will tell you that you are on the right track. We may be *in* this world, but we are not *of* this world. This understanding is the beginning of awakening, and it places failure, humble though it may be, at the heart of an important spiritual quest.

Can failure, then, save my life? you might ask. Yes, it can. Provided that you use it well. How failure can be put to good use is the story this book seeks to tell. As you will find out in due course, far from being the unmitigated disaster its maligners make it out to be, failure can work wonders of self-realization, healing, and enlightenment. It will not be easy, though, for failing is a complicated affair.

Failure is like original sin in the biblical narrative: everyone has it. Regardless of class, caste, race, or gender, we are all born to fail. We practice failure for as long as we live, and we pass it on to others. Just like sin, failure can be disgraceful, shameful, and embarrassing to admit. And did I mention "ugly"? Failure is also ugly—ugly as sin, as they say. Failure can be as brutal and nasty and devastating as life itself.

For all its universality, however, failure is generally understudied, neglected, or dismissed. Or worse: it is turned into something trendy by self-help gurus, marketing wizards, and retired CEOs with too much time on their hands. They all make a mockery of failure by trying—without any irony—to rebrand it and sell it as nothing less than a stepping-stone to success.

The failure-as-success peddlers have managed, among other things, to ruin a profound, appropriately dark saying by Samuel Beckett—you probably know the one. What they invariably fail to mention is that, in his next sentence, right after the phrase they quote ad nauseam, Beckett proposes something even better than "failing better"—*failing worse:* "Try again. Fail again. Better again. Or better worse. Fail worse again. Still worse again. Till sick for good. Throw up for good."[3]

Beckett was not Cioran's friend for nothing. He wrote him once, *"Dans vos ruines je me sens à l'aise"* (Amidst your ruins I feel at home).[4] To be "sick for good," to "throw up for good"—there is hardly a better way to describe our existential predicament. To the extent that, for Beckett, failure leads to self-realization, and to a healing of the fundamental sickness that comes with our next-to-nothingness, *In Praise of Failure* is a Beckettian book.

And how, you may ask, are we to tell real failure from fake failure, of the kind peddled by self-help gurus? It is simple: failure always humbles. If it doesn't, it's not real failure, it's just "a stepping-stone to success"—self-deception by another name. And that does not lead to healing but to even more sickness.

In Praise of Failure is not about failure for its own sake, then, but about the humility that failure engenders, and the healing process that it triggers. Only humility, a "selfless respect for reality," as Iris Murdoch defines it, will allow us to grasp *what is happening*. When we achieve humility, we will know that we are on the way to recovery, for we will have started extricating ourselves from the entanglement of existence.

So, if you are after success *sans* humility, you can safely ignore this book. It will not help you—it will only lead you astray.

As a rule, we fail to take failure seriously. Even the idea of examining failure more closely makes us uncomfortable; we do not want to touch it for fear of contagion. Which is itself touching, considering that we come into the world already infected by it.

All of this makes the study of failure ideal for a contortionist's job: we have to look for failure in the external world, but also within ourselves, in the darkest corners of our mind and heart. We will find it in individuals, but also in society as a whole; in nature as in culture. We have to track its presence in religion, politics, business, and pretty much everywhere else. Besides, the study of failure cannot but be undermined by its object: we look at failure with failing eyes, ponder it with an error-prone mind, and convey whatever we find in a language that is anything but perfect. Any study of failure is a study in failure.

And yet, there is something remarkable about our situation. For even as we find ourselves entangled in a failed world and are seriously flawed ourselves, we can *recognize failure*. Whenever we remark, "But this is not right," "This is not how it should be," we show that we know failure when we see it. We may be fallible, utterly imperfect creatures, but not enough so to ignore what failure is. Not only do we recognize failure—with some luck, we can domesticate it and make it our guide. Which is precisely my task in this book.

In a beautiful Gnostic poem, "The Hymn of the Pearl" (from Acts of Thomas), a young prince is asked by his father, "the king of kings," to go down to Egypt and retrieve a special object: "the one pearl, which is in the middle of the sea surrounded by the hissing serpent."[5] The prince obliges and takes to the road. Once he reaches his destination, we are told, while waiting on the shore for the opportune moment to snatch the pearl from the serpent, he is seduced by the Egyptians: "They mingled their deceit with me, and they made me eat their food." Under "the burden of their exhortations," the prince falls into "a deep sleep" and forgets everything: where he has come from, who sent him there, and for what purpose.

Eventually, the king—his father—takes mercy on the prince and sends him word: "Remember the pearl, on account of which you were sent to Egypt." That's enough to wake him. The prince recalls everything: who he is, where he has come from, and why. He retrieves the pearl and returns home with it in full glory, healed of all confusion and alienation.

The poem depicts the predicament of the Gnostic believer in the world. This is also *our* predicament, even though we may have to wake up and remember all by ourselves. The king has forgotten to send us word—if he hasn't died already. We have to grope our way back, guided by nothing but failure.

Since failure is boundless, and its manifestations legion, trying to map it out is not unlike attempting, as the little boy was doing in the famous Saint Augustine anecdote, to scoop out all the water of the sea, with a seashell, and deposit it into a small hole he had dug on the beach. The exercise seems doomed to failure, but that's hardly the point: the mad beauty of the attempt is what we are after.

"Though this be madness," observed Polonius of Hamlet, perhaps the most tragic failure in literature, "yet there is method in it." Since failure besieges and surrounds us, it would not be unreasonable to imagine that it comes in circles: concentric, tightening circles, with us right at the center—in the eye of the storm, as it were.

In this pursuit of failure, my method is to start from the outer ring and move, one circle at a time, toward the form of failure that is closest to us, and most intimate. I begin with the circle of external, *physical* failure, which I see as the most remote. "Remote" not in the sense of spatial distance, but more of spiritual dissonance: we are radically different from things, even though we live among them, use them, and depend on them. The failure of things affects us, and so does their flawlessness, which can dehumanize us. In this circle I will consider how Simone Weil's feeling of being maladjusted and "out of place" in the world led her to a lifelong project of self-transcendence and self-dematerialization. Weil's life is a study in radical humility: she would rather not be at all than offend God with her existence. Eventually, turning her back on the world, she extricated herself from its entanglement as inconspicuously as she could. When the bullfighter showed up, he could not find her: she had already vanished.

Next comes the circle of *political* failure. Politics involves us all to some degree, even the most apolitical among us; indeed, to stay out of politics is itself a political decision. The ring of political failure is closer than the previous one because the *polis* is not outside of us, it is part of us. Even rebels and anarchists live in relation to a political community and define themselves against it. Mahatma Gandhi, whose acquaintance we make in this circle, got seriously muddled in the politics of his day, even as he never stopped seeking purity. Out of a compulsive need for purity and perfection (which brought him into dangerous proximity with Robespierre and other political purists), Gandhi sometimes displayed alarmingly imperfect behavior. What redeemed him in the end may have been his other-worldliness. When the bullfighter showed up, he had trouble locating Gandhi—the Mahatma had always seemed to belong to another realm.

The next circle is that of *social* failure. Even if we decide to live alone, away from any human association, society still lingers within us—haunting our minds and our language. We are always socially entangled, and it is in this entanglement that we experience a particularly pervasive form of failure. To face social failure head-on, some people decide to embrace it as a personal vocation. E. M. Cioran, around whom much of the third chapter revolves, dedicated his life to actively doing nothing, making a total mockery of the founding myths of our wealth-obsessed and work-centered society. "Anything good we can have comes from our indolence, from our incapability of taking action, executing our projects and plans," he writes.[6] Cioran thought inaction was the only reasonable response to a meaningless existence. *La révélation de l'insignifiance universelle* was the all-consuming religion by which this atheist lived.[7] When the bullfighter showed up, Cioran made him laugh so hard that he forgot why he came there in the first place. And so did Cioran himself, apparently—thanks to his Alzheimer's disease.

Finally, closing in ever further, there is the circle of our *biological* failure—our own mortality. No matter how far we may try to run from death, it will inevitably catch up with us. Yet even if mortality is scripted in our DNA, we find it rather hard to process. To think of death is "to think the unthinkable," says Vladimir Jankélévitch. Perhaps as a way out, classical philosophers like Seneca were preoccupied with death less as a theoretical problem than as a practical concern: they believed that mastering our fear of death could help us lead a better life. I will consider here the strange case of Yukio Mishima, who plotted and executed what he thought to be a "beautiful death," placing himself firmly in the Japanese tradition of the noble failure. To defeat the bullfighter, Mishima turned himself into the bullfighter.

In Praise of Failure works with an evolving—indeed, expanding—definition of failure. Whatever success is, it normally involves a "succession" of states or events (the word comes from the Latin *succedere,* to come after). When something fails, that succession does not take place, and a sense of emptiness ensues. Failure is whatever we experience as a disconnection, disruption, or discomfort in the course of our patterned interaction with the world and others, when something ceases to be, or work, or happen as expected. As we move through our circles of failure—either directly, as a shattering personal experience, or indirectly, through imagination and contemplation—we come to know more and more of this disconnection, disruption, and discomfort. And such a state is the best starting point for any journey of self-realization.

We absolutely need the accumulative experience of disconnection, disruption, and discomfort if we are to come to terms with our next-to-nothingness. For it is only in the crucible of this experience that we can achieve humility, which gives us the chance to be healed of hubris and egocentrism, of self-illusion and self-deception, and of our poor adjustment to reality. The progression through these four circles of failure is not just any journey: it is a *cathartic* one. If reading this book leaves you disturbed, it means I have not completely failed. For failure is a profoundly disturbing experience—as disturbing as life itself.

Of all the journeys, the one in search of ourselves is the most difficult, the longest journey to make. You should not be too worried, though: having taken failure as a guide, you stand a good chance to succeed. After all, this is what the best doctors have always taught: that which can destroy you can also cure you. The serpent's venom is both poison and medicine.

IN A FALLEN WORLD

From God's point of view, the existence of the world is an embarrassment. This is what the Gnostics taught. Neither the world nor we were ever meant to exist. Nonexistence is a perfection of the highest rank; as soon as something comes into existence, it is degraded. In Gnosticism things don't exist—they *fall* into existence. Any Gnostic cosmogony would give an account of the event: what triggered it, the actors involved, and how bad the fall. This fall is also where the human drama starts.[1] It is, significantly, a drama of failure. For cosmic existence, the Gnostic argument goes, is the offspring of a *primordial failure*. "The world," we read in the Gnostic Gospel of Philip, "came about through a mistake." The one who made it "wanted to create it imperishable and immortal," but he "fell short of attaining his desire." For "the world never was imperishable, nor, for that matter, was he who made the world."[2]

As the work of the same incompetent craftsman that fashioned the cosmos, humans are in no better shape. In one way or another, humanity falls short of the promise suggested by its divine model. In some Gnostic narratives of creation, the maker of the world catches a glimpse of the archetype of the human being, which resides in "the intelligible brain of the true God of the highest circle."[3] He can barely see—let alone study—the model. Yet he is smitten and so blinded by passion that he does not realize he lacks the skills to bring such an ideal type into existence. The result is deplorable—so remote from the original that almost any trace of resemblance is gone. The maker shouldn't have tried in the first place, but now it's too late: humankind was brought to life, and failure is here to stay.

Take the myth of creation we find in Saturninus, a Gnostic author who lived at the time of Emperor Hadrian. Seven angel-makers, the story goes, had seen "a brilliant image (eikōn) descend from the supreme power, and had striven to detain it." They didn't have enough time to examine the object in any detail, but were immediately taken by what they had glimpsed: "Let us make man after the image and after the likeness." And so they did, to their regret. The result was humanoid, but since the creators were "too feeble to give him power to stand erect," the creature "lay on the ground wriggling like a worm."[4] That creature is us.

You cannot but ask yourself: Who is this clumsy creator, the originator of an embarrassment of such cosmic proportions? It is the demiurge, the god of all things imperfect—of corruption, decay, and darkness. The demiurge, in Gnostic theology, is opposed to the other God, the supreme power, the principle of light, "the unknown," "the hidden," "the nameless," or "the alien God," as Marcion called it.[5] The demiurge's bringing the world into existence as a failed act is present in virtually all the Gnostic cosmogonic narratives, which reinforce the same point, over and over: the creation of the world was an unfortunate event, which the demiurge should not have engaged in, because such work was beyond his capabilities. He was driven by passion, ignorance, and recklessness. The demiurge, writes a modern historian, "was flawed, limited, and a decidedly unreliable workman," yet this did not "deter him from creating mankind and the universe that we all still inhabit."[6]

Scholars of Gnosticism have variously drawn attention to the event. Kurt Rudolph refers to the "important episode" of world creation as the "presumption (hybris) of the Demiurge."[7] Hans Jonas talks of this divinity, unflatteringly, as "a blind and arrogant Creator," exercising mastery over a universe that is "the product,

like himself, of fault and ignorance."[8] Others refer to the creator
of the world as an "incompetent and profoundly malevolent demiurge."[9] The demiurge of the Gnostics is the most unlikely of divin-
ities: *the god of failure.* The only god we can truly understand, and
who can understand us.

Failure is so central to the Gnostics that they see evidence of it
everywhere they look. In an insightful study, *Les Gnostiques,* Jacques
Lacarrière foregrounds the notion. "Viscerally, imperiously, irre-
missibly," he writes, "the Gnostic feels life, thought, human and
planetary destiny to be a failed work, limited and vitiated in its most
fundamental structures." Every single thing in the world, "from the
distant stars to the nuclei of our body-cells," from its macro- to its
micro-levels, carries the "materially demonstrable trace of an original imperfection."[10] Last year's earthquake, the floods this spring,
plagues and cancer—these are all manifestations of cosmic failure.
There is no escape from it because failure is scripted into the flesh
of the world like a DNA of sorts.

In the Gnostic anthropology, humans share with the rest of
creation the same structural flaws, the same imperfections, the
same deficit of being. Failure reigns supreme over us all: it determines the working of our minds, the shape of our lives, the circumstances of our passing through the world. The "history of man,"
writes Lacarrière, "reproduces very closely the initial drama—and
the farce—of the cosmos." Like the universe itself, man is "a failed
creation, a lamentable imitation, the mere resemblance of a man."[11]
Man and cosmos alike bear the signature of the same clumsy
author: the god of failure.

In their everyday life, Gnostic believers were supposed to limit
the effects of this failed creation. They were urged not to make
money or own riches, gain or exercise power, marry or procreate.
Since the world was such a bad place, they should have as little to
do with it as possible. The resistance to procreation was perhaps
their most eloquent gesture: if one truly believes existence is bad,
why bring others into it? This notion was central to virtually all

movements of Gnostic inspiration, from the Manicheans of the Roman Empire to the Bogomils of the Balkans to the Cathars of medieval France and Italy. One of the main theses of Catharism was that "any sexual act, even between married persons, is wrong."[12] By giving in to your sexual desire and procreating, you're doing the work of the Devil, the Cathar equivalent of the demiurge. True Christians, as the Cathars thought themselves to be, don't engage in sex. That's how they can defeat the Devil and his traps.

In Praise of Clumsiness

From an early age, Simone Weil embodied a curious paradox: she was at once a child of extraordinary promise and a hopeless weakling, a prodigy and dangerously sickly.[13] Steel and dust. A perceptive doctor, who happened to treat her when she was a child, thought she was "too extraordinary to go on living."[14] Despite the prediction, Weil did go on living, but hers was to be a precarious existence, perpetually on the edge. "From infancy," observes a biographer, "chronic illness imperiled her life, a pattern of ill-health from which she never completely escaped."[15] In adulthood, she would associate this precariousness with some primal failure. Recalling her health troubles as an infant, Weil would remark, with characteristic self-deprecation, *"C'est pourquoi je suis tellement ratée"*—That's why I am such a failure.[16]

She may have meant it as a joke, but failure is no laughing matter. No sooner do you utter its name than it takes on a life of its own—before you know it, it has moved in with you. Weil's precariousness would stick with her, causing her increasing suffering, both physical and mental, as she grew older. Yet the more she suffered, the more she understood, and since she came to suffer beyond measure, her understanding became prodigious. The combination of extreme fragility and extraordinary insight, which the good doctor had noticed in the child, would eventually define her. Weil was only too aware of the connection. Referring to her crippling migraines, she told her mother once, "You oughtn't be sorry that I have had headaches, for without them there are many things I would not have done."[17]

Throughout her life, Simone Weil was fundamentally clumsy, and in her dealings with the physical world she had to make a significant amount of effort. Her clumsiness, recalled Gustave Thibon, "was only equaled by her goodwill—the latter ended by triumphing over the former."[18] It must have been one of the cruelest ironies: while intellectually and morally she was well above others, when it came to simple tasks that involved her body, she was below most. "Physically," a classmate recalls, when she was around ten years old, Weil looked like "a little child, unable to use her hands."[19] She could write only with much difficulty, and would regularly fall behind others in her class. For all her intellectual promise, her childhood was marked by a desperate effort to catch up with her classmates in all things practical, from writing and drawing to sports or just walking down the street. It was as though she had been hastily put together by a demiurge almost as clumsy as she was.

A former schoolmate observed that Weil looked as if she "belonged to another order of being, and her mind didn't seem to belong to our age or our milieu. She felt like a very old soul."[20] Even decades later, an encounter with her would have the same effect. Weil would invariably come across as awkward, her head dangerously in the clouds: "I had the impression of being face to face with an individual who was radically foreign to all my ways of feeling and thinking."[21] To her high school colleagues who didn't know her well she could appear as weird, even arrogant. "I knew Simone Weil at Henri IV," one of them remembered. She was "completely aloof and unsociable."[22] In the street, it was "only miraculously that she was not hit by cars."[23] Sometimes her otherworldliness could reach hilarious proportions. In her twenties, and a graduate of the École normale supérieure to boot, she would write her mother a letter asking, in all earnestness. "How do you eat bacon—raw or cooked? If you want to eat it with eggs on a plate, do you have to cook it first?"[24]

This must have been one of the few occasions when Simone Weil felt the need to eat something. Most of the time, she didn't. To her, eating seemed "a base and disgusting function," her friend and biographer Simone Pétrement recalled.[25] And you could tell. To those who encountered her, Simone Weil gave a distinct impression of *bodilessness*, to go with her otherworldliness. It was as though she was there, before your eyes, and yet she wasn't.

This ghostly quality, along with her unique demeanor, made her presence an unsettling experience. The poet Jean Tortel tried to convey her appearance: "A cone of black wool, a being completely without a body, with a huge cape, large shoes and hair which looked like twigs; her mouth was large, sinuous and always moist; she looked at you with her mouth."[26] Her presence was at once fascinating and disturbing. George Bataille, who stated, bluntly, that Weil's "undeniable ugliness was repellent," admitted that few human beings "have interested me more deeply." He fell prey to her paradoxical charm: "I personally felt that she also had a true beauty. . . . She seduced by a very gentle, very simple authority."[27]

Given her outstanding gifts, the École normale supérieure, one of France's top schools, was a natural choice. As a *normalienne,* after graduation she was expected to serve as a high school teacher, changing schools across France as needed. But Weil was the unlikeliest of teachers. When she went to take up one of her teaching positions, her overprotective mother by her side, the custodian took her for one of the incoming high school students and kindly asked her in which class she wished to enroll. In the common room, she would hardly interact with the other teachers. To provoke their bourgeois sensibilities, at staff meetings Weil would bring a Soviet newspaper in Russian (a language she did not know) and pretend to read it with concentration. In the cities where she taught, she was often labeled a "radical" and a "troublemaker," and respectable people were warned to stay away from "the red virgin."

When Weil first showed up in class, the students at the all-girls school didn't know what to do with their new teacher—she was so unlike any others they had had before or after. "So strange. At first, we laughed at her," one of them would remember. "She dressed badly and her gestures were awkward and graceless. She hesitated when she spoke. Her method was as odd as her appearance."[28] As soon as they got used to her unorthodox ways, however, they were won over by her brilliance and the dedication she put into her work. Eventually, they came to love her, and to respect her "gentle" and "simple" authority.[29] Weil's clumsiness was part of her charm. When, on one occasion, she came to school with her sweater on backward, the pupils discretely drew her attention to this, and "arranged things so that she could hide behind the blackboard, take the sweater off, and put it on right."[30] The girls behaved maternally toward their childlike teacher.

Considering Weil's clumsiness, it was a good thing that she chose an intellectual profession. We would be suspicious of a thinker who comes across as too savvy in the ways of the world. But the choice came with its own challenges. She felt privileged and could not stand the guilt of pursuing the life of the mind while others were laboring to feed, dress, or shelter her body. That was why, as Weil reached adulthood, she became determined to take up a physically demanding job, if only on a temporary basis. She knew she was not meant for it, but that only stimulated her. So, even as she graduated from the École normale supérieure, which sealed her membership in the French intellectual elite, and embarked on a teaching career, Weil looked for opportunities to do a stint as an unskilled factory worker.

A year-long leave of absence, in 1934, allowed her to do just that. The times were not ideal for guilty intellectuals playing factory worker: "In these days," she wrote to a former pupil, "it is almost impossible to get into a factory without credentials—especially when, like me, one is clumsy and slow and not very robust."[31] But eventually she got her factory job—more than one, in fact.

Weil had some harsh bosses, but most oppressive of all was her own sense of inadequacy and the feeling that, having to service the machines, she was being turned into a thing herself. For the duration of her employment (a little over a year), she lived in "the fear of not being able to meet the work quotas one must attain to stay in the factory."[32] The movements of her body, the tempo of her inner life, her whole existence in the factory, she discovered, were now dictated by the speed of the machines to which she was attached. And she fell painfully short in that department. "I am still unable to achieve the required speeds," she wrote several months into her employment. The reasons were always the same: "my unfamiliarity with the work, my inborn awkwardness, which is considerable, a certain natural slowness of movement, headaches . . ."[33]

When Charlie Chaplin's *Modern Times* was released, in 1936, Weil not only recognized its formidable artistic vision and philosophical import, but found herself, whole, in the story: the Little Tramp was her. The film, she realized, uncannily captured the experience of the modern factory worker who, instead of using the machines, was being used and abused by them—to the point of being eaten alive.[34] The poor worker became a tool at the mercy of alien forces: the assembly line, the factory, the whole capitalist system. Weil loved the film, even though watching it brought her no comfort: for what she saw on screen was a replay of her own anguish. Just like Chaplin's Little Tramp, the factory turned her into a thing. A cog in a machine—depersonalized, replaceable, disposable. What made her situation particularly painful was her fundamental inability to adjust herself to the rhythms and demands of the machine she was part of. She could not even be a cog, it turned out.

If you think that someone as clumsy as Simone Weil—and a pacifist to boot—would refrain from taking up arms in a time of war, you are wrong. No sooner did the Spanish Civil War break out, in 1936, than she jumped at the opportunity and joined the republican forces in Barcelona. She had an absolute duty to fight, she thought. This time her awkwardness added an element of black comedy to the drama. Having attached herself to an anarchist group, she left for the frontline. Like everybody else, Weil received a rifle, but her handling of it gave her away: she was so short-sighted and maladroit that, when this ragtag band of irregulars started target practice, none of those brave men wanted to be anywhere near her line of fire. Her clumsiness made her more dangerous than Franco's snipers. Later, when she described her exploits, she made light of their fears: "I am so nearsighted that I don't run the risk of killing anyone, even when I shoot at them."[35]

At one point, while she and her companions were all camping at the frontline, dinner was being prepared. So as not to give away their position, the cooks had dug a hole in the ground, started a fire in it, and placed a large pot over the coals. It took a while, but the method was relatively safe. Not for Weil. When dinner was almost ready, after all that slow cooking, she, hopelessly shortsighted and cloud-headed as she always was, stepped right into the pot filled to the brim with boiling oil.

The burns were severe, and the pain must have been unbearable. As her comrades tried to remove her stocking, parts of the skin remained attached to it. She was in no condition to fight, if she ever had been, and was promptly sent back to Barcelona. As she lay in her hospital bed, most of her former comrades were killed in combat.[36] What saved her life was her spectacular clumsiness.

Corps Étranger

When you are clumsy, your every contact with the physical world is a reminder that you have been brought into it in a state of incompletion: some part of you is missing or poorly made or improperly designed. You look like others and, in most respects, you are like them, except for the missing bit that sets you apart, which you experience painfully whenever you try to accomplish something using your body. The discomfort thus caused, and the attending embarrassment, shapes pretty much every aspect of your worldly existence.

To be clumsy is to be born with a thorn in the flesh, which you can neither pull out nor ignore. Yet if you manage to find a way to live with the thorn, or even befriend it, the rewards make up for the pain. For when you can't insert yourself smoothly into the flow of things, and any dealing with the world brings you so much discomfort, you are uniquely positioned to observe its course and study its workings. The insights are considerable: your clumsiness puts a distance between you and the world, and the depth of your insight is in direct proportion to that distance. The more painful it gets, the more discerning you become. At the limit, as the thorn becomes of a piece with your flesh, your understanding will have reached uncanny proportions. If it hasn't ruined you, it will have made you wiser than most.

The process is worth considering in some detail. It starts with an annoying feeling of inadequacy: as you try to apply yourself to some physical job or another, you find that your body is not up to the task. Our physicality is an integral part of the world, and we are meant to operate smoothly within it—like a fish in water, as they say. Not yours, apparently. In some important way, your body remains ill adapted to its environment. Some fateful mismatch puts it perpetually at the wrong angle: you can't place your hand where you should, or the hand does not talk to your eyes, or the eyes to the brain, you don't apply the right amount of pressure or else you press too much, you let an object go when you should hold it tight, or you hold it so tightly that you break it, or you fail in some other embarrassing way.

As you experience the unfolding of this mismatch, you come to see your own body in a new light: it appears to be lacking a necessary harmony with the physical world around you, and between its parts—each limb seems to be going its own way. It is as though your body—or some part of it—is acting up, rebelling, proclaiming its autonomy. This is how you discover a province of yourself that

you have little control of, a foreign enclave of sorts—a part of you
that is not really you. Certainly, you can try to train your body in
the hope that you will manage to subdue the rebellious faction, but
you realize that you will never fully succeed. Eventually, you will
have to learn to live with the enemy within.

Clumsiness is a peculiar form of failure: one that is at once yours
and not yours. It is *yours* because you are the one who does the
failing: owing to poor motor coordination, you are unable to accomplish something that most people have little trouble accomplishing.
And yet since this is due to a part of yourself that you can't fully
control—indeed, a rebellious part that is not you—it's *not* exactly
your failure. You suffer the consequences—shame, embarrassment, humiliation, or worse—just as Weil did throughout her life,
without much fault of your own.

This failure, which gradually colonizes the clumsy and determines the contours of their lives, is not properly a human failure;
it belongs to the things of the external world. And it is precisely
its brutal *thingness* that makes it so disturbing when found in
humans. Human as you are, you are supposed to have only "human"
failings—errors of thought or judgment, of memory or affection,
moral shortcomings, and so on. But when you exhibit a failure that
normally belongs to the physical world, a technical malfunction,
you become a unique spectacle that cannot fail to unsettle people.
You are positively *creepy*. Others will seek to stay away from you and
will end up seeing you as "out of this world." You are certainly out
of *their* world.

Weil knew this only too well: "I am not someone with whom it
is good to cast one's lot," she confided to her friend Simone Pétrement. "Human beings have always more or less sensed this."
Pétrement intuited the link between Weil's physical awkwardness
and her otherworldliness: her clumsiness "seemed to spring from
the fact that she was not made out of the same crude materials as
the rest of us."[37]

Naked

Remember the plane about to crash because of engine failure, and the revelations to which it gave rise? Such an experience allows us to realize that before facing annihilation, we face failure. Like few other human experiences, failure puts us in a unique position to understand who we are, and what our place in the world is. Above all, the experience of failure gives us a chance to see our *existence in its naked condition*. Our survival instinct normally leads us to see our existence in the world as solid, reliable, even indestructible. We come into the world with built-in mechanisms of self-deception that allow us to forget just how fragile our condition is, and how close we are to not being. Failure may not always pose an existential threat, but some encounters with it remind us sharply of our fundamental precariousness. The example of the plane whose engine has stopped working mid-flight tells you how flimsy the wall that separates us from the other side is.

We often take pride in being high-minded, spiritual creatures, whose materiality is largely irrelevant. As if to mock our pretensions, there can be something obscenely materialistic in any "brush with death": some faulty piece of equipment—a worn-out part, some defective item, a loose screw, anything—can be more than enough to put an end to everything. "Here lies a former angel done in by a leaky pipe."

Yet even as failure pushes us toward the edge of existence, mocking us in the process, it gives us a chance to look at everything with fresh eyes. The failure of things interrupts life's routines, our patterned existence, with a jolt. That machines (plane engines, cars, buildings, computers) fail when they shouldn't is intrinsically important to designers, architects, engineers, or manufacturers. That's not my concern here.[38] I am concerned not so much by why things fail as by what happens to those who witness that failure, and are changed by it. In failure, the precariousness of the world meets our own precariousness, and there are few things more defining for us than what occurs during this brief encounter.

One of the more difficult questions of traditional metaphysics is the so-called question of being, which asks, "Why is there something rather than nothing?" Translated into existentialist language, the interrogation takes on a more personal form: "Why should *I* exist rather than not?" The question is overwhelming for at least two reasons. First, because it is so oppressively personal: there is only one person in the world who can ask this question, and that's me. If I fail to ask it, the question will remain forever unasked, which may be worse than remaining unanswered. Second, because it is ultimately unanswerable. Certainly, I can toy with it and try to formulate *something*. Philosophy and literature, religion and science may give me some convenient, ready-made answers. Yet I remain painfully aware that, in the final analysis, the question "Why should *I* exist rather than not?" cannot be firmly decided one way or the other. Ivan Karamazov—one of the sharpest philosophers never to have existed—would call it a "cursed question." At the same time, I cannot afford not to ask it. I become myself in the very process of wondering "Why should *I* exist rather than not?" Not to ask it would be to deprive my existence of something vital, which structures, enriches, and eventually gives it meaning. There are different ways of asking this question: by writing a novel, sacrificing myself for something larger than myself, showing compassion to others. In the end, the fact that the question is unanswerable is not decisive; the answer lies in the very act of asking it, and we choose to do so as a result.

And here's where failure comes in. To be sure, it does not come to provide an answer; failure has never been in the business of answers. What it offers, instead, is a better position from which to ask that question. Which may be more important than an answer. Failure is the sudden irruption of nothingness into the midst of existence. When we experience failure, we start seeing cracks in the fabric of existence and the nothingness that stares at us from the other side. Failure reveals something fundamental about the human condition: that to be human is to perform a tightrope walk with no safety net. The slightest wrong step can throw you off balance and send you back into the abyss. As a rule, we perform our tightrope walking blissfully unaware of what we are doing, like a sleepwalker. To experience failure is to wake up suddenly—and to look down.

That's precisely the moment when failure turns out to be a blessing in disguise. For it is this lurking, constant threat—the abyss below—that should make us aware of the extraordinariness of existence: that we exist at all when there is no obvious reason why we should. Coming out of nothing, and returning to nothing, human existence is a *state of exception*. And failure, with the sudden prospect of nothingness that it reveals, is important because it helps us grasp precisely that. When we fail, we are forced to understand what we are exactly. Certainly, we are not much, but in many respects that's more than enough. For either you are or you are not; there are no degrees here, one cannot be "more or less." The sheer fact of existing in the world as a self-aware being gives you access to all there is to be known about what it means to be human. We come from the abyss, and the abyss is where we are headed, but simply falling into it is not a good option. We need to learn, on our own, how to find our way back so that we can find ourselves in the process. It's bad enough to "fall into existence," as the Gnostics would have it, but to exit it without knowing what this is all about is even worse. Failure can give us this precious knowledge.

Granted, this is no flattering knowledge: you find yourself nothing but a creature of chance, the icon of flimsiness, a brief flickering. You are cast in some cosmic farce, nothing but a plaything, a walking joke. Yet even as you gain this knowledge you realize the magnitude of your accomplishment: you see yourself *as you are,* you've reached a state of ontological nakedness—and you get the joke. Thanks to your experience of failure, you've broken the veil of self-deceptions, self-delusions, and self-defense mechanisms that normally keeps you hidden from yourself. Failure, with the sudden sense of threat it brings about, shakes you up so thoroughly that nothing prevents you now from really seeing. You look at yourself in the mirror and recognize yourself for what you are.

Failure has a bad rap, but it can be the most honest of friends: it doesn't flatter, doesn't make false promises, doesn't sell you unachievable dreams. Frightful in its frankness, it performs a crucial function in any process of self-realization: disenchantment.

The Cog and the Machine

When Simone Weil was six years old, and the First World War was being fought, she decided to go without sugar because, as she told her flabbergasted parents, "the poor soldiers at the front" could not afford any.[39] This was to be her signature gesture: if she thought someone was deprived of something somewhere, she wanted to experience the deprivation herself. Throughout her life, Weil displayed an uncanny capacity to empathize with the suffering, the vulnerable, and the underprivileged. She lived in unheated rooms because, she believed, workers could not afford to heat theirs; she ate poorly because that was how she thought the poor ate. When on one occasion her money disappeared from her rented room, her only remark was, "Whoever took it undoubtedly needed it."[40] Not only did she feel for others, she thought she had to push her life to its breaking point for them; in England, albeit seriously sick and exhausted, she didn't take the food she needed because, she believed, the French under occupation were deprived of theirs.

Ironically, this capacity for empathy could make Weil blunt, impatient, even intolerant toward others. In *Memoirs of a Dutiful Daughter*, Simone de Beauvoir describes her failed encounter with Simone Weil. It must have been in 1928. "A great famine had just begun to devastate China, and I was told on hearing the news she had wept," remembers de Beauvoir. "I envied her for having a heart that could beat right across the world." When she approached Weil, however, de Beauvoir was in for a shock. No sooner was small talk over than Weil declared, irrefutably, that the only thing that mattered was a "revolution that would feed all the people on earth." As de Beauvoir attempted to voice dissent, Weil cut her short: "It is easy to see you have never gone hungry."[41] And that was that.

It is not entirely clear what kind of revolution Simone Weil had in mind, but it was unlikely to be a communist one. She was increasingly critical of the Soviet Union and the Moscow-sponsored communist parties in Europe. At a time when few left-wing Western intellectuals would dare say anything against the Bolshevik regime, Weil articulated a remarkably lucid and prescient critique of the Soviet system. Whatever was accomplished during the Russian Revolution of 1917, she thought, was destroyed by the Bolshevik regime born out of it. The first communist state was the gravedigger of the first communist revolution.[42] Soviet Russia, in Weil's estimation, was under the control of a bureaucracy that had at its disposal an amount of power (military, political, judicial, economic) that the capitalist states in the West could never even dream of attaining. And the result? Nowhere, she wrote in 1934, is the working class "more miserable, more oppressed, more humiliated than in Russia."[43]

As Weil familiarized herself with the revolutionary milieu in France and elsewhere, she became convinced that the workers would fare much better *without* a communist revolution. "The revolution is not possible," she wrote in 1935, "because the revolutionary leaders are ineffective dolts. And it is not desirable because they are traitors. Too stupid to win a victory; and if they did win, they would oppress again, as in Russia."[44]

For all her criticism of revolutionary politics, Weil was not a reactionary. She cared for the workers as few of her fellow intellectuals did. Simone Pétrement recalls that while they were still in high school, Weil told her, looking tenderly on a group of workers, "It's not only out of a spirit of justice that I love them. I love them naturally. I find them more beautiful than the bourgeois."[45] Class guilt had fueled the leftist sympathies of generations of middle-class intellectuals in the West, and Weil had her share of it. A worker who got to know her well would recall:

> She wanted to know our misery. She wanted to free the worker. This was the goal of her life. I would say to her, "But you are the daughter of rich people." "That's my misfortune; I wish that my parents had been poor," she would say.[46]

Yet it was much more than just class guilt. Having realized that revolutionary politics would not help the working class, and that revolutionary leaders were either crooks or incompetent or both, Weil decided that the workers could only help themselves. Revolutions generate bureaucracies, and "bureaucracy *always* betrays," she said. If intellectuals truly want to understand and help the workers, there is one path they can pursue meaningfully: work alongside them, share their hunger, feel their pain, let themselves be crushed along with them.

Weil's decision to become an unskilled factory worker was driven by the same fundamental empathy toward the underprivileged that shaped her entire life. Working and living like a "beast of burden," she hoped, would give her the chance to experience human life at its most naked and brutal. And here she got more than she bargained for.

Barely a few months into her new existence as a factory hand, in January 1935, she wrote to a friend, "It is not that it has changed one or the other of my ideas (on the contrary, it has confirmed many of them), but infinitely more—it has changed my whole view of things, even my very feeling about life." Nothing would be the same again for her after *l'année d'usine* (the year of factory work). She would come out of it a changed person. "I shall know joy again in the future," she went on, "but there is a certain lightness of heart which, it seems to me, will never again be possible."[47]

The social reality burst open for Weil in the factory, and she could now see right through all the shallowness of revolutionary talk. As she was trying to keep up with the impossible work quotas, the overbearing bosses, her crippling migraines and her clumsiness, she realized that the leaders of the Bolshevik Revolution who were speaking so grandly in the name of the proletariat had no idea what they were talking about. From the perspective of the assembly line worker, it was all imposture and demagogy. The communist leaders, it appeared to her now, were no different from the bourgeois politicians they were trying to overthrow:

> Only when I think that the great Bolshevik leaders proposed to create a *free* working class and that doubtless none of them—certainly not Trotsky, and I don't think Lenin either—had ever set foot inside a factory, so that they hadn't the faintest idea of the real conditions which make servitude or freedom for the workers—well, politics appear to me a sinister farce [*une sinistre rigolade*].[48]

The most consequential discovery Weil made in the factory was the state of complete dehumanization that assembly line work brings about in the worker. In April 1935, in a letter to Boris Souvarine, she repeats what a female worker, who was servicing a conveyor belt, had told her: "After a few years, or even a year, one no longer suffers, although one remains in a sort of stupor." Weil found that intolerable. "This seems to me to be the lowest stage of degradation."[49] Even though she would not spend enough time in the factory to reach that stage herself, she could easily place herself in her fellow worker's shoes.

Eventually, it was her empathy for her fellow workers that helped her survive that year. Her fundamental need to *understand* brought some meaning to what otherwise seemed meaninglessness itself. "I don't feel the suffering as mine, I feel it as the workers' suffering," she told Souvarine. Whether "I personally suffer it or not seems to me a detail of almost no importance." The urge to "know and understand easily prevails." "I swore to myself," she writes in another letter, "that I would not give up until I had learned how to live a worker's life without losing my sense of human dignity. And I kept my word."[50]

L'année d'usine allowed Weil to make some important observations about what happens to human beings as they are reduced to a cog in a social machine. "Nothing is more paralyzing to thought," she would write in 1936, than "the sense of inferiority which is necessarily induced by the daily assault of poverty, subordination, and dependence."[51] If you happen to be assigned to a cog's position, you eventually become a cog—not just in others' eyes, but also in your own. The most difficult thing to retain in the factory, she discovered, was a sense of human dignity; everything there conspired to keep you in a "state of subhuman apathy."[52] Once you've surrendered to this state, anything can be done to you: you are no longer a person, but an object—at anyone's disposal.

When Weil summarized her factory experience, she singled out two lessons she had learned. The first, "the bitterest and most unexpected," was that oppression, beyond "a certain degree of intensity," does not generate revolt, but "an almost irresistible tendency to the most complete submission." The second was that "humanity is divided into two categories": those "who count for something" and those "who count for nothing."[53] Both these lessons would stay with her for the rest of her life.

New Eyes

There is another benefit we get from the encounter with the failure of things. When you experience it, not only are you yourself shattered, but so is your whole universe. Failure reveals not just the nothingness against which your personal existence is defined, but also a deficit of being in the world itself. When something breaks down in your proximity, you first question the faulty item, but then you may start questioning the solidity of things in general. You come to suspect, and for good reason, that there may be more nothingness hidden in things. And all of a sudden the world reveals itself in a different light. It now has a novel and complex face, which has been revealed to you by failure. You take a step back and re-approach it fully alert.

We often realize the presence of something only when it breaks down. We take our computer, or printer, or coffeemaker for granted—until it stops working. In a certain sense, it is only when these things fail that they start to exist for us and come into full view; they become visible after a measure of nothingness has crept into them. As long as you can use your car unproblematically to move from one place to another, you don't pay much attention to the car itself; gradually, as it keeps working as it should, you see less and less of it. But when it breaks down in the middle of the road, the car becomes suddenly, massively present. You cannot *not* notice it now: here it is, an imposing pile of steel and stuff, conspicuously not moving. Not unlike Heidegger's hammer, except on a grander and more annoying scale. Failure unsettles—it dusts things off, exposing them for what they are.

We would pay less and less attention to a world where everything worked flawlessly. If nothing unusual happens, if nothing breaks down, an increasingly thick veil of familiarity descends upon the world, and we become blind to it. We make use of some object or another, perform this or that action, and before we know it our life has become all routine—that is, parts of it have atrophied and died. Up to a point, this is normal. That's what life ordinarily does: it falls into patterns, allowing itself to partially atrophy in order to survive as a whole. But if this goes on for too long, routine takes over and life becomes a scripted exercise—nothing new, no change of rhythm and variation, just one endless season. When you die, you don't even notice because you've been dead for a while.

In other words, if there is something worse than failure, it's the absence of failure. Failure pricks us, and in so doing it puts us in touch with reality, brutal and painful as the contact may be. Failure comes with a degree of immediacy that sobers up even the most intoxicated among us. No matter how many times we experience it, it always manages to preserve its novelty. "Failure, even repeated, always seems fresh; whereas success, multiplied, loses all interest, all attraction," writes Cioran.[54] Failure gives us new eyes. The world is born again to the one who has experienced failure. Old presumptions are shattered, certainties fade away, reputable truths are put to shame—the screen of convenient labels, worn-out conventions, ready-made theories through which we are so used to looking at the world is suddenly torn apart. For a brief moment, before we come up with yet another screen—as we always do—we experience the world as a brand-new creation.

In failure, the world opens itself up to us, revealing some of its secrets. Failure gives us an acuity of perception and a clarity of vision that allow us to perceive the nakedness of things. In a world without failure, we would cease to have access to the real; we would look absent-mindedly at something recorded at some point in the past and then played and replayed, endlessly, before our lifeless eyes. That world would no longer be real. And neither would we.

"I, a Slave . . ."

As Weil was processing the significance of her factory experience, she started using a new term to describe it: *slavery*. Observing the workers' "complete submission," their "inhuman apathy" and increasing alienation, she could not come up with a better name for them than "slaves." From her study of the classical world, Weil knew what it meant for a human being to belong to another, and she found the modern worker to be a replica of the ancient slave. In addition to social degradation, which had always been the slave's mark, the factory worker was reduced to a nonthinking entity. The "absence of thought" required of the worker was "indispensable to the slaves of modern machinery."[55] Finally, slavery is the domain of "affliction" (*malheur*), which, as Weil wrote in *Waiting for God,* is "quite a different thing from simple suffering [*souffrance*]." Affliction "takes possession of the soul and marks it through and through with its own particular mark, the mark of slavery [*la marque de l'esclavage*]." [56] For the rest of her life, "affliction" would be central to her understanding of herself and of the world around her.

As an unskilled factory worker, Weil felt that she had become a slave herself. Toward the end of her factory experience, she internalized the slave condition to such an extent that she could see the world through an enslaved person's eyes, feel what the enslaved felt, and say the things they would say: "How is this that I, a slave, can get on this bus, use it by paying my twelve sous in the same way as anyone?" she once wondered, in all earnestness, as she boarded a bus to work. "What an extraordinary favor! If they had brutally forced me to get off . . . I think that it would have seemed completely natural to me. Slavery has made me completely lose the feeling of having rights."[57]

When *l'année d'usine* was over, Weil found herself shattered and devastated, yet oddly renewed. Writing to a friend in October 1935, soon after the end of her factory employment, and referring to it as "those months of slavery" (*ces mois d'esclavage*), Weil explained that she regarded the experience as a gift. Slaving for those machines enabled her "to test myself and to touch with my finger the things which I had previously been able only to imagine." In another letter, Weil makes a striking confession: "It seemed to me that I was born to wait for, and receive, and carry out orders—that I had never done and never would do anything else."[58]

She is talking here about the routines of factory work, but something more profound and more consequential seems to be emerging. It is the voice of a *new Simone Weil*—the mystic, the visionary, the deeply heretical religious thinker—born out of the experience of affliction. It was as a slave that she was degraded, but also as a slave that she would be redeemed. Thanks to a swift, spectacular move, Weil turned slavery on its head, and found glory in it. How is that possible? you may wonder. Slavery, Weil discovered, gives us direct access to the ultimate, redeeming humility. "There is no greater humility than to wait in silence and patience," she wrote in one of her notebooks. "It is the attitude of the slave who is ready for any order from the master, or for no order."[59]

As she pondered and internalized the meanings of slavery, affliction, and humility, Weil stumbled upon a central Christian idea: when he was incarnated, Jesus Christ took "the form of a slave" (*morphē doulou*), as we learn from Saint Paul (Philippians 2:7). Weil went into the factory to find out more about the social conditions of the modern worker in capitalism. Instead, she found Jesus Christ.

Weil may have been raised in a secular Jewish home, but her whole education was shaped by France's Catholic mindset. In the factory she started to use Christian notions, symbols, and images liberally to make sense of what she was going through.[60] First among them was affliction itself, which defines both the slave condition and the Christian experience. In her "Spiritual Autobiography," she describes how the "affliction of others entered into my flesh and my soul." Because of her profound empathy for the oppressed, she felt the suffering around her as her own. That's how she received *la marque de l'esclavage,* which she likens to "the branding of the red-hot iron the Romans put on the foreheads of their most despised slaves." That's also how she was transformed: "Since then," she wrote, "I have always regarded myself as a slave."[61]

An intense religious experience, which she had soon after her factory stint, sealed the transformation. Finding herself in a small fishing village in Portugal, she witnessed a procession of fishermen's wives. Touring the anchored ships, they sang "ancient hymns of a heart-rending sadness." Weil froze in place. There, a conviction was "suddenly borne in upon me that Christianity is preeminently the religion of slaves, that slaves cannot help belonging to it, and I among them."[62] Nietzsche was right, if for all the wrong reasons.

Perfection Is Overrated

To an important extent, we need things to work properly—to be predictable and dependable. We would succumb to despair if too many failed to do their job. A world where things perform their proper function is a hospitable place. And what makes it hospitable is precisely its reliability and predictability. There is a point, however, beyond which this very flawlessness starts to induce a serious form of alienation. For when things work flawlessly, without friction, less and less is demanded of us. In the long run, this effortlessness is our undoing. It's not just that we become increasingly superfluous (which would be bad enough), but that we become more and more *like the things themselves*. We unconsciously start copying them. Their predictability becomes ours, and so does their fundamental inertness. In the proximity of something that never changes its patterns, we too slide into a heavily patterned existence. At the limit, if nothing changes to solicit our attention, we become indistinguishable from those things, and lose ourselves in their midst. Hospitability is admirable, but when a place becomes too hospitable, it turns positively hostile.

From the onset of the Industrial Revolution, generations of factory workers cried "death to the machines," sometimes going so far as to destroy them or set them on fire, as with the English Luddites of the nineteenth century. The explanation that is usually given is both simple and simplistic: fearing unfair competition from the machines, the workers put them out of commission. But that can't be all. The machines still needed human operators, after all. The workers' reaction must have had something to do with their experience of working, for awfully long hours, surrounded by those machines.

In its optimal state, a machine repeats the same movements, flawlessly, ad infinitum. Yet such perfection is utterly inhuman, and having to adjust yourself to it is a profoundly alienating experience. The machine is patterned existence at its most oppressive.

A worker servicing the conveyor belt spends her days and years, her whole life, in "a sort of stupor." She *becomes* the conveyor belt. In a telling scene of Fritz Lang's *Metropolis*, there is a clash between flawless machinery and the all-too-human workers, who are brought to paroxysm by having to submit to machines, and becoming more and more machine-like in the process. In the end, the workers cannot take it any longer and rebel. Theirs is a profoundly human gesture, the opposite of machine-like behavior—machines never rise in rebellion. Once the workers have destroyed the whole operation, they dance and celebrate. They are fully human again—albeit poorer and more endangered, their lives more precarious than ever.

The physical alienation induced by mechanical flawlessness, bad though it is, is not the worst thing we face. If everything keeps working without a flaw, and nothing challenges us to think and act, a certain form of mental degradation sets in as well. The word we usually employ for such a situation—stultification—comes from the Latin *stultus* (stupid, foolish). Rational thinking did not come to us ex nihilo; it was born and has evolved to help us cope with life's demands. Eventually, we came to employ it for abstract reasoning as well. We now weave metaphysical systems and design complex mathematical models, but for most of human history, rational thought was something rather practical, a tool of adaptation. Since intelligence is not static, but a process, it stays alive only if we keep it in motion, which happens whenever we respond to a challenge. But something that works flawlessly is not likely to challenge us. In itself, this self-sufficiency may be awe-inspiring, splendid in its perfection, but it leaves us mostly out. In terms of everyday comfort, the benefits are impressive; economically, the arrangement could not be more profitable. But, in the long run, the human cost may completely bankrupt us.[63]

There has always been a paradox with machines. We devise them to solve difficulties and make our lives more comfortable, which they do, but only to bring about new difficulties. To solve these, we come up with new machines, which generate yet more problems. Eventually, we create so many machines, to solve so many types of problems, that we end up working full-time *for them*.

As a result, the modern worker's primary role seems to be that of feeding the machines. Charlie Chaplin's *Modern Times* captures this paradox masterfully: in one of the film's early scenes, the workers posted along the assembly line are the machines' dutiful servants. All day long they make sure the machines are well fed and don't lack for anything. In so doing, the workers reproduce the machines' movements and rhythms, to such an extent that they end up as human extensions of the machines themselves. To prevent workers from wasting precious time on their meager meals during the lunch breaks, the management considers adopting a special feeding machine, which would place food mechanically in their mouths, while they would keep servicing the machines. Sand-wiched between two layers of machines (those they feed, and those that feed them), the workers would be reduced to almost nothing, their very humanity squeezed out of them. Chaplin's character, Little Tramp, is used as a guinea pig. The experiment doesn't go according to plan, and Little Tramp goes crazy. We laugh most heartily, if only to hide our tears. For what we see portrayed on screen is our own dehumanization.

That was almost a century ago. Today, in the age of generalized automation and artificial intelligence, the issue has acquired a new and painful urgency. Not only do we surrender our work to ma-chines that run almost entirely by themselves, we also sacrifice important parts of our lives to them. Machines tell us what to buy and where, what to eat and drink, whom to date and marry, what to read and what kind of music we should listen to. They give us, unprompted, the latest news and social gossip, and they rush to satisfy what they take to be our intellectual and emotional needs. And, apart from a handful of experts involved in their programming, they don't need us. Machines are a world unto themselves. They feed and maintain themselves—they even teach themselves, learning from their own errors and ours.

Freed from toil and worries, we should be happy at last, hunting in the morning, fishing in the afternoon, cowboys in the evening, as Karl Marx once wanted us to be. But we are far from happy. We can no longer get away from the machines that make this possible. The machines (from the personal computer and smartphone to the internet itself) have permeated our lives so thoroughly that if, for some reason, we are severed from them, we are no longer ourselves. Our alienation is now complete.

Significantly, we find ourselves in a state more helpless than before we started using the machines. It is not just that, by giving in to them, we have ceased to practice some important skills, lost some of our mental sharpness, or forgotten how to use simpler, yet more demanding tools. It's much worse: we have *altered* ourselves. Our heavy reliance on automation and artificial intelligence is not just making us increasingly dependent on things over which we have little control—it is making us positively dumber. Surrounded by objects that run by themselves, we encounter little that challenges us to think. Trained and fed and taken care of by algorithms as we increasingly are, our mind is largely jobless. And when thinking is not employed, it atrophies and dies.

Thinking dies like an abused dog: famished and mistreated, all skin and bones, yet absurdly loyal to its abuser, till its last breath. As we become increasingly attached to our machines, we unwittingly start aping them. Eventually, not to be outdone, we tend to develop a whole new "machine self," one that ideally should live up to the machines' commandments: don't take lazy detours, as humans used to, go "straight to the point"; don't waste time with useless things (machines don't do anything useless); don't use ambiguous language (machines are always literal); and, above all, rid yourself of humor (machines don't laugh—they have no reason to). Eventually, if we spend enough time in their proximity, we will end

up as well-oiled, efficient, and dead inside as the machines themselves. *Human automata.* If the machines weren't the mindless
objects that they are, our over-the-top flattery might embarrass them;
but being what they are, they don't mind.

The ultimate irony of course is that, when a tool is fully automated, it's a feat of engineering and a demonstration of human intelligence. When a human being is automated, it becomes stupidity
embodied. Artificial intelligence begets the ultimate stultification.

Only a god, or the gift of failure, can save us now.

Heretic

Weil entered the factory a scholar determined to understand the
condition of the working class, and she came out a full-fledged
mystic. But—with Weil there is always a *but*—not necessarily a
Christian mystic. For all her intellectual sympathy toward "the
Catholic idea," and despite her stumbling upon Jesus Christ in the
factory, she would to the end of her life have serious qualms about
Christianity as a religion. She would never be baptized. "I am as
close to Catholicism as it is possible to be . . . without being a Catholic," she quipped.[64]

No sooner did Weil discover Jesus Christ than she became a
heretic. Her *Letter to a Priest,* in which she seeks the opinion of
a Dominican priest, Father Édouard Couturier, about some of her
philosophical reservations vis-à-vis Christianity, is a heretical manifesto like few others, making it abundantly clear why she could
never join the Catholic Church—or any other church, for that matter.

For starters, she could not accept the notion that Jesus Christ
was God's only incarnation: "We do not know for certain," she
writes, "that there have not been incarnations previous to that of
Jesus, and that Osiris in Egypt, Krishna in India were not of that
number." Dismissing the church's teachings about the uniqueness
of the Incarnation, Weil suggests instead that Christ is present in
this world "wherever there is crime and affliction," which would

make his presence more widespread than even the most daring Christian missionaries would ever dream: "Whoever is capable of a movement of pure compassion towards a person in affliction," she writes, ". . . possesses, maybe implicitly, yet always really, the love of God and faith." A good heathen can find more favor with Christ than a mediocre Christian, for he "does not save all those who say to Him: 'Lord, Lord.'" He saves instead all those who, "out of a pure heart" offer bread to a starving person, "without thinking about Him the least little bit."[65]

Weil's ecumenism is not political or diplomatic, but philosophical: "The various authentic religious traditions are different reflections of the same truth, and perhaps equally precious."[66] The spirit of Christianity, she thinks, existed long before Christ, just as it can manifest itself in places which the church has not yet reached. This would make the church quite irrelevant, but that must have been the least of her worries. Elsewhere in the *Letter*, she brings some serious accusations against the church (poor Father Couturier— what had he done to deserve this?). The root cause of the church's ills lies in that it is an institution, and as such shares the sins of all human creations: corruption, injustice, immorality. Specifically, the church's original sin was its double origin in the ancient world. "Israel and Rome set their mark on Christianity," Weil writes. Israel, by "causing the Old Testament to be accepted by it as a sacred book," and Rome, by turning it into "the official religion of the Roman Empire, which was something like what Hitler dreams of doing."[67]

The ancient Jews, she thought, got it all wrong when it came to God. They conceived of Yahweh in their own image and likeness, and since "they wanted power," the result was a bloodthirsty, vengeful, unhinged God.[68] "Jehovah made the same promises to Israel that the Devil made to Christ," she had observed in her *Notebooks*.[69] Weil didn't seem to realize—or to mind—that, even as she was writing such things, Hitler was making similar arguments against the Jews before shipping them to the gas chambers.

The Roman Empire didn't fare much better. It was, she writes in the *Letter,* "a totalitarian and grossly materialistic regime, founded upon the exclusive worship of the State, like Nazism."[70] Having wreaked havoc throughout the Mediterranean world, uprooting ancient civilizations and ways of life, and suppressing dissent of any kind, the Romans adopted Christianity only to use it for their own purposes; they betrayed Christ's Gospel as soon as they accepted it. In Roman hands, the church became a purely worldly affair, the unholy business of lawyers and statesmen. Their rigid, disciplinarian spirit came to pervade Catholicism to such an extent that not even its finest representatives, such as Thomas Aquinas, could escape it. "The Thomist conception of faith," Weil writes, "implies a 'totalitarianism' as stifling as that of Hitler, if not more so."[71] Poor Father Couturier!

The pursuit of worldly power has pushed Christianity into a crisis for nearly as long as it has been in existence. Almost since its inception, the church has suffered from "an intellectual malaise," concludes Weil. This is due to the way it has conceived "its power of jurisdiction and especially the use of the formula *anathema sit.*"[72] If one doesn't unconditionally accept its teachings and discipline, one doesn't count for much, and should expect the worst. Weil found this intolerable. An unhealthy obsession with discipline, a zeal for exclusion, and an expectation of complete submission have turned Christ's church into a terrifying "bureaucracy." She could not forgive the church not just for what it did, but for what it was.

Once she had presented her view of the church's major shortcomings, she proceeded to show how she would like it to be reformed. Scandalized as Father Couturier must have been, he was in for even more disturbing reading. For all its corruption over the centuries, Weil argues, there was something incorruptible at the core of the church: the sacrifice on which it was built. The most important thing about Christ was not his resurrection, as most Christians would believe, but his crucifixion. If his story had ended

there, Weil could not have been happier. "When I think of the Crucifixion," she writes elsewhere, "I commit the sin of envy."[73] What
she wanted was Christ's affliction and agony, not his glory. The
cross produces "the same effect upon me as the resurrection does
upon other people."[74] What Weil was after was not relief, but ever
more pain. Infinite anguish.

In the *Letter*, as well as in other texts, she points to some fixes.
Most important of all would be the removal of Christianity's toxic
roots: a church without Jewish and Roman ingredients was not
just preferable, but doable. Before the Roman conquest, Weil
thought, the various nations inhabiting the Mediterranean and the
Near East formed a superior civilization, profoundly spiritual and
philosophical in nature:

> I believe that one and the same thought inhabited all its best
> minds and was expressed in various forms in the mysteries
> and the initiatory sects of Egypt, Thrace, Greece, and Persia,
> and that the works of Plato are the most perfect written ex-
> pression which we possess of that thought.[75]

Christianity was born out of this *philosophia perennis,* only to be
kidnapped, at birth, by a cabal of Roman-Jewish conspirators. If it
is to be freed at last, it should receive shelter elsewhere: among
the Gnostics, Manicheans, and Cathars, who "seem to have kept
really faithful" to the great Mediterranean spiritual tradition. They
were the only ones who managed to escape the "coarseness of mind
and baseness of heart which were disseminated over vast territo-
ries by the Roman domination," and which still "compose the at-
mosphere of Europe."[76]

Weil singles out Catharism as "the last living expression in Europe of pre-Roman antiquity."[77] In Marseille, where she was waiting
to escape to the United States from Nazi-occupied France, and
where many a Cathar had lived in the Middle Ages, Weil befriended
a group of scholars and aficionados of Catharism, from whom she

learned new details about the medieval heresy. And the more she
learned, the more she loved it. Weil became completely taken not
just by the Cathars' doctrines, but by their way of life. She was
struck by the Cathars' total rejection of the Old Testament, by their
disregard for wealth and power, and by their overall disgust at the
ways of the flesh, all of which she had already embraced herself,
on her own.

By now the good Dominican father must have concluded that
Simone Weil was a lost cause for the church. In all fairness, Weil
was a difficult personality, whose overflowing spiritual life could
not be contained within the framework of any single religion. No
religious system (save perhaps for Gnosticism) would have been
capacious enough to accommodate such a luxuriant, convoluted,
and often unpredictable thinker.

Weil clearly had a religious calling, but hers was a heretic's
vocation. In other times, she might have ended up stoned to death,
burned at the stake, or drowned in a river for her ideas. In 1943,
she didn't need any outside persecution. She took care of the matter
herself—in the most Weilian manner possible.

Humility

Most of us, whether we know it or not, suffer from a peculiar condition: the *umbilicus mundi* syndrome, a pathological inclination
to place ourselves at the center of everything, and to fancy ourselves
far more important than we are. From a cosmic standpoint, there
must be something irrepressibly hilarious about *Homo sapiens*.
Most of the time we behave as though the world exists only for our
sake; we think of everything in terms of our own needs, concerns,
and interests. Not only do we appropriate other species—we devour
them. We don't just use the planet, we abuse it, voiding it of life and
filling it with trash. Out of greed or stupidity or both, we have subjected the natural world to such savagery that we may well have
damaged it beyond repair. We are as a rule indifferent to the

suffering of others, and incapable of relating meaningfully to them. Far from loving our neighbors, we exploit, mock, or resent them, when we don't simply ignore them.

What makes our situation particularly ludicrous is that, within the bigger picture, we are utterly insignificant creatures. Lilliputian tyrants. The smallest stone we pick up randomly from a riverbed has long preceded us, and will outlast us. We are no grander than the rest of the world; in fact, we are less than most things.

The good news is that there may be a cure for this condition. The failure of the plane's engine, of our car's braking system, or of the elevator's, can shatter us so thoroughly that, should we survive the experience, we will find ourselves transformed. What defines our changed existence is a new humility: failure has humbled us, and healing can come from there. The word "humility" has moral connotations, but rather than a virtue in the narrow sense, humility involves a certain type of insertion into the world, and a distinct way of experiencing the human condition. Humility is no ordinary virtue, as Iris Murdoch reminds us; it is "one of the most difficult and central of all virtues."[78]

In "The Sovereignty of Good," Murdoch offers what may be the best definition of humility, describing it as "selfless respect for reality."[79] Ordinarily, she thinks, we misrepresent reality because we have an oversized conception of our place within it; our "picture of ourselves has become too grand," and as a result we have lost "the vision of a reality separate from ourselves."[80] This misrepresentation harms *us* more than anything else. If we don't do anything to correct it, we will end up cut off from the world, inhabiting a reality of our own making. Humility offers us such a correction.

Some of the most endearing characters in Yasujirō Ozu's films are martyrs of humility. They would rather waste their lives than assert themselves. The greatness of the Japanese director's art, however, is that it not only depicts humility; it embodies and performs it. Thanks to his use of low camera angles, Ozu gives us access to another side of things, to their lowly dimension, which we—self-centered as we are—normally miss. This is the method of humility itself.

Just as in Ozu's films, where low camera angles bring forth a surprisingly rich face of the world, a humble position allows us to access a layer of reality that we don't ordinarily see. That's because our self-assertive drive places a screen between us and the world, and what we end up seeing is not the world itself, but our own fantasies of self-assertion—mere projections of power. It is only through humility, the opposite of self-assertion, that we can tear this screen apart and glimpse things as they are.

More than a form of behavior, then, humility should be seen as a form of knowledge. No wonder mystics and philosophers of different stripes have connected humility to a vision of truth. Purifying though it may be as a practice, this line goes, humility should be sought not for its own sake, but for the higher good it leads to. Bernard of Clairvaux likens humility to a ladder: you climb up it, one rung at a time (twelve in all), until you reach "the highest summit of humility" (*summae humilitatis*).[81] That's when you've finally found truth, for the sake of which you've done all the climbing. In his own words: "The way is humility, the goal is truth. The first is the labor, the second the reward."[82] Following in the same tradition, André Comte-Sponville defines humility as "loving truth more than oneself."[83]

There is something unique about the truth that humility gives us access to. It's not just that we acquire a better, more "truthful" understanding of how things are, even if that's no small feat. Something important is happening *to us* on the way there: we are being transformed as we climb the ladder and take in the view. When the humble reach the top, they find themselves possessed of a renewed sense of self—a reformed self. For those who happen to be believers, this is an epiphany of redemption: "Therein lies the greatness of the humble," writes Comte-Sponville, "who penetrate the depths of their pettiness, misery, and insignificance—until they reach that place where there is only nothingness, a nothingness that is everything."[84]

A Disappearing Act

As she entered the airy, light-flooded room, Simone remarked, "What a beautiful room in which to die." And it was in that very room that she did die, just a week later, on August 24, 1943. Not that she had the gift of prophecy, splendidly gifted though she otherwise was. But she had a hand in her death. The coroner's report concluded that the "deceased did kill and slay herself by refusing to eat whilst the balance of her mind was disturbed."[85] Technically true, but far from the whole truth. As often happens in such cases, the document conceals more than it reveals. Refusing to eat was something Simone Weil had been doing all her life, not just in these final days. She had lived off self-starvation—and thrived. As for her mind, while of an unusual cut, it was one of the finest of her time. It was not her mind that was out of balance; it was the world itself. Not just because of the war, but because, as Weil herself would argue, it is in the nature of the created world to be out of joint.

Death, then, is not something that happened to her in that "beautiful," meadow-facing room; she had been dying most of her life. She practiced death as a matter of philosophical conviction and personal vocation. Much of Weil's life was infused by a longing for annihilation, which structured her biography and gave it meaning and direction. "I always believed," she had written not long before, "that the instant of death is the center and object of life. . . . I never desired any other good for myself."[86]

The Mud Cure

The labor of humility is a complex, dialectical process. Let me focus here on just three of its phases. In a first movement, humility involves acceptance of our cosmic insignificance. The word itself comes from the Latin *humilitas* (lowliness), derived in turn from *humus* (earth). The truly humble regard themselves as dust, or even less than that. The insight is as old as spiritual life itself. Adam, the first man in the Abrahamic tradition, not only was made out of dust, but had earth in his name (*adamah*). Humility is what God wanted to instill in Job when he asked him, "Where were you when I laid the foundation of the earth?" (Job 38:4). Job could not answer because dust doesn't talk, especially not to God. Bernard of Clairvaux intuited something essential about humility: the humble can reach heavenly heights precisely because they lower themselves so drastically.

When the Stoics recommended "the view from above" as a form of philosophical therapy, what they meant was that one should embrace utter humility. To see yourself from above is to realize your insignificance on a large, cosmic scale. That's also what Lady Philosophy, in *The Consolation of Philosophy*, sought to teach a terrified Boethius waiting execution in his prison cell. Or what, more recently, Carl Sagan popularized so well. "Our posturings, our imagined self-importance, the delusion that we have some privileged position in the Universe," he writes in *Pale Blue Dot*, take a different meaning if we just look at the earth from some remote point in space.[87] Taking "the view from above" is the opposite of arrogance: it is to place ourselves within the bigger picture so as to understand how insignificant we truly are. Seen from such a distance, we are nothing but *humus*, if that. At its most fundamental, to be humble is to embody, in our dealings with the world and others, the insight that we are closer to nothingness than to anything else.

Embracing our cosmic insignificance is the zero-degree of our existence. At this stage, shattered by failure and overwhelmed by precariousness, we rightly feel crushed, flattened, reduced to dust. Humility, thus, places us where we belong. We are reduced to our true condition: next-to-nothingness. Yet this is no small feat: for along with losing our self-importance, we manage to get rid of the combination of self-deception and self-flattery that usually keeps us hidden from ourselves. The humble, although they are at the very bottom, are the ones who will make progress. "The humble man," writes Murdoch, "because he sees himself as nothing, can see other things as they are." He is the kind of person "most likely of all to become good."[88]

In a second movement, we come to the realization that, thanks to our being brought down to earth, we find ourselves in a better position: we are on firm ground. Granted, we have been crushed and defeated, but then we underwent a rebirth of sorts, and we can again stand on our own two feet. We also realize that there is no degradation at this stage, for, by embracing our cosmic insignificance, we are true to ourselves. We may be poor, but we are honest. And that's the best place to start: wherever we go from here, it will be a worthwhile journey. There is nothing healthier, for minds so frequently pulled up into the air by the force of their own fantasies, than to be drawn back down to earth once in a while. Hardened dreamers undertaking the mud cure are in for a feast. If the first stage, involving a crushing experience of failure, was traumatic, this one is rather serene. We are contemplators now, biding our time and enjoying the view. But don't be deceived: the ultimate lowliness can take us to new heights of insight.

The third movement is expansive. Having lowered an anchor into the world, and regained our existential balance, we can move on to other, bigger things. The dreams now have the necessary ballast to be dreamt properly. At this stage, humility is no longer an impediment, but an enhancement of action, should we so desire. There is nothing more daring than the act of the humble.

Humility is the opposite of humiliation—that's the chief lesson of this stage. There is nothing demeaning or inglorious about humility; on the contrary, it is rejuvenating, enriching, emboldening. Humiliation relies on the exercise of raw, external power; humility is all inner strength. Humiliation involves coarseness of mind (a truly intelligent person doesn't humiliate others), while humility is itself a form of intelligence. Whether aware of it or not, the one who humiliates is a reject. Humiliation is often born out of frustration. In contrast, humility is all about inwardness and intimacy. The humble know from within—they see everything, understand everything, forgive everything—and that places them in a position of significant strength. Humiliation exhausts itself in the act, and those who perform it usually reveal their impotence. Humility grows and thrives with practice, transforming everything around it in the process. True humility, writes the rabbi Jonathan Sacks, "is one of the most expansive and life-enhancing of all virtues." What it involves is not "undervaluing yourself," but an "openness to life's grandeur" and a "willingness to be surprised, uplifted, by goodness."[89] It is written that the meek shall inherit the earth.

Humility in response to the experience of failure is a promise of healing. Properly digested, then, failure offers us a medicine against arrogance and hubris. Against the *umbilicus mundi* syndrome— our debilitating tendency to imagine ourselves at the center of the world. It can heal us, should we care for a cure.

Endura

In Catharism there was a form of ritual death—*endura,* it was called—which consisted of self-starvation.[90] Cathar believers who embarked on it stopped eating so that they could separate themselves from the world of matter. By starving the body, the soul was to be purified, which would allow it to join the true, hidden God. The *endura,* writes the historian Le Roy Ladurie, was meant as "a purely religious act, designed to ensure salvation."[91] Simone Weil may have found out about *endura* relatively late in life, but she had been rehearsing the practice for most of her existence. A sympathetic, yet puzzled biographer speaks of her typical diet "based primarily on starvation."[92] What happened during the last months of her existence was not an accident, but the crowning performance of a lifelong project.

Weil's *endura,* like the Cathars', was not just a moment in the history of the body: it was a metaphysical act, a carefully planned effort to relocate from one order of existence into another. Just like the Cathars, Weil articulates a philosophical justification for her exit along largely Gnostic lines. Given the little she knew of Gnosticism, the commonalities are uncanny.[93] The grand scenario is pretty much the same: this world (a failed creation) came into existence somehow, but it doesn't really represent the true God; we find ourselves entangled in the thickness of matter, yet we sense this is not our real homeland; we are born with an urge to leave the place, which will guide our efforts to escape; finding our way back is a redemptive process that takes superior knowledge (*gnosis*).

God, writes Weil in her *Notebooks*, "abandons our whole entire being—flesh, blood, sensibility, intelligence, love—to the pitiless necessity of matter and the cruelty of the devil." Yet God makes an exception for "the eternal and supernatural part of the soul" (the "divine spark" of the Gnostics), which can lead us back to our primordial source.[94] A passage like this could have come from any Gnostic author of old:

> The Creation is an abandonment. In creating what is other than Himself, God necessarily abandoned it. He only keeps under his care the part of Creation which is Himself—the uncreated part of every creature. That is the life, the Light, the Word; it is the presence here below of God's only Son.[95]

The key phrase here is "the uncreated part of every creature." This is what, in Weil's view, constitutes the connection to our homeland, even as we spend our lives in exile. Just as in Gnosticism, we may be forced to live in a remote place, but we still preserve some memory, however vague, of where we have come from. This link allows us to move gradually toward light, even as we are entrapped in darkness. Weil maps out the journey from one point to the other: "Our sin consists in wanting to be, and our punishment is that we believe we possess being. Expiation consists in desiring to cease to be; and salvation consists for us in perceiving that we are not."[96] The journey doesn't just free us from the captivity of matter: it defines us.

In Weil's final years, especially in some of the essays that would comprise *Gravity and Grace,* she developed a mystical theology around the notion of "decreation." To "decreate" is to "make something created pass into the uncreated," thus bringing it closer to God. Decreation is the opposite of destruction, which is making "something created pass into nothingness."[97] A complicated potlatch game is thus forever being played between God and us. God makes the first move and creates us. Yet by doing so, God "renounces being everything." Our move, in response, should be to "renounce being something." That would be the right thing to do, for "we only possess what we renounce; what we do not renounce escapes from us."[98] God cannot do anything other than create us, yet we are ontological debtors, and should return the loan as soon as we can. "God gave me being in order that I should give it back to him," Weil observes.[99] Decreation is about giving back to God what is naturally his. In her *Notebooks,* Weil depicts the situation in unforgettable imagery:

> In relation to God, we are like a thief who has burgled the house of a kindly householder and been allowed to keep some of the gold. From the point of view of the lawful owner this gold is a gift; from the point of view of the burglar it is a theft. . . . It is the same with our existence. We have stolen a little of God's being to make it ours.[100]

Decreation is more than returning a favor in our game with God. It involves, on the one hand, restoring a fundamental balance between two regimes of existence: to "undo the creature in us" is to "re-establish order."[101] By giving God back what is properly his, we can bring our small contribution to the great restoration. In strictly human terms, on the other hand, an act of decreation is the greatest possible favor we can do for *ourselves.* Just being doesn't mean anything—it all depends on what we do with it. In Weil's view, we realize ourselves, paradoxically, only when we manage to withdraw from being and turn ourselves into transparent vessels of God. "I can easily imagine that God loves that perspective of creation which can only be seen from the point where I am. But I act as a screen. I must withdraw so that he may see it."[102] What higher good can one aspire to in this life than to make room for God himself? The less we are, the more and the worthier.

Hence the nihilist's prayer: "May God grant that I become nothing. In so far as I become nothing, God loves himself through me."[103] In her *Notebooks* we come across a more detailed version of the prayer, which makes for hair-raising reading:

> Father, in the name of Christ, grant me this. That I may be unable to will any bodily movement, or even attempt at movement, like a total paralytic. That I may be incapable of receiving any sensation, like someone who is completely blind, deaf and deprived of all the senses. That I may be unable to make the slightest connection between two thoughts, even the simplest, like one of those total idiots who not only cannot count or read but have never even learned to speak. That I may be insensible to every kind of grief and joy, and incapable of any love for any being or thing, and not even for myself, like old people in the last stage of decrepitude.[104]

But how does decreation work in practice? Weil has some answers, though they are oblique and have to be inferred from her biography. There is a sense in which her fundamental clumsiness can be related to her project of decreation. When your embodiment is a dubious affair, and your experience of the world around you a painful reminder that you don't belong, you may well start plotting a way out. Indeed, the fundamental mismatch that you discover in yourself as you experience your clumsiness may force you to see not just your personal situation, but the human condition itself in a new light.

Where some might be tempted to yearn for a path free of hardship and pain, Weil came to the conclusion that only affliction (crippling physical pain doubled by social degradation) can best show us the way back. "It is in affliction itself that the splendor of God's mercy shines, from its very depths, in the heart of its inconsolable bitterness," she writes in *Waiting for God*. Affliction is a helping hand God extends to us from an infinite distance, "a marvel of divine technique."[105] Weil benefited aplenty from that marvel. In 1942, barely thirty-three years old, she could say, "I am an instrument already rotten. I am too worn out."[106]

Weil badly wanted out, and thought she had gained her right to exit. In the final months of her life, her considerable physical suffering was matched by an acute sense of personal failure. In May 1942, she and her family managed to leave France for the United States. Yet almost as soon as she arrived in New York City, unable to adjust and devoured by guilt (the same old pattern: others were suffering while she was safe), she started making plans to return to Europe. In November, with great efforts and even greater hopes, Weil sailed to England, only to find out that her well-meaning, yet perfectly utopian projects (she wanted to be parachuted into France, and given a suicide mission behind enemy lines) were dismissed by the leaders of the French resistance in London. Charles de Gaulle thought her crazy (*"Mais, elle est folle!"* he famously burst out).

That's why, while those final months were productive intellectually and spiritually decisive, she was eaten up by an overwhelming feeling of uselessness. By the time tuberculosis set in, her life was already in shambles. She confessed in a letter, "I am finished, broken, beyond all possibility of mending, and that independent of Koch's bacilli. The latter have only taken advantage of my lack of resistance and, of course, are busy demolishing it a little further." She seemed ready to part ways with this world. To someone who was in the hospital with her at the time, she admitted as much: "You are like me, a badly cut-off piece of God. But I will no longer be cut off; I will be united and reattached."[107]

The next logical step was to stop eating, just as the Cathars did during *endura*. The more we feed ourselves off the flesh of the world, the more we fatten it. And, conversely, by no longer devouring the world, we come closer to God. Weil seems to have believed that if she stopped engaging with the material world, it would somehow collapse under the weight of its own irrelevance. Such thinking was popular among the Cathars, of whom Weil became one of the most receptive latter-day adherents. By taking too much care of our bodies, we prove ourselves spiritually misguided, she thought, like any good Cathar. The matter of the world, while perishable, projects an illusion of endurance. "Hunger (thirst, etc.) and all carnal desire is an orientation of the body towards the future. The whole carnal part of our soul is oriented towards the future," Weil writes in her *Notebooks*. "The life of the flesh is oriented towards the future. Concupiscence is life itself." To take too much care of our flesh is to keep feeding this dangerous illusion. Death puts things right because it "freezes" the future. And when we stop eating, we start dying: "Privation is a distant likeness of death."[108] In hunger we encounter the "uncreated" in us. The more we fast, the more we "decreate" ourselves.

There is also, Weil thinks, an unpardonable degree of arrogance in our feeding ourselves, incessantly, off the world around us. "It is the pride of the flesh to believe that it draws its life from itself," she writes. "Hunger and thirst oblige it to feel its dependence on what is outside."[109] We can cure ourselves of this dependence by embracing the most humbling of all human experiences—death. "Total humility," Weil writes, "means consent to death, which turns us into inert nothingness."[110] Death is what gives one's life structure and texture and closure. It's the moment of truth in anyone's existence: "Truth is on the side of death."[111] Everything important is on its side. "Death is the most precious thing which has been given to man," Weil wrote in *Gravity and Grace*. "That is why the supreme impiety is to make bad use of it. To die amiss."[112]

As Simone Weil lay dying in Ashford, Kent, a Mrs. Rosin, an acquaintance, visited from London. She was to witness her last moments. Simone was "very lucid and remained so until the end," Mrs. Rosin later remembered. "She was also very beautiful, ethereal, transparent. Everything material seemed destroyed in her."[113] It is unlikely that Mrs. Rosin, a simple soul, would have known anything about her friend's philosophizing on decreation and death as truth and liberation. That makes her testimony all the more remarkable.

All her life Simone Weil had been afraid of failing in her death, of "dying amiss." "While still a child she had resolutely determined to make something out of her life," Simone Pétrement recalled, and "she feared above all to fail or 'waste' her death."[114] Judging by this witness's testimony, she didn't. How could she?

In the Unsettler's Hands

Life, again, has a habit of settling down and falling into patterns. Even our most spontaneous and creative acts can end up in routine. The hottest, most fluid lava becomes stone. That's both unavoidable and fine. We would not get anywhere if we didn't develop habits and routines, which help us better channel our efforts and make our passing through the world a little less stressful. Yet if there is too much routine in our lives and too little to unsettle us, we end up dead inside. And death in life is the worst kind of death there is because of its monstrosity: it's neither death nor life. A human existence that is too channeled and routinized is not just impoverished, it is a positively bad life. You don't lead such a life, it leads you—nowhere.

That's why we badly need someone like Simone Weil. Not so much to show us how to exit existence (her disappearing act was uniquely hers), but to teach us how to live well—spiritually well:

that is, how to break the deadening patterns with which life continuously entangles us. We need Weil to show us how to keep our souls alert by living a more demanding rather than an easier life—by taking risks and leaps of faith and perilous steps, rather than settling down into comfortable routines. She was harsh with herself, as we should all be if we are to make spiritual progress. Such harshness is nothing but a superior form of kindness.

Weil is a great unsettler in the tradition of Augustine, Pascal, Kierkegaard, Nietzsche, and Cioran. Her story illustrates an ancient wisdom we seem to have forgotten: to save your life you have to be ready, at any given moment, to part with it. Face the abyss, look it in the eyes, and behave as if this were the most natural thing in the world. It's precisely at such moments, in that state of readiness, and thanks to the radical humility it brings forth, that you live to the highest degree.

2

THE RUINS OF
POLITICAL FAILURE

Failure, it's worth repeating, is a Dantesque, circular affair. Just as the grain of wheat has to pass through the millstones if it is to turn into something more refined, so we have to go through several circles of failure, each one of which will shake us properly and leave us badly wounded, but also make us a little sharper. All that pressing and grinding will not be in vain.

The first circle of failure involves our interactions with the world around us. Much though we way wish otherwise, we will be disappointed by our imperfections and confronted by our finitude as we navigate through a world where things are failing, in one way or another. At some level, however, the things that surround us are of limited concern. Their failure certainly affects us, but they remain foreign to who we are. No matter how often I use my car, however much I may rely on it in daily life, it will always remain fundamentally alien to me. Even some mechanical device that doctors place inside my body, such as a pacemaker, which I carry with me at all times and on which my life depends, remains external to who I am. Things and humans belong to different domains of existence, however much they mix and mingle.

The next circle of failure brings us into territory that is less foreign and more intimate: the *polis*. As social animals, we all live in a community, or "republic"—in the broad and original sense of the term (*respublica*), meaning "public thing." Compared with physical things, which remain external, the public ones cut into our lives and shape us more decisively. *Res publicae* are the countless ties that, visibly and invisibly, relate us to one another, thus forming a new and massive body—the body politic—amid whose entrails we find ourselves entangled.

Whether we like it or not, to be human is to be with others, to be involved in collective pursuits, and to invest a good part of ourselves in them. And since failure is essential to the human experience, being with others is often just another form of failing—sometimes tolerably, sometimes catastrophically, and always revealingly. For when this togetherness comes tumbling down and catches us amid the ruins, in that experience of grief and undoing we discover something defining about ourselves. The collapse leaves us shattered and wounded, but also with a better understanding of our limits, of what we can and especially what we *cannot* do together. We may never come out alive from the ruins, but if we do, we emerge as more refined material. In that respect, even the most catastrophic of political failures can have therapeutic value. That's how failure works, after all: the serpent's venom is both poison and medicine.

The Eroticism of Crowds

The film may be about one of the most singular individuals in recent history, but we rarely see him by himself. If there is something that singles him out, it is the fluid relationship he has with those around him. There he is, in one shot, mingling with the mass of people—shaking hands, chatting, smiling, faking empathy with a seasoned actor's skill. In another, he separates himself from the crowd, slowly emerging from the public like some natural secretion. He has achieved some degree of stature, and yet, whatever he is now, he owes to the relationship he has with the human mass around him. Later on, we see them—the crowd and him—together again, but the relationship is different: he is at the podium, in an elevated position, energetically addressing the people down below.

"Addressing" may not be the right word. To address someone is to engage in some form of communication conducted along rational lines. But what the speaker is doing to these people is anything but rational: he is not speaking to them, lecturing them, or even preaching. He is seducing them. The relationship is markedly erotic: what the crowd experiences in this man's hands is mindless, boundless, collective *jouissance*. They—the screwer and the screwed—have now become one, caught in an act of mystic-political copulation. The speaker is breathing heavily, and the crowd seems to be panting. He acts like a great, intuitive lover, always anticipating what the other wants, and offering them just that. And the crowd is not disappointed: it seems to be receiving a first-class political orgasm. They scream together, sweat together, and come together. The man's pronouncements may be empty, nonsensical even, but that matters little. Every single one of his utterings brings the aroused mass to new heights of pleasure.

By all indications, the pleasure is mutual. The exercise delights the speaker, too. Nothing is more of an aphrodisiac than power itself. Should he know that venerable Sicilian saying, he would gladly concur: *Cummannari è megghiu 'ca futtiri* (To lead is better than to screw). But most likely he doesn't—there is so much he doesn't know, after all. Just as he has reached the climax, the speaker must be realizing that he can now do *anything* he wants with his enraptured listeners: they will submit, with sweet abandon, to his most crazed fancies.

Something important is happening to these people. As they surrender themselves to the speaker's verbal priapism, they feel as though their lives have acquired meaning at last. What he gives them may be nothing but worn-out phrases, flat-out lies, ludicrous conspiracies, yet coming as they do from someone who has offered them such an intense emotional experience, they exude a strange coherence and somehow manage to make narrative sense—albeit in a way they wouldn't be able to explain. Thanks to him, there is now a promise of meaningfulness in these people's lives, and they would do anything to fulfill that promise. If the speaker tells them the earth is flat, they will smash anyone who dares say otherwise. Indeed, within a decade, many of these people will kill and be killed because of this man's words.

Adolf Hitler was certainly a histrionic figure, but his audience, captured on film in Leni Riefenstahl's *Triumph of the Will*, are real people experiencing genuine pleasure. The film is a documentary recording the 1934 Congress of the Nazi Party, in Nuremberg, attended by more than seven hundred thousand people. Since Riefenstahl was a meticulous director, the documentary involved much staging and careful planning, but those who appear on screen are not actors. They are housewives and factory workers, high schoolers and university students, farmers and professionals. And this being intellectual Germany, we should suspect that there must have been many decently educated individuals among the enthusiasts gathered in Nuremberg. It wasn't just that the country was *das Land der Dichter und Denker* (the land of poets and thinkers); the general population of Germany was among the most educated in the world. Simone Weil had visited Germany not long before and was impressed. The German working class, from which many of Hitler's supporters came, was one of the most politically advanced at the time. When Karl Marx envisioned a proletarian revolution almost a century before, it was the German proletariat he primarily had in mind.

At the same time, you could hardly find a more complete nohoper, by German standards, than the clownish fellow addressing these people. Hitler was ignorant and incompetent, uneducated and unpolished, when not plainly vulgar. Discerning people in Germany regarded him as a "half-insane rascal," a "bigmouth," and a "nowhere fool."[1] He had a poor work ethic, no clear profession, and no accomplishments in any field. He was the kind of do-nothing

Germans tend to laugh most heartily about. Here's Thomas Mann: "The fellow is a catastrophe . . . a man ten times a failure, extremely lazy, incapable of steady work; a man who has spent long periods in institutions; a disappointed bohemian artist; a total good-for-nothing."[2] *Nothing* came to Karl Kraus's mind when he thought of Hitler. Charlie Chaplin could play him so easily, and so memorably, in *The Great Dictator* precisely because he had a history of playing clownish figures. How was it, then, that such sophisticated citizenry could fall so badly for such a bad joke?

A half century earlier, Fyodor Dostoevsky had hinted at a possible answer in *The Brothers Karamazov*. His Grand Inquisitor observes, long before Viktor Frankl famously made the same point, that more than anything else—more even than food or shelter—humans need *meaning*. We are nothing without it. We will patiently endure the worst tortures, the deepest humiliations, so long as we know *why* we are going through all that. The "mystery of man's being is not only in living, but in what one lives for," says the Grand Inquisitor. "Without a firm idea of what he lives for, man will not consent to live and will sooner destroy himself than remain on earth, even if there is bread all around him."[3]

This explains why religion has played such a vital part in any human society: it gives people a clear sense of meaning. One of religion's fundamental functions lies in the hermeneutics that comes with it: no matter how badly you suffer, it helps you find something meaningful in your suffering. And that will make you not only accept the pain, but even ask for more. Such meaning is never abstract, but *embodied:* it's what makes people feel and move and act. John Gray speaks of religion as "an attempt to find meaning in events, not a theory that tries to explain the universe."[4] Few would put their lives on the line for a scientific theory or a philosophical idea, but those who have died for their faith are beyond counting.

Since what distinguishes all mature religions is their inexhaustible capacity to bring meaning into people's lives, it has always been tempting for the political to steal as much as it can from the religious: rituals, gestures, symbols, images, and language. By taking on some of religion's hermeneutic functions, political power hopes to consolidate its own prestige, authority, and control. When, as has been the case in the West for a while now, the religious begins to lose its relevance, the political does not hesitate to step in and instantiate itself as a major source of meaning in people's lives. That's how politics itself becomes a form of religion—"political religion," as it has been called.[5] And that spells serious trouble. With God in the shadows, people will flock to the charismatic politician who gives them even an illusion of meaning. They will swallow up anything from him, even the silliest bilge, and imagine him a savior.

This is precisely what we see in *Triumph of the Will*. Riefenstahl's Hitler is no ordinary human being: his arrival in Nuremberg by airplane, in the film's opening scene, is meant to suggest the image of a divine being's slow descent to earth. Here he is, coming down in full glory, the mustached messiah, redeemer of the German race. Hitler's histrionic streak (he practiced prodigiously in front of the mirror, and once described himself as "the greatest actor in Europe"[6]) must have come in handy. It helped him not only to keep up the pretense, but to solidify it. The complex ritual that follows—the crowd of worshippers, the screams, the pagan orgy—only cements the impression cunningly planted by the opening scene. It is a remarkable testimony, both to the power of art to transfigure reality and to the artist's political blindness, that Riefenstahl manages to transform a mediocre, kitschy Austrian comedian into such an otherworldly apparition.

We shouldn't blame Riefenstahl too much, though. Her audience also had a hand in the affair. For Hitler didn't materialize out of thin air: he was first born in the hearts of many Germans, out of their need for certainty in that most uncertain of ages. Longing for meaning, and praying for its coming, the Germans had unwittingly conjured up this fake messiah in their minds. Then, to everyone's misfortune, their prayers were answered. As they opened their eyes, they saw not the little fellow from Linz, but a heavenly figure who had come to save them from meaninglessness. Hitler's shallowness and colossal narcissism, far from undermining their faith in him, made it even stronger.

Such is the power of faith—even when it is misplaced. People "who do not have a good religion," observed Milton Mayer, "will have a bad one." They just cannot do without it. "They will have a religion; they will have something to believe in."[7]

"A Very Disappointed Man"

As he lay dying, failure stared him in the face. With mocking eyes, a slippery manner, and an unmistakable air of complicity, failure was there, right behind his assassin. Nathuram Godse may have pulled the trigger, but it was failure that made it so easy for him to kill Mohandas Gandhi.[8] It was failure, too, that made Gandhi so vulnerable, turned him into a sacrificial victim, and then finished him off. Once the bullet's job was done, the perceptive observer could have seen failure slowly drawing closer, and shutting the Mahatma's eyes. Perhaps even dropping a tear of compassion. That's how Gandhi died, on January 30, 1948, by a fanatic's hand and in failure's shadow.

That's also how Gandhi lived: in the long shadow of failure. His final, fatal encounter with it must not have surprised him. If anything, he would have been surprised had failure *not* showed up. In the summer of 1947, while trying to address the communal violence that had engulfed parts of the country, Gandhi confessed to a close associate, the anthropologist Nirmal Kumar Bose, "I don't want to die a failure. . . . But it may be that I am a failure. . . . I am groping for light, but I am surrounded by darkness."[9] Things didn't get any clearer after that. On January 30, 1948, hours before his assassination, he admitted to an American journalist, "I can no longer live in darkness and madness. I cannot continue."[10]

And for good reason. The India Gandhi had envisioned was nowhere in sight, even though the British had left and the country had been granted independence. The dream of a great India had turned into the nightmare of a country divided against itself—"vivisected" was the word he used—partitioned into two new political entities containing myriads of squabbling Indias, each one angrier and unhappier than the next. This unleashed mass violence of catastrophic proportions, with millions of people killed or wounded, and even more displaced. The word "holocaust" would be used, more than once, to describe what happened in the aftermath of Partition. For decades Gandhi had been trying to teach Indians the superiority of nonviolent resistance—*satyagraha*—over the use of brute force. Now it looked as though he had only managed to stir up their interest in the latter.

For a man who had made nonviolence (*ahimsa*) the centerpiece of his philosophy, political program, and public career, such an outcome could not have been but a resounding failure. The irony must not have been lost on Gandhi. Earlier in his career, one of his concerns had been that Indians lacked a "fighting spirit." Foreigners (Afghans, Mughals, British) could rule India for centuries for the simple reason that Indians had allowed them to do so. Indians were too "soft," the complaint went. "You cannot teach non-violence to a man who cannot kill," Gandhi used to say.[11] Now, many seemed determined to prove him wrong: not only *could* they kill, they did so with gusto. The piles of uncollected corpses Gandhi could see all around him in the streets of Calcutta (Kolkata), and elsewhere, offered empirical proof.

India had gained its longed-for independence, but it had lost so much in the process that some started to wonder if the price was too steep. For Gandhi, India's independence was not *swaraj* (self-rule) as he had understood the notion, and he could see no role for himself within it. When, on August 15, 1947, India's political elites gathered in New Delhi to celebrate the event, he was conspicuously absent. He had little to celebrate. Just a few days before, an article in the *Times of India* offered a glimpse of Gandhi on the brink of independence. It is a fine study in failure:

> Mr. Gandhi today is a very disappointed man indeed. He has lived to see his followers transgress his dearest doctrines; his countrymen have indulged in a bloody and inhuman fratricide war; non-violence, khadi and many other of his principles have been swept away by the swift current of politics. Disillusioned and disappointed, he is today perhaps the only steadfast exponent of what is understood as Gandhism.[12]

Sometimes it seemed as if he was not even that. At one point during the independence negotiations with the British viceroy, in August 1946, an exasperated Gandhi reportedly slapped the table and thundered, "If India is to have her bloodbath, let her have it."[13] Little did he know how vast that bloodbath would be, or that he himself would be washed away by it.

As the violence unfolded, there were omens. While visiting Amritsar, he was startled to hear, "Go back, Gandhi!" instead of the usually enthusiastic welcome. For India's Muslims, he was a Hindu, despite all his attempts at ecumenism. To many Hindus, he was a traitor, because of his ecumenism. For most of India, during those bloody days, he was largely irrelevant.

And he knew it. "If India has no more use for nonviolence, can she have any for me?" he wondered.[14] It turned out he was right: he had become expendable. More and more frequently, in the months before January 1948, mobs would shout, *"Gandhi mordabad!"* (Death to Gandhi!). Gandhi had always had a good feel for the crowds—for their changes of disposition, for the way they showed their love or hatred. He sensed the life of a crowd in the same intimate way a lover senses his beloved's body.[15] So he must have known what *Gandhi mordabad!* really meant: that his whole political program was in tatters. All those decades of intimacy had come to naught. Rarely had failure spoken more clearly amid so much chaos and confusion.

Judged by his own standards, Gandhi's life, while apparently well lived, seems badly spent. He didn't die in clashes with the police in South Africa, in the early stages of his political career, or while carrying the wounded during the Boer War; he didn't die during any of his repeated imprisonments, or while trying to pacify angry crowds, or challenging them, as he often came to do latterly. He didn't even die of starvation, much as he tried. He died the most ignoble of deaths—as brutal as it was ordinary. Gandhi was killed, stealthily and swiftly, by an assassin's bullet, as an animal is done away with in the slaughterhouse. The man certainly deserved a better death, which may explain failure's presence at the scene of the crime, and its complicit gaze, as it recorded his fall.

The Fragility of Democracy

But this can't be right, I hear you saying. Hitler was uniquely evil, and dictatorships are exceptional situations. People everywhere want to live free rather than under tyranny, don't they?

They certainly do. People have dreamed of living "in freedom and dignity," as they say, for almost as long as they have lived together. Democracy seems to be the image of decency itself. Its core idea is disarmingly simple: as members of a community, each of us should have an equal say in how we conduct the business of living together. "In democracy as it ought to be," Paul Woodruff observes in his history of Athenian democracy, "all adults are free to chime in, to join the conversation on how they should arrange their life together. And no one is left free to enjoy the unchecked power that leads to arrogance and abuse."[16] Can you think of anything more reasonable? But who says we are reasonable?

History—the only true guide we have on this matter—has shown us that true democracy is rare and fleeting. It flares up almost mysteriously in some fortunate place or another, and then fades out just as mysteriously. Genuine democracy is difficult to achieve and, once achieved, fragile. In the grand scheme of human events, it is the exception, not the rule.

And for good reason. Highly desirable and disarmingly simple as democracy is, it doesn't come to us as a matter of course. It is telling that, even as he tries to explain what the democratic ideal is, a historian of democracy feels the need to bring up "unchecked power," "arrogance," and "abuse." Fundamentally, humans are not predisposed to living democratically. One can even make the case that democracy is unnatural because it goes against our vital instincts and impulses. What is most natural to us, as to any living creature, is to seek to survive and reproduce. And for that purpose, we assert ourselves—selfishly, relentlessly, savagely—against others: we push them aside, step over them, overthrow them, even crush them if necessary. Whether we like it or not, this *libido dominandi* (the urge to rule) lies at the core of who we are. How we live and how we die, what we think and what we feel, the way we represent ourselves and the world around us—all are marked by our built-in thirst for power, the chief manifestation of our survival instinct. Nietzsche's philosophizing on the topic scandalizes us only because we recognize ourselves so thoroughly in it.

The urge to rule over others, even to annihilate them if need be, has defined *Homo sapiens*. We certainly collaborate with others, but in most instances only to assert ourselves more efficaciously. Like other animals, we seek collaboration not out of altruism, but to increase our chances of survival. Behind our well-mannered façade and social sophistication, we remain the same *Homo rapiens* that we were thousands of years ago. Civilization is only a mask, and a precarious one at that. Shake the modern human just a bit, and along with the mask, off will come all pretensions. What you will see is human nature in its naked state, governed by the animal force to stay alive. This force, observes Simone Weil, is "as pitiless to the man who possesses it, or thinks he does, as it is to its victims; the second it crushes, the first it intoxicates."[17] A few years after the victory of the Bolshevik Revolution, which was supposed to bring about the most advanced human society imaginable, Stalin confessed, with admirable frankness, "The greatest delight is to mark one's enemy, prepare everything, avenge oneself thoroughly, and then go to sleep."[18] One wonders whether the caveman was capable of such refined savagery.

If there is one place where our self-assertion is on full display, it is politics. In the *polis,* we betray our true nature more than anywhere else. We are not called "political animals" for nothing. Our political behavior should be studied by zoologists, not by social scientists. The "social organization of chimpanzees is almost too human to be true," writes primatologist Frans de Waal. "Entire passages of Machiavelli seem to be directly applicable to chimpanzee behavior."[19] It is the "unreasoning and unreasonable human nature," writes another zoologist, Konrad Lorenz, that pushes "two political parties or religions with amazingly similar programs of salvation to fight each other bitterly," just as it compels "an Alexander or a Napoleon to sacrifice millions of lives in his attempt to unite the world under his scepter."[20] World history, for the most part, is the story of excessively self-assertive political animals in search of various scepters. It doesn't help matters that, once such an animal has been enthroned, others are only too eager to submit to their whims. And what a sweet surrender! *The Triumph of the Will* gives us a glimpse of how the process works.

This is, roughly, the background against which the democratic idea emerges. No wonder that it is a losing battle. Genuine democracy doesn't make grand promises, nor does it seduce or charm. It only aspires to a certain measure of human dignity. Democracy is not erotic; compared to what happens in populist-authoritarian regimes, it is a rather frigid affair. Who in his right mind would choose the dull responsibilities of democracy over the instant gratification of a demagogue? Frigidity over boundless ecstasy? And yet, despite this, the democratic idea has come close to embodiment a few times in history—moments of grace when humanity managed to surprise itself. In its ideal form, democracy has not succeeded yet, but people have never stopped trying. It's one of the dreams that has kept history alive.

One thing that is needed for democracy to emerge is a strong sense of humility. A humility that is at once collective and personal, public and internalized, visionary yet true. The kind of humility that is comfortable in its own skin—one that, because it knows its worth and limits, can even laugh at itself. A humility that, having seen many an absurd thing and learned to tolerate it, has become wise and patient. To be a true democrat, in other words, is to understand that when it comes to the business of living together, you are no better and no smarter than the person next to you, and to act accordingly. The illiterate plumber and the Nobel Prize winner are on an equal footing in a real democracy: each of their votes has exactly the same weight. If they err—and, being human, they always do—their errors should not disqualify them, but bring them closer together. As Camus put it, democracy is "the social and political exercise of modesty."[21]

While nondemocratic regimes often claim perfection (they never tire of promising a "perfect society," "perfect social order," "perfect virtue," and whatnot), democracies posit fallibility at their core. "Democracy was born out of a reverent awareness of human folly," observes Woodruff.[22] To live democratically is to embrace imperfection, to deal in failure, and, in general, to entertain very few illusions about human society. Only such humility would make genuine democracy possible.[23] If democracy is so hard to attain in practice, it is because it is nearly impossible to produce this kind of humility on a large scale. Democracy fails when it doesn't make enough room for failure—when people can't help seeing themselves as better than they really are. Which is most of the time.

All the more reason to praise the ancient Athenians.[24] Somehow, they stumbled upon the intimate link between democracy and humility. When they came up with what turned out to be one of the most radical inventions in human history, *isonomia* (equality before the law), they knew they were going against some strong human instincts. Nonetheless, they determined that, since all male Athenian citizens were equally entitled to rule, and the number of ruling positions was limited, the most reasonable way to appoint public officials was by lot (*sortition*). Equality reveals itself in randomness. For those who established democracy in Athens, elections (in our sense of the word) would have struck at the heart of the democratic idea, for they would have allowed some people to assert themselves against others. Individual wealth, prestige, family influence, and titles counted for little in the newly democratic Athens: what mattered was Athenian citizenship. By traditional standards, the notion must have appeared outrageous. One can only imagine how Athens's old elites—the aristocrats and the wealthy, the well-connected and the well-bred—must have reacted.

The founders of Athenian democracy imagined just that. That's how they came up with another fundamental institution of their democracy: *ostracism*. When some of their fellow citizens were becoming a trifle too self-assertive, and their hunger for power was too conspicuous, the Athenians could vote them out of the city for a period of ten years by inscribing their names on bits of pottery (*ostraka*). This was an unusual punishment: the ostracized paid with exile not for something they had done, but for what they *might* do if left unchecked. Democracy, aware of its own fragility, could not afford to take risks, and chose preemptive action instead. Athenians knew that they were too flawed and weak to resist political seduction (their complicated affair with Alcibiades gave them ample proof of that), and they denied themselves the pleasure. Democracy, as a human construction, is of a vulnerable constitution— better not to put it to the test. Ostracism is the perfect example of a political institution designed with built-in failure.

This made politics in democratic Athens look like a curious social game: you had to be, at once, visible and invisible, present and absent. You were expected to show you were a good, concerned citizen, and yet doing so too ostentatiously could be your undoing, for it would come across as *hybris,* excessive self-assertion, bringing you the kind of notoriety no one really wanted in Athens. "The list of those ostracized read like an Athenian *Who's Who,*" quipped one scholar.[25]

The whole institutional arrangement points to the ultimate precariousness of Athens's democracy. Its founders seem to have believed that, once the citizens had agreed upon the rules of the democratic game, the rest would take care of itself. No transformation was needed in the people themselves; all they had to do was play by the rules. One example will suffice. To make it difficult, if not impossible, to bribe juries, democratic Athens operated with large numbers of jurors (another case of built-in failure). At Socrates's trial, there were 501 of them. It's unlikely that anyone could have tried, let alone succeeded, to corrupt them all. What the founders of the Athenian democracy failed to anticipate, however, was the possibility that the Athenians would *corrupt themselves* by letting themselves be deceived, becoming prey to demagogy, and eventually behaving like a mob. Outwardly, they respected the rules, and democracy seemed to work, and yet the whole thing started to rot inside. That Plato could not find anything good in democracy, seeing it as essentially mob rule, may have something to do with how his master ended.

When the Athenians killed Socrates, they acted perfectly democratically; by existing standards, the trial was flawless. Yet its outcome shows that democracy hadn't caused a significant transformation *within* the people of Athens. The change was only external: it had brought about a new political game in town, while the players remained fundamentally the same. Just making the Athenians formally equal before the law didn't change who they were. They remained the same self-assertive, power-hungry, revenge-driven political animals as before. It was just that, Athens being Athens, they practiced the bloody sport of politics behind a more respectable façade. *Isonomia* was a formal condition of democracy, and the Athenians failed to bring forth a new humanity with which to fill that form.

Paul Woodruff thinks that the shortcoming of Athenian democracy could have been addressed by significant access to education. The "great failure of Athenian democracy," he writes, was "its failure to extend access to education beyond the moneyed class."[26] Had the Athenians known better, they would have been better citizens, and their democracy would have been saved. Knowledge is virtue, according to this line of thought, and Socrates himself was one of its strongest advocates. In his footsteps, Woodruff sees education (*paideia*) as a profound, transformative experience that should make us better human beings. The self with which you leave school is different from the one with which you entered it. The assumption may be correct—education can indeed transform people. The question remains, however: Is it realistic to think, or even to hope, that there is a school in this world capable of effectuating, on a sufficiently large scale, such a radical transformation as to kill the arrogant, power-hungry animal that lies at the core of who we are?

Humbler Than the Dust

There is another reason why failure was at Gandhi's side on that January evening in 1948. They had a close relationship that went back decades. If there was something Gandhi knew intimately, better than he knew himself perhaps, it was failure. It had frequently been at his side. Whenever he had success—and the Mahatma was by some measures one of the most successful men of his time—failure would be there to belittle him and hold him down. When he failed—and, as with any great man, Gandhi's failures were many—this shadow stalker was also there: to pull him up and set him back on his feet, to shame him into action and self-reform. Just two years before his death, Gandhi admitted, "I can learn only by my mistakes. . . . I can learn only when I stumble and fall and feel the pain."[27] Gandhi was largely a self-taught man; he could dispense with fancy schooling and famous professors. But there was one teacher he could not do without, and it was failure.

In 1925, Gandhi, in his mid-fifties, started publishing (in Gujarati and English) an account of his life so far: *An Autobiography; or, The Story of My Experiments with Truth*. When the text reached South Africa, where he had spent most of his public career up to that point, a friend from Pretoria found it difficult to recognize Gandhi in his self-portrait. "I wished," she wrote to him, "you had not given us that picture of yourself. The Mr. Gandhi I have known is much nicer."[28]

Inadvertently perhaps, Gandhi's South African correspondent stumbled upon one of the key features of the Gandhian approach to life: settle for nothing but failure. Failure can be used as a technique for living. To lead a good life, you need to posit yourself as a site of perpetual disappointment: you start from the worst person you could possibly be, and then, gradually, build yourself up from there. By this method, your life acquires worthiness to the extent that you can extract it from failure. The more you fail, the better your chance to realize your worth.

The original Gujarati word for autobiography is *atmakatha*: the story of a soul. That's precisely what Gandhi offers in his book: a detailed account of how his "failed experiments with truth" over many decades shaped his soul, structured his self, and eventually made him who he was. A crucial issue here is, where does this journey start, exactly? To play it safe, Gandhi thought he should descend to the lowest rung he could possibly reach, and in doing so he sets quite a high standard. "The seeker after truth should be humbler than the dust," he writes. "The world crushes the dust under its feet, but the seeker after truth should so humble himself that even the dust could crush him. Only then, and not till then, will he have a glimpse of truth."[29]

In the introduction, Gandhi is quick to mention his "Himalayan blunders" and promises not to "conceal or understate any ugly things that must be told." He hopes to "acquaint the reader fully with all my faults and errors."[30] And Gandhi delivers. Nothing is left untold in his book. Everything—even the most embarrassing episode—is properly confessed, described in painful detail, and repented for. Lest there be any ambiguity, various chapter headings make Gandhi's judgment of himself abundantly clear. "A Tragedy" (two chapters, in fact) details his meat-eating experiment. "My Father's Death and My Double Shame" connects Eros and Thanatos in a particularly self-torturing and guilt-centered fashion. "A Himalayan Miscalculation" recalls the setback he experienced during one of his *satyagraha* campaigns. Just as other people would brag about their accomplishments, the Gandhi of the *Autobiography* seems to take pride in his errors, pitfalls, and shortcomings.

Even as a child Gandhi showed precocious signs of failure. It was, he writes, "with some difficulty that I got through the multiplication tables. . . . My intellect must have been sluggish, and my memory raw." For all his occasional scholastic promise, he "could only have been a mediocre student." The future charmer of crowds and breaker of empires was an excessively shy person; he avoided all company "lest anyone should poke fun."[31] And did I mention that he was a coward? According to the *Autobiography*, he was an outstanding one. Before he made war against the British Empire, Gandhi had to deal with a different kind of enemy:

> I used to be haunted by the fear of thieves, ghosts and serpents. I did not dare to stir out of doors at night. Darkness was a terror to me. It was almost impossible for me to sleep in the dark, as I would imagine ghosts coming from one direction, thieves from another and serpents from a third.[32]

Gandhi underwent an important personal transformation in London, where he studied for three years (from 1888 to 1891) to become a lawyer. But that doesn't mean his relationship to failure ended. If anything, the affair took on a new intensity. Upon his return to India, Gandhi embarked on a promising career as a "briefless barrister," first in Bombay (Mumbai) and then in his native Rajkot. His first case in court stands out for its eloquent brevity. A defendant had engaged the London-educated lawyer at the small causes court. Gandhi showed up, fancy lawyer's dress and all, ready to make a splash. Then the moment came when he had to cross-examine the plaintiff's witness. "I stood up, but my heart sank into my boots," he recalls.

> My head was reeling and I felt as though the whole court was doing likewise. I could think of no question to ask. The judge must have laughed, and the vakils no doubt enjoyed the spectacle. But I was past seeing anything. I sat down and told the agent that I could not conduct the case.[33]

In his private life, the Gandhi of the *Autobiography* was an impatient, even abusive husband. It took him decades to settle into a decent relationship with his wife, Kasturba. Before that, his main recipe for solving marital crises involved kicking Kasturba out of their marital home. He didn't fare much better as a father, either. The Mahatma may have been, metaphorically, the "father of India," but his actual parenting left much to be desired. "I did not prove an ideal father," he writes in what may have been an understatement. The world looked up to Gandhi as its teacher, and he may have taught it a thing or two. Yet, strangely enough, he failed to educate his own children: "It has been their, as also my, regret that I failed to ensure them enough literary training." Gandhi was not necessarily indifferent to his children's formal education, but he "certainly did not hesitate to sacrifice it" for what he thought was a higher purpose: his all-absorbing career in the service of others.[34] "Others" apparently did not include his own offspring.

The *Autobiography*'s inventory of failures is as extensive as it is refined. Gandhi could have called the book "The Story of My Experiments with Failure." It is meant not so much to give a faithful account of Gandhi's journey as to provide him with an answer to life's pressing questions: how to live with failure; how to make the most of it; how to turn failure into the source of a more meaningful life. There is no point in fleeing failure, he thinks; it will always catch up with you. Failure has the pervasiveness of water: nothing is safe from its reach, no one remains untouched. The Gandhi we see here is swimming in failure, and sometimes coming close to drowning.

Yet the space between nearly drowning and drowning itself, narrow though it may be, is more than enough. Almost drowning can be a formative experience, as enriching and transforming as it is life-threatening. As you are gasping for air, you find yourself touching the limits of your earthly existence—you can feel it in your lungs. Yet sometimes this experience is exactly what you need to wake up: morally, spiritually, existentially.

Gandhi's "experiments with truth" are public confessions of failure, but that is precisely the point of his whole project. If you are to find your footing, you have to fail first—fail often and fail greatly. And if all that failing doesn't crush you, then you stand a chance. A chance not to succeed, but to reach self-realization, which for Gandhi was the one thing worth living for. Failure, then, is not to be passed over in silence, sugarcoated or otherwise dismissed. It must be confronted in its all ugliness. Hence the failure therapy Gandhi undertakes in the *Autobiography*.

Like Saint Augustine's *Confessions,* or Rousseau's, Gandhi's book is performative self-writing at its cruelest—more self-flagellation than literature. No fall is too insignificant, no shame too embarrassing to admit. Gandhi uses the pen to act upon himself—to inflict pain, to shame himself, to do penance. He was a believer in the regenerative powers of confession and frequently recommended it to others. Whether his falls were great or small, his blunders "Himalayan" or otherwise, his harshness with himself had a clear purpose: self-reform. One may be forgiving with others, but never with oneself. "Saints should always be judged guilty until they are proved innocent," observed George Orwell in his "Reflections on

Gandhi."[35] Few followed Orwell's advice more enthusiastically than Gandhi himself.

"I have always held," he writes toward the end of the *Autobiography,* that "it is only when one sees one's own mistakes with a convex lens, and does just the reverse in the case of others, that one is able to arrive at a just relative estimate of the two."[36] Yet when you proclaim that your life is your message, as Gandhi did, you place yourself in the most difficult of positions: you lay yourself bare, in all your nakedness, for all to judge. And you are stuck. You have nowhere to go, for you've just denied yourself the right to privacy. As a contemporary noted, "Gandhiji *had no private life,* as we Westerners understand the expression."[37] If your message is to make any sense, you have to articulate it in its entirety. To say that "my life is my message" is to acknowledge at some level that your life is no longer yours.

And here is where the true difficulties begin. For "my life is my message" is an open invitation for others to stare at you, to size you up and assess you as mercilessly as they see fit. The Gandhi of the *Autobiography* may be harsh with himself, but since he is doing the narration, he still has control over the narrative; he can frame the story in this way or that, direct the reader's gaze, distract or keep us busy. There is no such thing as an innocent narrator. Yet the life you narrate and the life others see unfolding are two different lives. The failure you admit to, however openly and contritely, and the failure others will find in you are distinct. In this respect, to his critics and even to his followers, Gandhi has proven to be a gift that keeps on giving. There was more and deeper failure in Gandhi than he himself was ready to admit or able to narrate.

A Case of Misplaced Faith

But all of that is ancient history, you may object. We don't live in Socrates's Athens, but in a very different world. Yes, our world is quite different from Socrates's. But if anything, this makes our situation worse.

Twenty-five centuries after Socrates's death by democracy, we seem to have learned at last that conversions through humanist education on a large scale are next to impossible. *Paideia* (defined as a rigorous and comprehensive training in the liberal arts) is one of the finest things one can experience in life, and does involve a radical transformation when done properly. "The whole secret of the teacher's force," wrote Emerson, "lies in the conviction that men are convertible. And they are. They want awakening."[38] But by its nature this form of education is an individual exercise; it works only in limited numbers, and—when successful—creates highly individualized people. The transformation that is brought about by *paideia* takes place within the individual, and only indirectly, in severely diminished form, in society. Statistically, whatever the thinkers of the Renaissance and revolutionary period may have hoped, it's just not possible to cause, by education alone, a radical transformation in society at large. While *paideia* may produce responsible, democratically minded citizens, there will never be enough of them to trigger the kind of radical collective conversion needed for a true democracy.

Here we have some proof. Large-scale access to higher education over the last half century hasn't resulted in a more enlightened citizenry in the West so much as a significant decrease in the intellectual quality of the education itself. The more people who get a college education, the less demanding it becomes, and the shallower the outcomes. The system produces enough decently trained professionals (doctors, engineers, teachers), but it doesn't affect the inner lives of these people in such a way as to cause a major change in society. The profound humility that genuine democracy presupposes—the notion that you are no better than the next person and that, for all your education, you may be wrong and the other right; the acute awareness of your *libido dominandi* and the internalized need to keep it in check—is not something to be expected upon graduation from the modern university.

Populism and authoritarianism are flourishing today in places with remarkably high educational levels. For all the self-flattering talk about civic-mindedness and political engagement, the citizenry in the West is in no better shape than it was one hundred years ago. And we seem resigned to the situation. Derek Bok, a former president of Harvard University, observes casually that, at American universities, the arts and sciences faculties "display scant interest in preparing undergraduates to be democratic citizens, a task once regarded as the principal purpose of a liberal education."[39] It appears that we have to learn to live with this conundrum: democracy remains only a dream without an education capable of transforming human nature, yet such a transformation does not seem possible on a large scale.

What makes our predicament even worse is that, while ancient Athens had a reasonably good rooting in religious traditions, which satisfied the Athenians' collective need for meaning and belonging, we live in a world where the demise of the old gods has left people at once spiritually orphaned and politically adrift. Our radical secularization has shattered a frame of reference that, for millennia, made people's lives meaningful by addressing their spiritual needs and giving them a sense of cosmic belonging. The "death of God" has changed everything, especially those things (politics, for example) that didn't seem to have much to do with God. The traditional frame of reference has been broken into countless bits and, however hard we try, we just can't piece it back together. Deprived of such a frame, many of us are left in a Brownian state of motion, swinging endlessly between self-worship, compulsive consumerism, social manipulation, and political demagoguery— anything that might give our lives an illusion of meaning.

Umberto Eco relates the proliferation of conspiracies, for example, to a desperate need for meaning that secularization can't satisfy. In *Foucault's Pendulum,* as elsewhere, he engages with Karl Popper, for whom the "conspiracy theory of society" was born of "abandoning God and then asking: 'Who is in his place?'"[40] Whatever imperfections philosophers may have found in the old notion of God, it served reasonably well as an authoritative source of meaning—social and epistemic, individual and collective—in this world and the next. However harsh he may have seemed, the old God promised a sense of cosmic order, and thus a measure of existential comfort. When that order vanished, it took away the ground from under people's feet. Nietzsche rightly talks of the "death of God" as an event of catastrophic proportions. To come up with a new source of meaning, of a similar authoritative power, would take nothing less than an *Übermensch*.

If God could no longer serve as a source of meaning, then anything would do. Chesterton's apocryphal aphorism captures the drama: "When people stop believing in God, it's not that they believe in nothing, it's that they believe in anything." But to believe in *anything at all* spells serious trouble, as we are starting to understand. When people are "starved for" meaning, someone remarks in *Foucault's Pendulum,* they will devour even the most unpalatable of conspiracies: "If you offer them one, they fall on it like a pack of wolves. You invent, and they'll believe."[41] No matter how crazy the stories, a rudderless crowd will blindly gorge on them.

We need stories because we need meaning, which is narrative in nature. If collective meaning is no longer generated by sacred stories, then we will look for it in the most profane of places. In populist politics, for instance. Populist politicians don't need to tell the truth or keep promises or even be honest. They only need one thing: to know how to tell stories. The more captivating their concoctions, the better their chances to gain emotional control over the crowd. That's why populists are so often histrionic figures: comedians are some of the most effective storytellers there are.

"If you want to understand modern politics," writes John Gray, "you must set aside the idea that secular and religious movements are opposites."[42] At its core, populist politics is a case of misplaced faith: a charismatic leader, even of dubious morality and no civic credentials, comes to embody a promise of meaningfulness for a spiritually starved community because he tells them the stories they need to satisfy their hunger for meaning. If he manages to make them believe that he can offer them such a redeeming narrative, they will swallow anything: the most outrageous of lies, the most idiotic plots and conspiracies. And they will remain eternally grateful for that. "What convinces masses are not facts, and not even invented facts," writes Hannah Arendt in *The Origins of Totalitarianism,* "but only the consistency of the system of which they are presumably part."[43] In such situations consistency is not a matter of logic, but of emotions. And few things are more consistent than the emotional exchange between a histrionic populist and his followers: *everything* makes sense within this universe. Politics already appeared to Simone Weil as "a sinister farce." Since her time, things have only got worse.

"Hitler, My Friend"

There is a distinct "otherworldliness" to Gandhi's life and work, which renders him at once fascinating and disturbing. The man seems to have lived among us while being at the same time positively from another world. When Winston Churchill called him a "half-naked fakir," he meant it as an insult, but Gandhi took it as a compliment. If he wanted to make a career, it was not really in law, politics, or even spinning yarn, but something completely different: "I have been long trying to be a Fakir and that naked—a more difficult task."[44]

Most often Gandhi's aspiration to be a fakir got him in trouble. It was not exactly comfortable being around this metaphysical interloper. Mahadev Desai, Gandhi's faithful secretary and disciple, once versified, "To live with a saint in heaven is bliss and glory / To live with a saint on earth is a different story."[45]

Truth be told, Gandhi could at times be a very pragmatic person. "Inside the saint, or near-saint," writes Orwell, "there was a very shrewd, able person who could, if he had chosen, have been a brilliant success as a lawyer, an administrator or perhaps even a businessman."[46] He came from the Bania subcaste, whose members had a reputation for business acumen and exquisite negotiation skills. Yet Gandhi could also display spectacular bouts of naïveté, cluelessness, even blindness. Faced with obvious instances of political evil, he was capable of singularly stupid judgments.[47] In the question of the Armenian genocide, the great man took the side of the Ottomans. While the Japanese army was raping China at length, he advised the Chinese not to fight back:

> It is unbecoming for a nation of 400 million, a nation as cultured as China, to repel Japanese aggression by resorting to Japan's methods. If the Chinese had non-violence of my conception, there would be no use for the latest machinery for destruction which Japan possesses.[48]

As Hitler was wreaking havoc in Europe, Gandhi proved to be remarkably supportive. In May 1940, he said, "I do not consider Herr Hitler to be as bad as he is depicted. He is showing an ability that is amazing and he seems to be gaining his victories without much bloodshed."[49] Future generations of Germans, he thought, would "honor Herr Hitler as a genius, as a brave man, as a matchless organizer and much more."[50] For good measure, he wrote Hitler personal letters, addressing him as "Dear Friend" and urging him to adopt nonviolence. His friend didn't have a chance to reply, as he was busy ramping up the Holocaust. But Gandhi was never one to give up easily. In December 1941, he again poured praise on his silent German friend: "He has not married. His character is said to be clean. He is always alert."[51] To be fair, Gandhi didn't neglect the Jews. He urged them to pray—for Hitler. "If even one Jew acted thus, he would save his self-respect and leave an example which, if it became infectious, would save the whole of Jewry."[52]

Half a world away from Europe, and overwhelmed by his own country's problems, Gandhi was hardly in a position to understand what was going on in Nazi Germany. But that didn't prevent him from embarrassing himself with such pronouncements: "The Jews of Germany can suffer Satyagraha under infinitely better auspices than Indians in South Africa." Even after the war, when there could be no doubt as to what happened, and what the "alert" Herr Hitler had been up to, Gandhi did not revise his views significantly. The Jews, he said, "should have offered themselves to the butcher's knife. . . . It would have aroused the world and the people of Germany."[53]

"Democracy Is for the Gods"

After Athens's radical experiment in equality, democracy surfaced elsewhere, but often in forms that the ancient Athenians would have had trouble recognizing. Today's much praised American democracy would by Athenian standards be deemed oligarchic. It's the wealthy few (*hoi oligoi*) who typically decide not only the rules of the political game, but also its winners and losers. Ironically, the system favors what the founding fathers desperately wanted to avoid when they opted for democratic representation in the first place: the arrogant, oppressively self-assertive political animal. Recent developments have shown that even the American system would be easy enough to dismantle. Much easier, in any event, than we would like to think.

We should not be surprised, though. "If there were a people of gods, it would govern itself democratically," Jean-Jacques Rousseau wrote two and a half centuries ago in *On the Social Contract*. "So perfect a form of government is not for men."[54] Democracy is so hard to find in the human world that most of the time when we speak of it, we refer to a remote ideal rather than a fact: something that people attempt to put into practice from time to time, yet never adequately and never for long—always clumsily, timidly, as though for a trial period. So far, the trials have ended mostly in failure.

Yet even as these attempts have failed, they have occasionally reduced the amount of unnecessary suffering in the world. Which is more than enough reason to choose democracy over its alterna-tives. *Less suffering*, humble though it may sound, is in fact a rather difficult goal. If we managed just that, we would accomplish a great deal. For less is so much more. Some of the most ambitious moral reformers, from the Buddha to Saint Francis of Assisi, asked nothing more of us: just show less greed, less self-assertion, less ego. Instead of talking endlessly about "making the world a better place"—usually an excuse either to do nothing or to wield power over others—we should perhaps try a little harder and make the world a less hor-rific place. A tall task, no doubt, but one worth trying.

If the trials and tribulations of democracy teach us something, it is that, no matter how noble our dreams, how high our aspira-tions, we should always be ready to settle for less. Such humility would do us much good.

A Million Dead

Since the boundaries separating Gandhi's personal life from the public life of India were porous at best, his failures were never his private affair; they involved his country as well. For Gandhi the pol-itician, a million dead Indians, for example, wasn't such a bad thing, provided their deaths served a good purpose. "I have made up my mind," he said in 1942, "that it would be a good thing if a million people were shot in a brave and nonviolent resistance against the British rule."[55] Death can accomplish many a great thing, and be put to excellent use—all you need is someone who knows how to master it. Gandhi thought he was such a master of death. "My heart now is as hard as stone," he declared during the Salt March. "I am in this struggle for Swaraj ready to sacrifice thou-sands and hundreds of thousands of men if necessary."[56]

The British officials were "shocked," as one historian puts it, to hear Gandhi "talk coolly of the number of deaths that would re-sult if they did not accede to his demands and riots or communal strife broke out in some Indian city."[57] Perhaps they shouldn't have been that shocked—they had been warned, after all. Didn't Gandhi write in *Hind Swaraj*, "That nation is great which rests its head upon death as its pillow"?[58] In his defense, Nathuram Godse, Gandhi's assassin, referred precisely to this feature of Gandhi's political persona. For Godse, as he explained late in life, the Mahatma was "a violent pacifist who brought untold calamities on the country in the name of truth and non-violence."[59]

In 1915, soon after he moved back to India from South Africa, during evening prayer at a newly established ashram near Ahmedabad, while extolling the virtues of discipline and resilience, Gandhi proclaimed to the ashram's dwellers that

> he looked forward to the day when he would call out all the inmates of the Ashram, who had been trained in those disciplines, to immolate themselves at the altar of non-violence. Unmoved he would watch them fall one after another before a shower of bullets, without a trace of fear or hatred, but only love in their hearts. And then, when the last one of them had fallen, he would himself follow.[60]

Here we come across one of Gandhi's most characteristic failures: his cavalier attitude toward the death of others, the nonchalance with which he would deploy other people in his own battles, making them martyrs for a cause they were not always sufficiently informed about. A great charmer of people, he sometimes could not help charming his followers to death. He was not unaware of the uncanny power he had over others. "I do not know what evil is in me," he confessed at one point. "I have a strain of cruelty in me . . . such that people force themselves to do things, even to attempt impossible things, in order to please me."[61] The prophet of passive resistance could not always resist the temptation to abuse this power.

The Problem with Revolutions

The notion that human society can be transformed by *paideia* is for the hopeful and the patient. One needs a great deal of optimism, and even more patience, to believe that books and teachers will one day turn power-hungry animals into model citizens working self-lessly for the general good—wolves into vegetarian activists. For the impatient, there is another way to try to make this change: burn down the house and start everything from scratch—remake humanity altogether. Not *paideia,* but *revolution.* The belief that something like this is possible and feasible is another thing that has kept history alive—if a bit too alive sometimes.

In *The German Ideology,* Karl Marx and Friedrich Engels spell out how the process works in practice. Having established the need for an "alteration of men on a mass scale," they specify that this is something that "can only take place in a practical movement, a *revolution.*" Then they detail the double function of revolution as a highly disruptive, violent historical act.[62] The "revolution is necessary," they write helpfully, "not only because the *ruling* class cannot be overthrown in any other way, but because the class *overthrowing* it can only in a revolution succeed in ridding itself of all the muck of ages and become fitted to found society anew."[63] Marx and Engels wrote *The German Ideology* in 1846. Though they were speaking of a communist revolution yet to happen, they were not prophesying it ex nihilo: they were projecting an imagined future based on events that had happened just a generation before, which were all about "founding society anew."

The French Revolution was, at its core, a project of radical novelty. In the hot summer of 1789, the whole system of social and political institutions that the French had relied on for centuries was found to be not just oppressive and unjust, but irrational. The ancien régime became suddenly something to be ashamed of, needing to be replaced by new, rationally designed, forward-looking institutions. Hence the Revolution's first commandment: "You shall reinvent everything." And everyone seemed to obey it. Tabula rasa, starting from a clean slate, would soon become a national addiction. Georges Danton, who, like most French revolutionaries, drastically reinvented himself, put it best: "We have to look again at everything, recreate everything." The Declaration of the Rights of Man, which had just been adopted, "is not without faults, and it deserves to be reviewed by a truly free people," Danton said.[64] Only a permanent revolution was revolutionary enough.

The idea of a clean break with the past came from the Enlightenment philosophes, but experiencing such a break in real life was another matter. As you follow the unfolding of revolutionary events in France, you sense not only the tremendous excitement generated by what those people were attempting, but also the widespread anxiety, the distress and trepidation. There's at least a hint of that in the words of Philippe Le Bas, a radical member of the National Convention (the first government of revolutionary France), right after the execution of Louis XVI. Le Bas had voted for the king's decapitation, and now he was waking up to the full realization of what he and his fellow revolutionaries had done: "The road back is cut off, we have to go forward, whether we want to or not, and now one can really say, 'live free or die.'"[65] There was no longer anything for the revolutionaries to fall back on if their bold experiments failed. Most of the old social forms, political rituals, and public practices had been abandoned, and pretty much everything had to be remade anew—from the calendar to the measurement system to public education. Nothing was off limits for these dreamers. The members of the Society of the Friends of Truth, one of the political clubs that mushroomed in revolutionary Paris, dreamed of "remaking the universe" itself, and of "creating a new religion of humanity."[66]

It was the revolutionaries' relentless quest for novelty, some worried, that made their project not just impractical, but positively dangerous. Few of the Revolution's critics were more penetrating, in this respect, than Edmund Burke. When his *Reflections on the Revolution in France* came out, in November 1790, its subject matter was still in progress, yet Burke managed to capture what was really at stake. He thought that the revolutionaries' fundamental mistake came from their indiscriminate rejection of the past: "You chose to act as if you had never been moulded into civil society, and had everything to begin anew. You began ill, because you began by despising everything that belonged to you. You set up your trade without a capital."[67]

Reason alone, Burke suggests, is feeble and imperfect, never in enough supply, and easily overwhelmed by the complexity of the tasks at hand. We should not rely too much on it when it comes to the more serious matters of life: "We are afraid to put men to live and trade each on his own private stock of reason, because we suspect that the stock in each man is small. . . . The nature of man is intricate; the objects of society are of the greatest possible complexity."[68] Reason is admirable, but relying on it alone can lead to irrational outcomes.

The spectacular failures that followed in quick succession—the Reign of Terror, the rise and rule of Napoleon Bonaparte, the Restoration (a nasty hangover after such a glorious party)—seemed to confirm Burke's criticisms. In this respect, as in others, the French Revolution anticipated more recent attempts at a complete separation from the past such as the Bolshevik Revolution in Russia, Mao's Cultural Revolution in China, and the Khmer Rouge regime in Cambodia. In all of these cases, a high price was paid for a rather banal lesson: there is more to humanity than mere reason. We are a complex mixture of rationality and emotion, logic and imagination, common sense and prejudice. Seemingly insignificant details such as local culture and attachments, peculiar customs and traditions, irrational though they may be, have at least as important a role to play in any society as the abstract plans devised by philosophers. The baggage of emotion, memory, and culture may be just ballast, but sailing without it is reckless. In Arthur Koestler's *Darkness at*

Noon, the old Bolshevik Rubashov, while awaiting execution in his prison cell, observes, "We have thrown all ballast overboard; only one anchor holds us: faith in one's self."[69]

Did he just say "faith"? Coming from a radical rationalist like Rubashov, this is quite an admission. When the vehemently anti-Catholic Robespierre, realizing that no society could do without some form of organized religion, came up with a cult of the Supreme Being, he too conceded more than he may have liked to. Just a few years later, when Napoleon mended ties with the Catholic Church, he showed that he understood human nature much better than the revolutionaries did. Not that he believed in God, but he knew that the French wouldn't believe in him unless he exhibited some faith. This was cynical, but not delusional. "They will say that I am a Papist; I am nothing; I was a Muslim in Egypt, I'll be a Catholic here for the good of the people."[70] Faith has its reasons that mere reason will never understand.

The quest for radical novelty was not the worst thing about the French Revolution. A bigger problem was the means employed to attain it: *terror.* One function of revolution, as you may recall, is to cleanse us of "the muck of ages," so that we can "become fitted to found society anew." A cleansing so thorough that it would amount to a rebirth. We can't enter a new age of humanity while still clinging to our old filthy selves. Hence the Revolution's second commandment: "You shall kill!" For blood, it turns out, is an excellent cleansing agent.

While believers in democracy (ancient and modern) hope that such transformative cleansing will come from good rules and institutions, even if it takes centuries, revolutionaries have little time, and even less patience, for long-drawn-out historical processes. They firmly believe that they can achieve a remaking of the human material within the shortest time. Certainly, the methods have to be brutal, but when we consider the loftiness of the goal, any price is worth paying.

And the goal of the French Revolution *was* lofty: those people dreamed of nothing less than a "Republic of Virtue," which would put an end to human history as we know it. Nothing less than a perfect society would satisfy them. The Revolution was meant to transcend its particular time and space, becoming a major turning point in the unfolding of the human story. This was no ordinary politics—it was eschatology in action. "The French Revolution," Alexis de Tocqueville would observe, "was a political revolution that proceeded in the manner of religious revolutions."[71] And when one is doing Heaven's work on earth, ordinary standards do not apply. Anything is permitted: abuse, murder, the extermination of *les ennemis de la Révolution* (real or imaginary), regicide, even genocide. When the achievement of human perfection is at stake, paying attention to legal technicalities or ethical niceties is the worst kind of treason.

The Reign of Terror, then, was born, ironically, out of a great love of humanity. Those people were *terroristes* only because they were such passionate philanthropists. The unfolding of the Terror showed the thickening of a link between the *purity* of the revolutionary ideals and the *violence* of the means employed to realize them; the nobler their aspirations, the more blood on their hands. What permitted the "temporary suspension of the law," and especially of "the rights of man," François Furet observed, was "the loftier need to establish society on the virtue of the citizens."[72] Their vicious methods were demanded precisely by their relentless pursuit of virtue.

The outcome was large-scale devastation. The Revolution claimed hundreds of thousands of victims: guillotined, decapitated by sword or axe, butchered by mobs, drowned in rivers, set on fire, broken by the wheel. But numbers are usually lousy speakers. Sometimes the testimony of one eyewitness can be more eloquent than the most detailed statistics. "It is completely impossible to express the horror of the profound and somber silence that prevailed during these executions," recalled François Jourgniac Saint-Méard, an army officer with royalist sympathies who survived, almost miraculously, the September 1792 massacre, with which the Reign of Terror made its debut. That silence

> was interrupted only by the cries of those who were sacrificed, and by the saber blows aimed at their heads. As soon as they were laid out on the ground, murmurs arose, intensified by cries of "long live the nation" that were a thousand times more terrifying to us than the terrible silence.[73]

The Theory and Practice of Fakirism

Eventually, it was his otherworldliness—his fakirism, if you will—that defined Gandhi. In Sufi Islam, a *faqīr* is someone who leads a life of complete self-renunciation and dedication to others; he has no personal interests, no desire for worldly goods, and can do without personal possessions. The *faqīr* usually lives off alms or else thin air. The word comes from *faqr* ("poverty," in Arabic). Sufi fakirs had for a long time been part of the Indian religious landscape, having shaped the spiritual lives not only of Muslims, but of Hindus as well. They were held in reverence by both groups. That's why when Churchill called Gandhi a "fakir," Gandhi was flattered. How could he not be? The most powerful man of the British Empire had just referred to him as a "spiritual master." If he had any qualms, it was that he was *not fakir enough*.

While still in South Africa, Gandhi had made a conscious decision to live a fakir's life. First, he embraced the calling to be poor: fakirs don't own anything. That was easy enough because, as he would say later, the "uses of poverty are far sweeter than those of riches."[74] He put an end to his legal practice and disentangled himself from other worldly affairs. He stopped wearing fancy European dress and traveled only in third class. For good measure, he decided that those close to him would be just as poor (fakirs by association), and duly informed his family that from now on they would have to do with much less than before. When his son Manilal voiced a desire for a formal education and a career, his father cut him short: "We are poor and wish to remain poor."[75] Fakirs don't have worldly careers—fakirism itself is the best career.

When you strive to be a fakir as Gandhi did, it's not enough to be poor—others have to see it. You are a fakir for nothing if you don't make a show of it. To show his poverty, Gandhi would abandon more and more items of clothing till people started to worry, wondering where he would stop. Similarly, he would take less and less food. As Gandhi was looking for ways to reduce his material needs, he stumbled upon a golden rule: whatever you use beyond the bare minimum is theft. He said,

> If I need only one shirt to cover myself with but use two, I am guilty of stealing one from another. For a shirt which could have been of use to someone else does not belong to me. If five bananas are enough to keep me going, my eating a sixth one is a form of theft.[76]

No fakir could have put it better. As with the Sufi fakirs of old, poverty for Gandhi was not just about minimalist living—it was a path to self-transcendence. You become a fakir not just because you don't like this world, but because you are in love with another. Gandhi chose to have less because he wanted so much more.

There was just one thing Gandhi had to take care of before he fully qualified for fakirism: his sexuality. Fakirs are not bothered by the demands of the flesh. This step was not so easy because, by nature, Gandhi was a highly sexed, unusually passionate person. So his battle with the flesh was an uphill struggle. Yet in the end he did win, if by drastic measures. After much self-examination and discussion with friends, Gandhi decided that he would stop sleeping with his wife and become a *brahmachari* (celibate, for religious reasons). He didn't feel the urge to discuss the matter with the wife herself before making his decision. Always the gentleman, however, he informed her of his decision as soon as he took it.

When Failure Is Not an Option

When it comes to revolutionary violence, there is hardly a more emblematic figure than Maximilien Robespierre. Upon meeting the former lawyer from Arras, Mirabeau famously exclaimed, *"Cet homme ira loin car il croit tout ce qu'il dit"* (This man will go far because he believes everything he says). In a society where speaking was a fine art pursued largely for its own sake, Mirabeau's *bon mot* was more of a warning than a compliment.

Before the Revolution, what distinguished Robespierre was that there was nothing distinctive about him. The man was blandness itself. After 1789, it was precisely this blandness, as François Furet pointed out, that allowed him to dissolve himself so completely in the stream of revolutionary events and become of a piece with it. He had no life of his own, no private existence, no passions or interests outside the Revolution. "Robespierre's self and the Revolution cannot be separated," observes Ruth Scurr. Caught together in the maelstrom, Robespierre and the Republic "became one and the same tyrant."[77] To defend the Revolution to the bitter end became second nature for Robespierre, as many of his fellow revolutionaries learned to their chagrin. Since the failure of the Revolution was not an option, any means were justified, in his view, as long as they contributed to its success. Which, ironically, is always a recipe for failure. And the more the Revolution seemed to fail, the more determined Robespierre became not to see or accept it.

Deeming himself morally pure (he was not known as *l'Incorruptible* for nothing), Robespierre put himself in charge of revolutionary France's moral purity. "He was not much interested in money, nor . . . in sex." He was not "commercially minded, not a connoisseur of thrills."[78] That made his behavior at once highly principled and utterly devastating. Robespierre was correctness embodied, from how he dressed and carried himself in society to how he sent people (his own friends included) to the guillotine. Had he been just a touch laxer, the fate of the Revolution might have been different. If there is something worse than a corrupted politician, it's an incorruptible one.

A good child of the Enlightenment, Robespierre used reason as a guide for action. He derived the norms of his behavior, pedantically, from the principles of universal morality, rooted in the postulate of a Supreme Being. It was this rational grounding of his existence that made him impervious to any human feelings. Once he understood where the dangers to the Revolution came from, he acted against them as implacably as a mathematician leading a proof to its logical conclusion. Like a high priest of old—and just as chastely and humorlessly—Robespierre uttered his pronouncements and performed everything his holy office required, human sacrifices included. When the Marquis de Condorcet observed that the Revolution "is a religion," and that Robespierre, "leading a sect therein," is a "priest at the head of his worshippers," he showed not only insight, but also first-hand knowledge.[79]

The solution Robespierre favored was terror. Without terror, he thought, "virtue is impotent," and without virtue the whole project becomes meaningless. "Terror is merely justice, prompt, severe, and inflexible," and since justice needed to be done, terror could not be stopped.[80] In Robespierre's hands, murder became a purely logical affair. To kill someone, one ordinarily needs some form of emotion (hate, anger, fear). Robespierre, a man of reason, was above emotions. His decisions to execute *les ennemis de la Révolution* were not born out of revenge or hatred; they were the implacable outcome of a reasoning process. Forgiveness would have been synonymous with malfunction for this human machine—it would have been, above all, a failure of reasoning, which he would have found intolerable. And this made Robespierre all the more frightening. For him, as François Furet reminds us, "the bloodiness was abstract, like the political system: the guillotine was fed

by his moral preachings."[81] In this respect, as in others, Robespierre embodies one of the great ironies of the Enlightenment
project: when pushed too far, reason turns into its opposite. A political project that needs a bloodbath for its implementation—
however noble the goal, however compelling the justification—is
anything but rational.

The most graphic illustration of this irony is the guillotine
itself. In an important sense, the machine was the visible embodiment of the Enlightenment: not only did the device involve the
rigorous application of modern science (a guillotine maker needed a
good grasp of Newtonian physics to calculate the blade's weight and
angle, the height of the frame, and so on), but its sheer existence
was the materialization of a philanthropic, progressive idea.

Dr. Joseph-Ignace Guillotin, who did *not* invent the guillotine
(the machine had been in existence, in other forms), was a sensi-
tive and thoughtful humanist, who, in late 1789, proposed a series
of measures aimed at reforming the criminal justice system in
France. Punishment during the ancien régime had been a cruel, degrading, and uneven affair. Hanging, reserved for commoners, took
many long minutes to bring death about; one had to die several
deaths before meeting one's end. Members of the nobility were
slightly luckier: their execution was by beheading—with a sword
or axe. But it was swift only if the executioner was skillful. Execution by breaking on the wheel was particularly gruesome. That's
why, out of concern for his fellow citizens, Dr. Guillotin came up
with the notion of a uniform, less painful, and more rapid method:
"decapitation by a simple mechanism." Such a "philanthropic
beheading machine," as it was called, had been used with good
results before—all they had to do was perfect it.[82] Which they did,
eventually turning guillotining into a fine art.

When it was finally adopted, in April 1792, the machine worked
wonders. It ran so well, in fact, that it left people disappointed: no
sooner were the condemned brought in than they were dispatched.
Just as the good Dr. Guillotin had predicted: "the head flies off . . .

the victim is no more."[83] This meant that there was almost no public spectacle, no orgiastic cruelty—and, therefore, no fun. Dr. Guillotin's "philanthropic beheading machine" turned out to be a first-class killjoy. By taking away the highly intoxicating mixture of emotions that had immemorially attracted people to public executions, it spoiled everything. The idea of "humane punishment" must have struck the revolutionary audience not just as a cruel joke, but as singularly stupid: it was like steak without meat, sex without a partner, alcohol-free spirit. Those brave sans-culottes didn't want painless executions—they showed up there precisely to enjoy the spectacle of real, prolonged, serious pain. Not some swift, "philanthropic" dispatch, but a slow, protracted death. "Humane executions" were never a match for the "passion for punishment and terror, nourished by a deep desire for revenge" that the sans-culottes felt abundantly in those days.[84] That's how the revolutionaries broke what might have been the Revolution's third commandment: "You shall not disappoint the mob!"

A lemonade seller from Paris, a lady of admirable *terroriste* sentiment (she said she "would like to eat the heart of anyone opposing the sans-culottes") expressed the collective disappointment with both the speed and accuracy of the guillotine: "There's a lot of talk about chopping off heads, but not enough blood is flowing."[85] In fact, the blood *was* flowing, plenty of it, but since the operation was conducted in such a neat manner, it gave the opposite impression: the guillotine was moving faster than the spectators had time to take in. To quell the popular thirst for blood, more and more people had to be brought to the machine and done away with, but to no avail.

Execution by hand, apart from gratifying the audience, would have slowed down the pace of the process, keeping the Terror in check. Instead, the dizzy speed of the machine called for more and more death sentences. And no matter how many were pronounced, and there were plenty, the audience's disappointment remained. Before they knew it, the revolutionaries were knee-deep in blood, and the audience kept asking for more.

When the guillotine was first proposed, Abbé Maury argued against it and the "routine decapitation" that it would bring about. It was not that he preferred the punishment methods of pre-revolutionary France, but he worried that such a quick dispatch "might deprave the people by familiarizing them with the sight of blood."[86] He was more right that he could have imagined.

In every single one of its details, the guillotine was an admirably designed and perfectly rational device; it had the stamp of the Enlightenment all over it. And yet it was irrationality at work. The guillotine worked without failure, and that flawlessness may have been its biggest problem.

That typical Enlightenment problem, let me add in passing, has stayed with us ever since. A higher rate of failure, more faulty equipment, a less competent bureaucracy, and in general less flawlessness would have saved many a life at Auschwitz, Treblinka, and elsewhere.

Over the Top

Gandhi was nothing if not a perfectionist. In all these things—diet, dress, sexuality—he was never content if he managed to do something just well; he always wanted to take it one step further. Which is sometimes the best way to ruin everything. Here's George Orwell, again: "No doubt alcohol, tobacco and so forth are things that a saint must avoid, but sainthood is also a thing that human beings must avoid."[87]

For someone who managed with so little eating, Gandhi's obsession with food is puzzling. Food is everywhere in Gandhi: in his published texts and his correspondence, in his sermons and private chats. His *Autobiography* is to a large extent a book about food: about Gandhi's vegetarianism, which was for him much more than just a diet; about how little he ate and the many things he would not eat; about his lifelong experimentation with different diets and the comparative merits of each. While studying in London, at the end of each day he listed religiously whatever he had eaten: how many bananas and oranges, how many nuts and raisins—and how bad his indigestion had been.

Gandhi's culinary obsession grew in direct proportion to how little he ate; with age, his aversion to eating became increasingly more sophisticated. "The process of eating is as unclean as evacuation," he would say, "the only difference being that, while evacuation ends in a sense of relief, eating, if one's tongue is not held in control, brings discomfort."[88] Like Simone Weil, Gandhi thought there was something disgusting about the sheer ingestion of food. He could fly into a rage and subject his servant-disciples to long lectures if they made a portioning mistake—for example, by giving him twenty-five raisins to eat for breakfast, instead of nineteen as agreed. Gandhi was a fastidious non-eater.

Non-dressing was no less important for Gandhi than non-eating. His lifelong striptease project started in London, where he must have been at his most dressed-up. No sooner did he arrive there than he decided to reinvent himself and become a proper English gentleman. He gave up his Indian dress and went on to purchase whatever he thought it took to make him look English: from a silk top hat to the flashy tie to the leather gloves and the silver-mounted stick. Meeting this fancy dresser in London one day, another Indian student was left with the impression that Gandhi was "more interested in fashion and frivolities than in his studies."[89]

His English gentleman appearance didn't help him find clients in India, though. Perhaps to put an end to his losing streak, in South Africa he decided to change the hat for a complicated turban of his own design. The trick apparently worked, because clients started coming. When he showed up in court, however, the combination puzzled the judge: Gandhi was now neither English nor Indian, though he eventually came to be known as "the coolie barrister." As he embarked on his fakir's career, Gandhi decided it was better to be Indian than English, so he dropped his European clothes and adopted the simple dress of the laborers he was now representing politically and in court: knee-length white cotton tunic, bare feet, shaved head (except for a patch on the top). At last, he dropped "barrister" from his title, and, dressed like a coolie, he essentially was one.

That worked for a while until, back in India, Gandhi started to feel oppressively overdressed. The one shirt became one too many. That's how he finally switched to his signature loincloth (*dhoti*)—not so much a dress item as a way to signal how undressed he was. Thankfully, he stopped there, as there was not much else to drop.

"My loincloth is an organic evolution in my life," said Gandhi. "It came naturally, without premeditation."[90] The confession is admirable, but not exactly true. When it came to Gandhi's dress, as with so much in his life, nothing was "without premeditation." Everything he did or said was usually much deliberated, pondered, and rehearsed. An "exceedingly shrewd tactician and strategist," as a biographer describes him, this perfectionist would never have forgiven himself had he left anything to chance, especially his public persona.[91] Gandhi's appearances were all high-class performances, and if they seemed spontaneous, it was only because he was such a gifted actor. When we look at photos from that time, we see a performer fully aware of himself, looking at us from the frame both boldly and expectantly. In 1931, he met King George V, at Buckingham Palace, wearing only a loincloth. When a journalist questioned the appropriateness of the attire, Gandhi reportedly countered, "But the king was wearing enough for the both of us." That made people laugh heartily, exactly as he had planned.

Gandhi knew that, if he was to change the hearts of his fellow Indians, he could do so not through arguments and speeches, but only by offering himself—his whole and naked self—to them. And much depended on the manner in which this offering was made. That's why the way he dressed was so important to him. His was a most demanding striptease show because it was at once a sartorial, a political, and a spiritual exercise. Gandhi's loincloth, for all its material precariousness, tied him firmly not only to the millions of downtrodden Indians who could not afford much else, but also to the immediately recognizable appearance of the Indian *sadhu,* the mendicant holy man living off alms and working for the spiritual edification of the people.

As the maintenance of naked fakirs goes, Gandhi's was a pretty expensive affair. For someone who was not supposed to have many needs, the size of his army of aides, assistants, disciples, and private secretaries was remarkable. As he grew older, his demands on his staff only grew in number and complexity: some had to carry his books, others to read to him, some to take dictation, others to mail the letters, some to attend to his bath, others to put him to bed, and others still to cook his elaborately frugal meals. In the long run, Gandhi's few needs almost ruined his family's finances. As a friend, the poetess and wit Sarojini Naidu observed, "It cost a great deal of money to keep the Mahatma living in poverty."[92]

Gandhi's *brahmacharya* was a similarly complicated affair. Not having sex was not enough for this perfectionist; he had to take the matter one step further. So he started a vigorous campaign against any form of sexual activity, licit or illicit, within or outside marriage. "Adultery does not consist merely in sexual intercourse with another man's wife," he wrote. "There can be adultery even in intercourse with one's own wife."[93] An exception could in theory be made for the situation when the sexual intercourse is "the result of a desire for offspring." But since the sexual act was evil and impure in itself, Gandhi wasn't really inclined to allow exceptions. It is, he writes, "the duty of every thoughtful Indian not to marry. In case he is helpless in regard to marriage, he should abstain from sexual intercourse with his wife."[94] Better extinct than tainted.

In general, in matters of intimacy, Gandhi operated by his own rules. Finding himself naked in the presence of women was never a problem for him: "I have never felt any embarrassment in being seen naked by a woman."[95] Woman friends made ideal conversation partners when he had to discuss such hot topics as involuntary ejaculation. The length Gandhi would go to reveal—and expose—himself was sometimes breathtaking.

Terror: A User's Manual

The other function of revolutionary violence, aside from transformative cleansing, you may recall, is eminently pragmatic: a violent revolution is needed, Marx and Engels tell us, because "the ruling class cannot be overthrown in any other way." Those in power have to be forced out—literally. Indeed, revolutionaries need violence not only to seize power, but just as importantly, to keep it. Which is not easy in times when all power seems up for grabs.

Even though Robespierre displayed "immense talent as a tactician," and often outmaneuvered his adversaries as professional politicians do, ultimately the first function of revolutionary violence (cleansing) prevailed in his case.[96] He didn't use terror primarily for petty political purposes, but for a higher, almost spiritual end. He believed, in the words of a biographer, that he was "the instrument of Providence, delivering France to her exalted future."[97] Robespierre placed terror at the core of a larger scenario of collective redemption and self-transcendence, whereby human beings (himself included) would be purified and elevated to another level of historical existence, even if many were to be destroyed in the process, just as he eventually was. In his hands, terror acquired an inhuman, truly terrifying dimension.

And that seems to have been the case with *la Terreur* more generally. For all the corruption and dirty politics involved (of which there were plenty), there remained something oddly idealistic about that enormous bloodbath. As the sans-culottes turned into a bloodthirsty mob, calling out for social vengeance, they coalesced into one enormous, uncontrollable wildfire. Thus incensed, their actions were ferocious beyond measure, mindlessly cruel, and so destructive as to be almost sublime. You can call it anything but "petty." Such extraordinary combustion couldn't last too long.

Eventually, having consumed everything (including the Revolution itself), the wildfire had to die out. But what a conflagration it was! We still feel its heat, more than two centuries later.

The Bolshevik Revolution was a different affair. There was a genuine revolutionary moment in the Russian Empire (largely in the Saint Petersburg area) in the winter of 1917. A great, spontaneous uprising effectively put an end to Russia's own ancien régime. The resulting governing coalition was expressive of the country's new political situation. The Bolsheviks' involvement at this stage was rather limited. Lenin was in Switzerland, Trotsky was in the United States, and Stalin was largely insignificant. Not only were they not involved in the events, but they seem to have been taken by surprise by them. In January 1917, weeks before the February Revolution, while addressing a socialist youth gathering in Zurich, Lenin came across as resignation embodied: "We old-timers may not live to see the decisive battles of the coming revolution," he reflected.[98] So much for sharp revolutionary vision. The February Revolution allowed the exiles to return to Russia, where they busily plotted over the next several months and did their best to subvert the work of the new government.

What the Bolsheviks overthrew in October was not tsarism, but a provisional government brought about by the February Revolution. Theirs was not a revolution, but essentially a coup d'état. In the words of historian Richard Pipes, governmental power was "captured" by "a small minority."[99] Generations of historians from the Soviet Union and elsewhere would speak ad nauseam of "the Great October Socialist Revolution." In fact, the Bolshevik coup was such a minor operation that it "passed unnoticed by the vast majority of the inhabitants of Petrograd," let alone the rest of the country. "Theaters, restaurants and tram cars functioned much as normal while the Bolsheviks came to power."[100] Russians should have seen it coming, though. In the summer of 1917, as he was preparing the coup, Lenin was quite explicit about what the Bolsheviks were up to: "We see countless instances of how the better organized, more conscious, better-armed minority imposed its will on the majority and conquered it."[101] So much for spontaneous revolutionary change.

The Russian "working class," in whose name the Bolsheviks seized power, was conveniently invoked and ritually mentioned, but never truly involved. For a very simple reason: it did not exist. Largely agricultural at the time, the Russian Empire was not sufficiently industrialized to have a working class worthy of the name. The Bolshevik leaders found themselves in the business of miracle-working: stirring up a proletarian revolution in a country without a proletariat. Lenin was the first to recognize the awkwardness of the situation: "We are dealing with a country where the proletariat represents a minority," he reflected.[102] Indeed, in late 1917, industrial workers made up about 1.5 percent of the population, and only around 5 percent of them were members of the Communist Party.[103] One of the very few revolutionary leaders of proletarian origin, Alexander Shliapnikov, once congratulated Lenin on being "the vanguard of a nonexistent class" (only to pay later with his life for his irony).[104]

The Bolsheviks tried the usual propaganda tricks, but they knew that this couldn't work out in the long run. Their only hope was that a victorious communist revolution in some advanced European country (Germany, for example) would somehow revive theirs, which at this point appeared to have been stillborn.[105] When revolutionary attempts in Munich and Budapest fizzled out, the Bolshevik leaders realized that there was only one way they could stay in power: sheer force. What a fake revolution needs to keep up the pretense is a highly effective, ruthless secret police. Only the latter's success can disguise the former's failure. That's how the Bolshevik political police, the Cheka, came into existence.

"I believe that the formation of the Cheka was one of the gravest and most impermissible errors that the Bolshevik leaders committed in 1918," recalls Victor Serge, an important Marxist intellectual and genuine revolutionary, who was to be one of the Cheka's many victims.[106] The creation of the secret police may have been an "error" in the eyes of an idealist like Serge, but for the Bolshevik regime it was a stroke of political genius. The idea came from Lenin himself. In September 1918, he wrote, "It is necessary secretly—and *urgently*—to prepare the terror."[107] Learning from the mistakes of the Provisional Government, which they had been able to overthrow so easily, the Bolsheviks set up a vast apparatus of surveillance, policing, and repression. "The strength of the French Revolution," said Trotsky in 1917, "was in the machine that made the enemies of the people shorter by a head. This is a fine device. We must have it in every city."[108] Not to be outdone, Lenin asked rhetorically, "How can you make a revolution without firing squads?"[109] Trotsky couldn't have his guillotines, but the Cheka's firing squads rarely stood idle under the new regime. In its first two months alone, almost fifteen thousand people were executed, which was more than twice the number of those executed in the entire last century of tsarist rule.[110]

And the more people the new regime executed, the more self-assured it became. Lenin declared cockily, in 1920, "We did not hesitate to shoot thousands of people, and we shall not hesitate to do that [again]."[111] As Simone Weil would observe about a decade later, the Bolshevik regime wasn't just a continuation of the tsarist autocracy—it was the perfection of it. The tsarist regime's "real forces," such as "the police, the army, the bureaucracy," she wrote, "far from being smashed by the Revolution, attained, thanks to it, a power unknown in other countries."[112] The Bolsheviks meant business.

In the business of Soviet state terror, everything revolved around four words: "enemy of the people." Being thought to be an enemy of the people was the worst thing that could happen to anyone living in the Soviet Union. If you wanted to survive, you had to do everything possible to avoid the label: engage in compromises and cowardly acts, betray friends and family, preemptively label others "enemy of the people." And who was an enemy of the people, exactly? That may have been the most difficult question to answer in the country. When Lavrenty Beria, future chief of the secret police, said "an enemy of the people is . . . [anyone] who doubts the rightness of the Party line," he didn't answer so much as show that this was not a question, but an effective tool of political control.[113] For the party line (whatever it was) could change at any time—from one day to the next, between lunch and dinner. Indeed, it seemed to be part of the plan *not* to have a clear party line—this way no one could feel safe. The point was not to coerce people to believe in this thing or that, but to break them morally by forcing them to swallow *anything*, including the absurd—especially the absurd. The Bolshevik regime didn't necessarily want their indoctrination. What it wanted, above all, was their mental incarceration and moral paralysis. This was an important distinction, which Orwell would illustrate, with harrowing detail, in his novel *1984*.

To do its job, the Cheka employed a vast network of snitches, spies, informants, and collaborators. They were everywhere—"in factories and offices, in public places and communal apartments." When the Great Terror reached its peak, in the late 1930s, "millions of people were reporting on their colleagues, neighbors, friends."[114] And if that were not enough, the Cheka even inserted itself inside the family. Children were often recruited to spy on their parents. "Wives doubted husbands; husbands doubted wives." People weren't sure "what to believe when a relative was arrested."[115]

And the arrests never stopped. To be arrested, to anticipate arrest, or to worry about a loved one who had been arrested was a defining feature of life under Stalin. Arrests were no longer a social fact, but—and that's precisely what state terror sought to accomplish—they came to occupy people's minds, shape their conscious and unconscious life, and color every aspect of their subjectivity. Even their sense of humor. In 1937, Margarete Buber-Neumann recalls, there was a popular joke in Moscow:

> "They've taken Teruel. Have you heard?" It was the time of the Spanish Civil War. "You don't say so. And his wife as well?" "No, no. Teruel's a town." "Good heavens! They've started arresting whole towns?"[116]

Gandhi's Utopia

The site of Gandhi's self-realization was the ashram: a form of communal living he started in South Africa and then perfected in India. An unlikely combination of Buddhist monastery, Tolstoyan village, New Age commune, and messianic Utopia, it was a uniquely Gandhian affair. The ashram allowed Gandhi to put into practice some of his more radical ideas: perfect equality, *brahmacharya*, truthfulness, nonviolence, the end of untouchability, and the nobility of manual labor, from spinning and cooking to toilet cleaning.

In good utopian tradition, Gandhi's ashram was a tough place to be. It was hierarchically divided into three classes: controllers, novitiates, and students. The Mahatma was at the top, though a better way to put it would be to say that he was omnipresent. The control was absolute, the discipline military, and the expectation was always for unconditional submission. An all-season bootcamp, only with less food and more prayers. In a country that had (and still has) a rather flexible sense of time, Gandhi's ashram was supposed to work with the precision of a Swiss clock: reveille at 4:00 AM, prayers at 5:00 AM, manual work from 7:00 to 8:30 AM, lunch at 11:00 AM, and so on. There was little room for maneuver and no freedom in the usual sense. Infringement of ashram rules (being late for prayers, for instance) could result in expulsion. In the absence of dedicated intelligence-gathering services, the ashram had to do with old-school methods: vigilant surveillance and plentiful gossip.

Demands for private life would have seemed out of place in Gandhi's ashram. Everything had to be done in the open, even the most embarrassing tasks. Gandhi wanted full access to the most intimate aspects of the ashramites' lives. Have you felt any sexual urges lately? Any sinful cravings? Report them to Bapu. Have you undressed a fellow ashramite with your mind's eye, wittingly or unwittingly? Go and get your punishment. Bapu developed a special interest in the ashramites' restroom activities. "Did you have a good bowel movement this morning, sisters?" he would ask his two close female disciples, Abha and Sushila, by way of greeting them every morning.[117] In turn, he would expose and deliver himself—to the last inch of his body—to the hungry eyes of the ashramites, who could not have enough of him. As a woman ashramite would remember later, Gandhi "was completely unselfconscious about urinating and defecating, rather like a child. . . . If any of us wanted to talk to him, we could go in and out as we pleased."[118] If an ashramite wanted more intimacy with Bapu, all they had to do was feign constipation. Since that was one of his favorite conditions, he would drop everything and personally perform an enema on her. Gandhi's bath-taking, however, was a more limited-access affair: as a sign of special favor, he would allow selected female ashramites to bathe him. For all the similarities, the dwellers of Thomas More's Utopia would have blanched at Gandhi's community.

It was in this deliciously weird setting that Gandhi wanted to establish "the Kingdom of Heaven on earth."[119] For the ashram was not only the place where Gandhi practiced his fakirism, but also where he pushed it to its breaking point: his mission was no longer to realize himself, and enlighten those around him, but to enlighten India as a whole—and, through it, the world at large. "If I found myself entirely absorbed in the service of the community," Gandhi writes in the *Autobiography*, the reason was "my desire for self-realization." He had turned "the religion of service" into his own religion, and felt that "God could be realized only through service. And service for me was the service of India."[120]

After Gandhi's return to India from South Africa, one senses in his language and thinking, and even in his behavior, increasingly messianic undertones.[121] The ashram, for all its modest appearance, was the place where the ideal India was rehearsed and was to come into existence. Gandhi's project was not so much political as anthropological. What he envisioned was not new political institutions, but a *transformed humanity*. If it worked in the ashram, it would succeed in India; and if it worked in India, it should succeed anywhere. "If one man gains spiritually," Gandhi wrote, "the whole world gains with him; and if one man fails, the world fails to that extent."[122] What Gandhi was ultimately after was planetary fakirism.

This helps explain the extraordinary demands Gandhi placed on the practitioners of *satyagraha:* utmost purity, complete poverty, selflessness, truthfulness, and above all, *brahmacharya* (absolute chastity). Without *brahmacharya,* thought Gandhi, *satyagraha* is impossible: "Only he who can observe complete brahmacharya can complete training in non-violence."[123] Politically meaningful action can only be the fruit of a properly channeled sexuality. Gandhi sketched a theory of power that tied the sublimation of sexual desire to the efficacy of service to others. "All power," he said, "comes from the preservation and sublimation of the vitality that is responsible for the creation of life. If the vitality is husbanded instead of being dissipated, it is transmuted into creative energy of the highest order."[124]

With deep roots in classical Indian spirituality, Gandhi's theory may explain his inordinate interest in sex. To do anything worthy, this theory goes, we need to transcend ourselves—defy and deny the biology in us. That is especially true of politics. Hence his exhortation: "Those who want to perform national service . . . must lead a celibate life, no matter if married or unmarried."[125]

A Person and a Thing

Margarete Buber-Neumann, a German communist who fled to the Soviet Union after Hitler came to power, was arrested in 1938. She didn't do anything wrong, and she didn't have to: she was sentenced as the wife of an "enemy of the people" and ended up in a camp in Kazakhstan. When Hitler and Stalin made their deal, she was promptly handed over to the Gestapo and taken to a Nazi camp. In her memoir, *Under Two Dictators,* Buber-Neumann compares the two systems, with a special emphasis on camp life in each.

Originally designed to neutralize political undesirables, the labor camps soon became a major economic force in the Soviet Union. They were "at the heart of the Soviet economy," concludes historian Anne Applebaum, and she is not alone in this assessment.[126] The Gulag, writes Orlando Figes, was a "vast archipelago of labour camps and construction sites, mines and railway-building sites, a slave economy that cast a shadow over the entire Soviet Union."[127]

The camps were not really meant to "reeducate" people, as the official line would have it, but to break and enslave them. The millions of inmates (*zeks*) spread throughout Russia constituted an enormous pool of virtually free slave labor, which the Soviet authorities put to profitable use.[128] "Slave" is hardly a metaphor here: for all intents and purposes, these people were the property of the Soviet state, which did as it pleased with them. In *One Day in the Life of Ivan Denisovich,* Alexander Solzhenitsyn (a slave himself) has Shukhov, the protagonist, calculate the exact amount of time that belongs to a *zek:* "Apart from sleep, the only time a prisoner lives for himself is ten minutes in the morning at breakfast, five minutes over dinner, and five at supper."[129] The result was complete dehumanization. As another *zek* observed, once someone has been in the camp, even if he's eventually freed, "he cannot make himself whole again."[130]

Eugenia Ginzburg, another slave, recalls a camp guard telling her, "Enemies are not people. We're allowed to do what we like with them."[131] And so they did. In the camp, writes Buber-Neumann, you are "a thing, an object to be mauled unceremoniously."[132] In the official Gulag documents, the *zeks* were referred to not as persons, but as "units of labor."[133] Maxim Gorky—that tender, artistic soul—could not use such rough language, and called them "half-animals" instead.[134] Some of Russia's finest people, its best minds, ended up like this. Between 1929 and 1951, the brilliant writer

Varlam Shalamov spent some seventeen years in various camps across Russia, where he lived the life of a thing, or—in Gorky's endearing words—half-animal. At the age of thirty, he recalls, "I found myself in a very real sense dying from hunger and literally fighting for a piece of bread."[135] More amazing than the length of his imprisonment is that he survived it. Others were not so lucky: Isaac Babel, Pavel Florensky, Osip Mandelstam, and countless others.

The differences between life inside the camps and life outside should not be exaggerated. It wasn't just that, with so many people arrested, there was always a busy traffic between inside and outside. There was also a profound continuity, and a symmetry of sorts, between the two, which didn't escape the more perceptive observers. "Life inside the camps," wrote Vasily Grossman, "could be seen as an exaggerated, magnified reflection of life outside. Far from being contradictory, these two realities were symmetrical."[136] Eventually, the whole country became one enormous labor camp, where the Bolshevik regime performed its work of annihilation. Joseph Conrad had called tsarist Russia an "empire of nothingness." The new regime made sure that Soviet Russia would not fall behind its predecessor.

The Bolsheviks viewed the French Revolution as a model of sorts; in their more arrogant moments, they pretended that they had taken over where the French had left off. But the contrast could not be sharper. While in France revolutionary violence was, by and large, a spontaneous occurrence, a cruel, yet genuine act of collective reckoning, in Russia terror was, for the most part, engineered in the upper circles of the party and used, cynically and pettily, as a tool of political subjugation. The French Revolution made thousands of victims, but somehow it didn't manage to kill hope. The Bolshevik Revolution, with its millions of dead and enslaved, ended all hope. History, which has its own sense of immanent justice, has treated the two events accordingly: while the former, for all its mindless cruelty, is still associated with a new age of liberty, equality, and human rights, the latter is indistinguishable from all the trappings of totalitarianism: a large surveillance apparatus, millions of informants, arbitrary arrests, the labor camps, to say nothing of the millions of corpses the Bolshevik regime left across Russia, and beyond.

Compared to the savage conflagration of the French Revolution, the Bolshevik Revolution was a pretty lame affair. The work of small-time arsonists who set their homes on fire to collect the insurance money. But the bodies piled up all the same.

The Three Evils

Exactly what kind of India was Gandhi plotting in his ashram? For good or ill, that country never came to pass, so we don't know for sure.[137] But we have a glimpse of his brainchild in *Hind Swaraj*, which he published in 1909. The book is as short as its job is tall: designing the India of the future. Before turning to the future, however, Gandhi needs to settle accounts with the India of the present. The country may nominally be ruled by the British, but in fact it's subjected to the tyranny of a far worse enemy. "India is being ground down," he writes, "not under the English heel, but under that of modern civilization."[138] So his target in the book is not so much the British Empire as the type of civilization it represents.

Gandhi cannot forgive modern civilization for bringing three evils to India. They are worse than plague, locusts, and venomous serpents. The three calamities have "impoverished the country so much so that, if we do not wake up in time, we shall be ruined." The three atrocious evils, in Gandhi's estimation, are *railways*, *lawyers*, and *doctors*. In their distinct ways, these devilish tools of subjugation have brought India to its knees.

Take the railways. They have "spread the bubonic plague," proclaims Gandhi. How could that happen? For a very simple reason: without trains, "the masses could not move from place to place." The railways are, therefore, "the carriers of plague germs."

If that was not bad enough, the railways could also cause famines to strike more often. How so? Because, thanks to the "facility of means of locomotion," people can "sell out their grain and it is sent to the dearest markets." If only Indian farmers kept their grain unsold, much disaster would be averted.[139]

The lawyers pose no less a danger to Indian society. Their trade is wicked, their skills of a dubious nature, and their sins countless. They have, Gandhi believes, "enslaved India . . . accentuated Hindu-Mahomedan dissensions and . . . confirmed British authority." Above all, lawyers are useless. They are "men who have little to do," writes the London-educated lawyer, contemptuously. "Lazy people, in order to indulge in luxuries, take up such professions." Should Indian lawyers realize the toxicity of their calling, and stop doing whatever they're doing, India would suddenly find itself in much better shape: "If pleaders were to abandon their profession, and consider it just as degrading as prostitution, English rule would break up in a day."[140]

Doctors, finally, are no better than lawyers. Granted, unlike attorneys, doctors are not idlers, but their deeds are no less impure. We should be suspicious of the medical profession, admonishes Gandhi, first of all, because it is "certainly not taken up for the purpose of serving humanity." People choose to practice medicine only to "obtain honors and riches."[141] (Those rapacious MDs, always ready to make a killing!) Second, because their job is repulsive by its nature. Consider the abominations going on in modern hospitals:

> Hospitals are institutions for propagating sin. Men take less care of their bodies and immorality increases. European doctors are the worst of all. For the sake of a mistaken care of the human body, they kill annually thousands of animals. They practice vivisection.[142]

Elsewhere, Gandhi writes that hospitals are "the instruments of the Devil." Modern medical science is nothing but "the concentrated essence of Black Magic." Just think of what we would be like without them: "If there were no hospitals for venereal diseases, or even for consumptives, we should have less consumption, and less sexual vice among us."[143] One doesn't go to see a doctor, Gandhi seems to suggest, because one had visited brothels. It's the other way around: one goes to see prostitutes because one has seen a doctor.

The trouble with modern civilization, Gandhi believes, is that it is singularly focused on the human body. This civilization has developed in the West to take care of material needs, and that has made it excessively worldly and materialistic—and, ultimately, immoral and irreligious. Nothing could redeem Western civilization in Gandhi's eyes. The scientific progress it has made possible? That only feeds its materialism. Democracy? God forbid! "It is a superstition and ungodly thing," he writes in *Hind Swaraj,* "to believe that an act of a majority binds a minority."[144]

By contrast, Indian civilization—India of the past and future—is all about the cultivation of the spirit. Indians may be unadvanced scientifically and technologically, but their superior morality and spirituality make up for what they lack elsewhere. "The tendency of the Indian civilization is to elevate the moral being, that of the Western civilization is to propagate immorality. The latter is godless, the former is based on a belief in God."[145] To be fair, Gandhi asserts the absolute superiority of India's civilization not only over Western civilization, but over virtually all other civilizations, Eastern or Western, ancient or modern:

> I believe that the civilization India has evolved is not to be beaten in the world. Nothing can equal the seeds sown by our ancestors. Rome went, Greece shared the same fate; the might of the Pharaohs was broken; Japan has become Westernized; of China nothing can be said; but India is still, somehow or other, sound at the foundation.[146]

Gandhi wrote these pages while he was away from India. He had left for England when he was still a teenager, before having had any chance to know his country. Then, no sooner did he return from London than he moved to South Africa. While there, he visited India a few times, for varying lengths of time, but without getting to know it in any meaningful way. The more time Gandhi was spending abroad, the more enamored with India he became. Not only does distance cause enchantment, but it completely recreates the object of our affection. Like all lovers, Gandhi could say silly things. At close quarters, when our focus sharpens, everything turns out to be quite different, as Gandhi was to find out, to his sorrow, in the coming years.

Gandhi's anti-Western and antimodern stance is not without its irony: the writers who influenced his religious, political, and philosophical outlook most vigorously, from Leo Tolstoy to John Ruskin, came almost exclusively from the modern West. His years in London were decisive for his formation as an intellectual, lawyer, and activist. Even his discovery of Indian spirituality he owed to Western writers: he first read the *Bhagavad Gita* in London, in Edwin Arnold's English translation.

The Worst Thing

"Tamara was only twenty-one; a dark-eyed beauty with delicate features and fine limbs." That's how Margarete Buber-Neumann recalls one of her camp friends. Tamara was young and beautiful and full of life. To her misfortune, she was also dedicated to the Bolshevik regime, and served it loyally and enthusiastically, if perhaps a bit naïvely.

> There was a literary circle at her university and she was one of its leading lights. . . . The students discussed literary problems and read aloud from their own works. . . . One day

> Tamara read a poem she had written entitled "Hymn to Freedom." Shortly afterwards she was arrested by the GPU [secret police] and charged with "Preparation for terrorism."[147]

Without having done anything wrong, Tamara was sentenced to eight years of forced labor and shipped to a camp, her young life all but destroyed. "The worst thing is that they arrested my father as well, and now Mother's all alone," she told Buber-Neumann, overwhelmed by guilt.[148] That was Stalin's signature act: along with the suspect, for good measure, family members were arrested, too. Tamara's drama was the drama of millions who went through what she did. The Gulag literature, from Solzhenitsyn to Shalamov to Buber-Neumann herself, gives us some sense of that, even though no literature can capture such senselessness.

Yet something else happened there—something more difficult to document and write about because of the considerable shame involved. Someone must have informed on Tamara, and when the report that led to her arrest was written down, the informer's own life was ruined as well, in a different way. Since the secret police relied heavily on informers, a large section of the population became accomplices to the regime's terror. Some were blackmailed and did it unwillingly; others were offered incentives and did it for gain. Others still, plenty, in fact, *volunteered* to inform—to exact revenge on someone, get rid of a love rival, obtain the suspect's apartment, curry favor with the regime, advance their careers, move up the social ladder, or whatnot. There is no way to undo such self-degradation. Outwardly, these people survived, some even thrived, but at a price so steep that they became totally bankrupt inside.

In the long run, the mass collaboration with the totalitarian regime was one of the most devastating effects of the communist regimes in Russia, Eastern Europe, and elsewhere. It wasn't enough that the system ruined people's lives, arresting them arbitrarily, taking away their children, executing them for imaginary crimes, or working them to death in labor camps. It killed the souls of many more, who stayed behind. With every denunciation made, willingly or under pressure, the informers descended one step lower.

If this was not bad enough, the large-scale collaboration made it difficult to draw a clear line between victimizer and victim, oppressor and oppressed. Pretty much everyone was in it. You could cross the line without even realizing it, several times a day; you could be the regime's victim in the morning and its unwitting collaborator in the afternoon. The "line separating good and evil," observed Solzhenitsyn, "passes not through states, nor between classes, nor between political parties either—but right through every human heart—and through all human hearts."[149]

The long-term result was moral hell. One of its subtler features is that you don't live in it—it is the hell that *lives in you;* it shapes every minute of your conscious life and eventually defines you. You wake up with it, live all day with it, and go to bed with it. "Communism is like AIDS," says filmmaker Krzysztof Kieslowski, who lived the experience in communist Poland:

> You have to die with it. You can't be cured. And that applies to anyone who's had to do anything with Communism regardless of what side they were on. It's irrelevant whether they were Communists or anti-Communists or entirely uncommitted to either political sided. It applies to everybody.[150]

The German Ideology was first published in 1932 by the Marx-Engels Institute in Moscow. By then, Moscow had become the mecca of a new religion—"scientific socialism," they called it. Lenin's holy relics were kept there. The names of Marx and Engels were chanted, ritually, countless times a day, across Russia and beyond, their faces displayed, like the icons of old, for all to behold and worship. The two godless prophets must have turned in their graves.

As for getting rid of "all the muck of ages"—when we finally emerged from that grand cleansing experiment, we were more covered in muck than ever. If fire was the privileged element of the French Revolution (one can still imagine a phoenix rising from its ashes), the Bolshevik Revolution seems to have had a strong preference for mud.

Self-Transcendence?

For all his own failing, Gandhi was ready to blame *himself* for the failures of others—his sons, his associates and disciples, India at large, the whole world. As a teacher, he tells us in his *Autobiography*, he thought he was responsible for the failures of his charges. Whenever a moral failure occurred in the ashram, he first blamed himself for it, before chastising the culprit. Sometimes, on such occasions, he undertook fasting for moral cleansing and purification. Taking the blame was for Gandhi not just some pedagogical trick (even if it was that too), but an important part of his self-realization project.

In this, Gandhi was inspired by a fifteenth-century Gujarati poet and mystic, Narsinh Mehta, who taught that "he who understands the pain of others is one of God's own." The way to the highest always passes through the lowest; one can't be in God's proximity unless one first recognizes oneself in the humiliated, in those whom others treat as dirt. "If I have to be reborn," Gandhi said once, "I should be born an untouchable, so that I may share their sorrows, sufferings and the affronts leveled at them, in order that I may endeavor to free myself and them from that miserable condition."[151] Gandhi identified himself with others so profoundly that often, if some wrong was committed in the world, he felt he had a part in it. When someone "commits a crime anywhere," he reflected, "I feel I am the culprit."[152] Later he wrote, "Whenever I see an erring man, I say to myself: 'I have also erred'; when I see a lustful man, I say to myself, 'So was I once'; and in this way I feel kinship with everyone in the world."[153] He was not a Mahatma ("great soul") for nothing.

The communal violence that preceded, accompanied, and followed the Partition gave Gandhi plenty of opportunity for self-identification with others and painful self-reflection—and self-blame. On January 2, 1947, he noted in his diary, "I can see there is some grave defect in me somewhere which is the cause of all this. All around me is utter darkness."[154] On January 9, 1948, while massacres were taking place in the Punjab, Calcutta, and elsewhere, he admitted, "I am responsible for all this."[155] This was the background for his experiments with young girls. The episode stands out for the scandal it caused; it embarrassed even his closest disciples, alienated his associates (some of whom quit), and has puzzled his admirers ever since. Ramachandra Guha, an otherwise friendly biographer, sees it as Gandhi's "strangest experiment."

As the political situation in India was deteriorating, a notion entered Gandhi's mind that the communal violence all *around* him was related to some failure *within*. That such things were happening he took as a sign that something important was missing in his own life: his *brahmacharya* was untested, he decided. If only he could pass the test, the violence might stop. It was not enough that for decades Gandhi hadn't had sex with anyone, or that he managed to control himself so completely that he could feel no desire. He wanted his desire to control itself, without the mind's intervention.[156] Untested, his chastity was not chaste enough, and his moral purity endangered. Gandhi chose to test his chastity by sharing his bed with young girls, selected from among his followers or even relatives (at least two of his nieces were involved). They would sleep, usually naked, next to him, in the same state of undress. There was nothing explicitly sexual about this, even as sex was at the core of the whole thing.

Gandhi's *brahmacharya* experiments were another instance of his lifelong effort to transcend himself. What's unique about Gandhi is not that he lived for self-transcendence, but that he thought he should take the whole world with him in this project. V. S. Naipaul, in an insightful essay, called Gandhi a "failed reformist."[157] But that may be the wrong way of reading the Gandhian project. Gandhi didn't simply want to "reform" the world, he wanted to remake it. And in so doing he failed. How could he not? The task was too much for him—it would be for anyone. Yet when you fail like this—not on a purely personal plane, but by taking on the failures of the whole world—your failure is no longer yours and probably no longer a failure. Rabindranath Tagore grasped Gandhi's predicament early on:

> Perhaps he will not succeed. Perhaps he will fail as the Buddha failed and as Christ failed to wean men from their inequities, but he will always be remembered as one who made his life a lesson for all ages to come.[158]

Could it be, then, that through his radical self-effacement Gandhi turned failure into its opposite? Gandhi succeeded, as tragic heroes often do, in pushing the boundaries of the human condition, and opening new vistas on to what humanity can be. He was crushed in the process, as tragic heroes always are. And left us all guessing, as tragic heroes sometimes do.

The Trouble with Perfection

Political failure works more insidiously than the failure of things, and—since the *polis* is us—it is all the more devastating. Some part of us dies with every political catastrophe we witness.

While there can be something oddly invigorating about the failure we experience in our relationship with the physical world, political failure, on top of the pileup of corpses it often leaves behind, is morally crippling and intellectually humiliating.

The most humiliating of all is that, when all is said and done, we typically fail to learn from it. Consider the worst political atrocities you know of—destructive wars, ethnic cleansing, mass rape, genocide, anything. They will almost certainly happen again.

All humans are mortal, but the Hitlers and the Stalins of this world never truly die—they only change names. We know everything about their deeds, but this will not prevent others from committing them again. On the contrary. Not only did Stalin know of Robespierre's Reign of Terror, he did everything he could to outdo him. And he succeeded. Knowing about the Armenian genocide did not prevent Hitler from organizing his own—if anything, it inspired him. Just as detailed historical knowledge of Hitler's Holocaust did not stop the genocides in Bosnia, Rwanda, and elsewhere. It is happening again, in one form or the other, in some part of the world or another, even as you read this.

The only saving grace, if that's what it is, lies in the brutal knowledge that this kind of failure brings about: the revelation of a world of power-hungry political animals, busily asserting themselves against one other, and crushing everything in their way. The spectacle of a humanity seriously undermined by the workings of its own survival instincts.

This is precious, uncommon knowledge, which few teachers will dare share with us, and yet it is something vital if we are to make any progress. Detachment from the domain of power has been part of any spiritual tradition worth its name, whether religious or secular, philosophical or otherwise. One cannot be spiritually elevated and politically entangled at the same time—at once sick and healthy. Gandhi's case shows dramatically what happens when the separation cannot take place because the sage and the politician reside in the same person. The higher his spiritual aspirations, the more painful his political entanglement. No wonder that at the end of his life he reached a point where all he could see was, by his own admission, "darkness and madness."

Since we are meant to live with others, any effort to separate ourselves from the body politic involves going against our nature and tears us apart. But do it we must if we are to reach a higher understanding. Political failure can offer us such a chance. For should we look intently enough into the landscape of loss and devastation that we face when a radical political project (utopian attempt, totalitarian government, bloody revolution) has bitten the dust, we will make out an unmistakable warning: "Be careful what you wish for!" "Republic of virtue," "classless society," "ideal state," "perfect community"—they are all admirable, as lofty as they are well-meaning, but we should never lose sight of what they are: *political fictions*. Not some mended version of the real world, but a wild act of imagination—a world unto itself, almost completely cut off from political reality.

The trouble with Utopia is not that it's impossible to put into practice (strictly speaking, it may be possible), it is that it is fundamentally alien to what we are. We are seriously imperfect creatures—flawed and error-prone and corruptible. Decency itself requires us to place this notion at the core of whatever we pursue, politically, in the world. But since we also lack decency, most of the time we don't do that, as our repeated political failures and the attendant pileup of corpses demonstrate. And so, out of an obsessive need for perfection and a misguided quest for purity, we end up muddled in ever more imperfection. Mistaking fiction for reality is not just naïve, it is highly dangerous. When you take them for something else, fictions come to haunt you with a vengeance.

Such failures, humbling us profoundly as they do, reinforce an important and simple lesson: we are closer to nothing than to anything else. By trying to be perfect and be everything, we miss the chance to achieve what might actually be within our reach.

3

WINNERS AND LOSERS

We all know him. He features in many of the stories we tell our-selves. We may have even had a glimpse of this person, but seeing him is not that important. At some level, he performs his function best when he is not there—when he is only invoked, mocked, gos-siped about, or scorned. For all his vivid presence in our lives, we wouldn't say we are close to him. In fact, we try to steer clear of him as much as we can. For his condition seems contagious, and God forbid his predicament rub off on us. We certainly need him, but only insofar as we need someone against whom we can define ourselves: whatever we are, we are not him. Thanks to this simple mental exercise, we manage to convince ourselves that we are better off by default: whatever problems we may have, we don't have his problem; no matter how bad our afflictions, we don't suffer from his. And who is this exactly? He is the worst kind of person one can be: *a loser.*

A loser is the ultimate social failure. And the way a community constructs its losers and failures is never innocent. Tell me how you define social failure, and I will tell you a few things about yourself—about your biggest dreams and your worst fears. In the United States, we are particularly good at constructing losers—it's a national industry. Losers seem to come with the American Dream, as its dark, shameful, ugly side. In an interview late in life, Arthur Miller, whose *Death of a Salesman* could be seen as a kind of hymn to loserdom, reflected on how America's obsession with success only accentuates the high cost of social failure. "People who succeed are loved because they exude some magical formula for fending off destruction, fending off death," he says. "It's the most brutal way of looking at life that one can imagine, because it discards anyone who does not measure up. It wants to destroy them. . . . It's a moral condemnation that goes on. You don't want to be near this failure."[1] You don't want to be in the proximity of the loser, and yet your success does not have much meaning in the absence of the loser's concomitant failure.

Each organized society generates its own type of losers— something in which, as in a magic mirror of sorts, it unwittingly projects and reveals itself. There is a certain light-heartedness, for example, in the way ancient Athenians engaged with the figure of Diogenes of Sinope. The Cynic seems to have been their favorite loser. Most Athenians certainly didn't want to be *like* him, but they would gladly amuse themselves by spending time with him. When someone asked Diogenes what kind of wine he liked best, he allegedly quipped, "Somebody else's."[2] Apparently, the Athenians offered him the opportunity to enjoy that particular vintage. As legend would have it, Diogenes's presence was in such demand in Athens that he could be fussy about where to go. Once he is said to have turned down a dinner invitation on account of the host's manners: the last time he had been there, he explained, the host didn't thank him properly.[3] Such examples, while apocryphal, suggest that Athenians needed Diogenes at least as much as he needed them. He may have been a loser, but he was one by choice, and as a matter of philosophical calling. No matter how scandalous his eccentricities, the Athenians were willing to play along. That was part of the way they constructed and engaged with their social failures.

To be a loser today is a different business altogether. We don't want to be anywhere near them, and yet we are obsessed with them, most likely because we are terrified by the possibility of becoming one ourselves. To be a loser shapes—negatively, yet decisively—the way we see ourselves and our place in society. Failure is rarely indifferent to us. It unsettles and disturbs—there is something dark, even morbid about it. And that is revealed in the way we relate to those our society constructs as losers.

There was a time, some two centuries ago, when a loser was someone who simply lost something—in a fire, for example, or a business venture gone bad. Not so anymore. Today a loser comes with an unwritten warning: "Stay away." As Scott Sandage suggests in *Born Losers: A History of Failure in America*, failure "conjures such vivid images of lost souls" that it is difficult to envision a time "when the word commonly meant 'breaking in business'—going broke."[4]

For us a failure is not someone who makes mistakes—big or small, occasional or frequent. Not even someone who fails in some way or another. Everyone fails, but not everyone is a failure. To be a failure is not a matter of practice, of intelligence or morality, but of being. Failure is who you are, not what you do or say or think, almost as if you were predestined to be this way. It is an aura that you just cannot shake. There may be an element of lifestyle choice involved, but in North America, Europe, and much of today's "civilized" world, to be a failure is to be cursed. Nothing can save you from it, no matter what you do or say or think. Your damnation is ontological.

The previous circle—that of political failure—concerns us because, like it or not, we are part of an organized community. And yet we could conceivably carve out a space apart from the reach of politics, should we so desire. Not an easy task, but the thing can be done—after all, many a sage has achieved it in the past, and has showed us how to do it. The circle of social failure, by comparison, is significantly tighter: regardless of where you are, on which side of the divide, you can feel its firm embrace. You feel it when others decree you to be a loser, just as you do when you participate, however remotely, in decreeing others as losers. You just can't escape it.

The Philosopher of Failure

For some, he was one of the most subversive thinkers of his time—a twentieth-century Nietzsche, only darker and with a better sense of humor. Many, especially in his youth, thought him to be a dangerous lunatic. Others saw him just as a charmingly irresponsible young man who posed no dangers to others—only to himself, perhaps. When his book on mysticism went to press, the typesetter (a good, God-fearing man), realizing how blasphemous it was, refused to touch it. The publisher washed his hands of the matter and the author had to publish his blasphemy elsewhere, at his own expense.

Emil Cioran was a Romanian-born French thinker and author of some two dozen books of savage, unsettling beauty.[5] He is an essayist in the best French tradition, and though French was not his native tongue, some think him one of the finest writers in that language. His writing style is whimsical, unsystematic, fragmentary; he is celebrated as a master of aphorism. For Cioran, however, the "fragment" was more than a writing style: it was a way of life. He called himself *un homme de fragment.* He was deeply suspicious of systematic philosophy; to concoct "philosophical systems" was a charlatan's job, he thought. He wanted to be a thinker pure and simple—*Privatdenker,* he called himself, reaching out for a better word—not "philosopher."

Cioran often contradicts himself, but that's the least of his worries. With him, self-contradiction is not even a weakness, but the sign of a mind alive. For writing is not about consistency, nor about persuasion or keeping the reader entertained. Writing is not even about literature. For Cioran, as for Montaigne several centuries earlier, writing has a performative function: you write to act upon yourself—to pick up the pieces after a personal disaster or to pull yourself out of a bad depression; to come to terms with a deadly disease or to mourn the loss of a close friend. You write not to go mad, not to kill yourself or others. In a conversation with the Spanish philosopher Fernando Savater, Cioran says at one point, "If I didn't write, I could have become an assassin."[6] Human existence, at its core, is endless anguish and despair, and writing can make it a bit more bearable. One writes simply to stay alive and to stave off death: *"un livre est un suicide différé,"* Cioran writes in *The Trouble with Being Born* (*De l'inconvénient d'être né*), published in 1973.[7]

Cioran wrote himself out of death over and over again. He composed his first book, *On the Heights of Despair* (*Pe culmile disperării*, published in 1934), when he was twenty-three years old, in just a few weeks, while suffering from a severe bout of insomnia. (Insomnia, he said repeatedly, was "the greatest drama of my life."[8]) The book—which remains one of his finest—marked the beginning of a strong, intimate link in his life between writing and sleeplessness:

> I've never been able to write otherwise than in the midst of the depression [*cafard*] brought about by my nights of insomnia. For seven years I could barely sleep. I need this depression, and even today before I sit down to write I play a disk of Gypsy music from Hungary.[9]

That Cioran is an unsystematic thinker doesn't mean his work lacks unity. In fact, it is kept tightly together not only by his singular writing style, but also by a distinct set of themes, motifs, and idiosyncrasies. Among them failure figures prominently. Cioran was in love with failure: its specter haunts his whole oeuvre. Throughout his life, he never strayed away from failure. He studied its many incarnations from varying angles and at different moments, as true connoisseurs do, and looked for it in the most unexpected places.

Not only individuals can end up as failures, Cioran believed, but also societies, peoples, and countries. Especially countries. "I was fascinated with Spain," he said once, "because it offered the example of the most spectacular failure. The greatest country in the world reduced to such a state of decay!"[10] Failure, for Cioran, is like the water of the Taoists: it seeps everywhere and permeates everything. Great ideas can be soaked with failure, and so can books, philosophies, institutions, and political systems.

The human condition itself is just another failed project: "No longer wanting to be a man," he writes in *The Trouble with Being Born,* he is "dreaming of another form of failure."[11] The universe is one big failure, and so is life itself: "Before being a fundamental mistake," he says, "life is a failure of taste which neither death nor even poetry succeeds in correcting."[12] Failure rules the world like the capricious God of the Old Testament. One of Cioran's aphorisms reads, "'You were wrong to count on me.' Who can speak in such terms? *God and the Failure.*"[13]

Born a Loser

The loser is so by decree, then. The situation, unsettling as it may be, is not new—we have looked into this abyss before: the old theological doctrine of predestination is precisely about such an ontology of damnation. How the successful in our society relate to our losers brings to mind the way in which the "reprobates" were treated at the hands of various communities of the "elect." Since the doctrine of predestination may help us find our footing when it comes to understanding how success and failure work, it is worth having a closer look at some key moments in its historical development.

In Saint Paul's Epistle to the Romans, there is a passage (Rom. 9:18–24) that proponents of predestination of different stripes consider a foundational text. The premise—involving God's omnipotence and freedom—seems innocent and reasonable enough:

> So then [God] has mercy upon whomever he wills, and he
> hardens the heart of whomever he wills. You will say to me

then, "Why does he still find fault? For who can resist his will?" But who are you, a man, to answer back to God? Will what is molded say to its molder, "Why have you made me thus?"[14]

Paul's next move takes us into positively terrifying territory. Pushing the pottery metaphor to its breaking point, Paul speaks now of God as a playful artist, a *Deo ludens* fond of dramatic effects. The text, in short, is about how God creates man only to take delight in his destruction, much as a whimsical artisan would approach his output:

> Has the potter no right over the clay, to make out of the same lump one vessel for beauty and another for menial use? What if God, desiring to show his wrath and to make known his power, has endured with much patience the vessels of wrath made for destruction, in order to make known the riches of his glory for the vessels of mercy, which he has prepared beforehand for glory?

A "vessel of wrath made for destruction"—who could say no to such destiny? Who would not be tempted to serve as a vessel for "menial use," not only in this world, but for all eternity? Granted, we may be reading too much into Paul's text; he may have had other things in mind. Yet his ruminations have made history.

John Calvin has a special place in this history. He used the Pauline text to develop a doctrine of predestination of his own, one of frightening coherence, with lasting impact. In his *Institutes of the Christian Religion,* Calvin talks of predestination in several places. A full chapter (book 3, chapter 20) is dedicated to "Eternal election, by which God has predestined some to salvation, others to destruction." It was precisely this doctrine that, for a long time, made Calvinism so feared and so loved, at once repulsive and attractive.

For starters, Calvin speaks of "the lofty mystery of predestina-tion" to warn his readers that it is not for the faint-hearted nor for the feeble-minded.[15] The topic may attract us only, perversely, to lead us to perdition. This realm—"the sacred precincts of divine wisdom," he calls it—can ruin even its most passionate pursuers. Calvin refers here to a "kind of knowledge, the ardent desire for which is both foolish and dangerous, nay, even deadly."[16]

Once he has taken these precautionary measures, Calvin can start dealing with predestination in earnest. As expected, he makes use of Saint Paul's metaphor. The image of the "vessels of mercy" prepared for glory and the "vessels of wrath made for destruction" is conspicuous in his text. The human condition Calvin depicts often looks like a site of devastation. First, a definition:

> We call predestination God's eternal decree, by which he com-pacted with himself what he willed to become of each man. For all are not created in equal condition; rather, eternal life is foreordained for some, eternal damnation for others. There-fore, as any man has been created to one or the other of these ends, we speak of him as predestined to life or to death.[17]

Not only is the Pauline distinction preserved in Calvin's text, but Calvin even borrows some of Paul's language. Sometimes the two voices echo one another, at other times they mix to become almost indistinguishable, and still at other times Calvin's voice emerges even stronger than Paul's in picturing a humanity crushed by God's *decretum horribile*.

"What of those," Calvin wonders, whom God "created for dis-honor in life and destruction in death, to become the instruments of his wrath and examples of his severity?"[18] What of them, indeed? They are of course meant for destruction, but for their crushing, Calvin's God employs devilish inventiveness. Intent as he is on breaking those unsightly vessels, God makes sure they have no chance to escape their fate—by mistake, for example, or by sneaking in along with the "vessels of mercy." The two types need to go their separate ways for fear of contamination.

Much of the predestinarian thinking is driven by an obsessive quest for purity, and Calvin's God goes a long way to make sure all chaff is kept safely away from the wheat: "That they may come to their end, [God] sometimes deprives them of the capacity to hear his word; at other times he, rather, blinds and stuns them by the preaching of it." This sophisticated holocaust is a matter of divine justice, Calvin assures us: it is God as "Supreme Judge" who "makes way for his predestination when he leaves in blindness those whom he has once condemned and deprived of participation in his light."[19] No trace of Paul's *Deus ludens* here. Calvin's God doesn't play games.

Calvin emerges in these pages as a radical theologian, and his radicalism is a sight to behold. Something frighteningly alien permeates whatever he says. As a matter of both philosophical method and personal calling, Calvin looks on the human world from an infinitely remote perspective. The judgment he passes from there is not his, but God's. No matter the issue at stake, Calvin always takes God's side: God is always right, by necessity so, while man is always wrong. "For the damned to complain of their lot would be much the same as for animals to bemoan the fact that they were not born as men," observes Max Weber. "For everything of the flesh is separated from God by an unbridgeable gulf and deserves of Him only eternal death, in so far as He has not decreed otherwise for the glorification of His Majesty." Calvin's interest is "solely in God, not in man." God "does not exist for men, but men for the sake of God."[20]

Calvin's radical method has a dual effect on his theology. First, it allows him to push his thinking to its ultimate logical consequences. We may disagree with Calvin or dislike his conclusions, but we have to admit that he is an awfully consistent thinker. If he was mad, as many of his critics liked to think, there was rigor and discipline to his madness. Second, Calvin's method renders his thinking *monstrous,* in the original sense of "dreadful." Calvin's legal training must have come in handy when he laid down his doctrine. Never has a more passionate case been made for capital punishment—for one's destruction not only in this world, but in eternity. In any given situation, Calvin takes on the prosecutor's role, never that of the defense lawyer. Then, before you know it, the prosecutor turns executioner—God's exterminating angel. The victim has no say in the process. There is nothing she could possibly utter in her defense, not even that God's judgment was passed on her before she could do anything, before she even existed— indeed, before the world itself existed. If anything, the condemned should consider herself blessed to be part of such a grand system of divine justice. For "God's hidden decree," Calvin writes, "is not to be searched out but obediently marveled at."[21]

Where does Calvin's divine "madness" come from? you may wonder. It must have started with an overwhelming experience of grace. In such cases, as Weber observed, there is a strong feeling of "certainty that that grace is the sole product of an objective power, and not in the least to be attributed to personal worth." That power only is in charge. The human subject is too weak, too sinful, and in general too insignificant to deserve such a gift: the overpowering "gift of grace" could not possibly owe anything to his "co-operation," nor could it be related to "achievements or qualities" of his "faith and will."[22] The human subject, fundamentally unworthy, can be something only to the extent that it submits to that power. Calvin's understanding of predestination, though it concerned the human species as such, had its roots in a very personal experience of God.

As you read through Calvin's text, you cannot help but think that human reason, pushed to its breaking point, turns against itself. You look in vain for any traces of doubt in Calvin's thinking, room for nuance or alternative readings. Perhaps God only predestined some to salvation, without necessarily condemning others to perdition? No, answers Calvin, the predestination is double: "God adopts some to hope of life, and sentences others to eternal death."

Or maybe God doesn't really cause our damnation, but just "allows" some of us to be damned? No, it cannot be. "God willed, not only permitted Adam's fall and the rejection of the reprobate." Is it really possible that in our election or damnation individual merit doesn't make any difference whatsoever? It's not only possible, it's mathematically certain:

> We assert that, with respect to the elect, this plan was founded upon his freely given mercy, without regard to human worth; but by his just and irreprehensible but incomprehensible judgement he has barred the door of life to those whom he has given over to damnation.[23]

We've reached what is probably one of the most devastating points of Calvin's theology of predestination—theology at its cruelest. That God condemns some human beings to destruction, harsh though it may be, would still make sense if we could see it as some form of punishment. By deed or thought or speech, we may have offended God, such a line of thinking goes, and he is within his right to punish us, disproportionate though the punishment may be. Yet, while Calvin thinks that the condemnation of the reprobate is a matter of justice, he also makes it clear that our individual merits are irrelevant. He writes that Jacob is "chosen and distinguished from the rejected Esau by God's predestination, while not differing from him in merits." Whatever we do, however diligent we may be, our conduct wouldn't gain us election, just as the worst sins we may commit are not enough to doom us. Rejection, Calvin writes, "takes place not on the basis of works but solely according to God's will."[24]

All our efforts are in vain, then. God has already made up his mind to condemn us. A reprobate is reprobate not because of what he does or thinks or says, but because of who he is. Reprobation is not a matter of personal integrity or practice, but of being. In our language, the reprobate is a total loser.

Winners in the Land of Failure

Cioran could speak so well of failure because he knew it intimately. He first encountered it in his native land, among his fellow Romanians. Cioran was born and grew up in Transylvania, a province that had long been part of the Austro-Hungarian Empire and had only lately, in 1918, been incorporated into the kingdom of Romania. People here have always displayed a strong work ethic; seriousness, discipline, and self-control are held in high esteem. Transylvanians are born Kantians: they do what they've got to do, whether they like it or not—silently, humbly, without concern for recognition or rewards. But when Cioran went to college in Bucharest, in the late 1920s, he effectively stepped into a different country. Here the winning skills were other: idleness, procrastination, the fine art of doing nothing. Wasting one's life was a vocation. The most successful people in Bucharest were the chatterboxes holding court in the city's cafés, spewing sophisticated nonsense and leaving the impressionable agape.

At first, Cioran was taken aback. "Here in Bucharest, one can only succeed through flattery and self-debasement," he wrote to a friend back home.[25] Soon, however, he came to appreciate the consummate idleness of the Bucharest intelligentsia. Moreover, he discovered that he had certain elective affinities with them. As an undergraduate philosophy student, Cioran encountered some of the city's best performers. The mix of intellectual brilliance and a striking sense of personal failure that some exhibited fueled his admiration. To the future nihilist, these people's deep commitment to a life of doing nothing was awe-inspiring:

> In Bucharest I met lots of people, many interesting people, especially losers, who would show up at the café, talking endlessly and doing nothing. I have to say that, for me, these were the most interesting people there. People who did nothing all their lives, but who otherwise were brilliant.[26]

For the rest of his life, Cioran would remain indebted to this land of failure that was his country of birth. Romanians seem to have a privileged relationship to failure. Just as the Inuit allegedly have countless words for snow, the Romanian language has many associated with failure. One of the verbal constructions most often used in Romanian, which Cioran cherished, is *n-a fost să fie*—literally, "it wasn't to be," with a strong implication of predestination. When some fine project bites the dust, Romanians are neither outraged nor determined to try again; they just drop casually, *N-a fost să fie.* A bridge has collapsed, a ship has sunk, an invading army couldn't be stopped, their response is the same: *N-a fost să fie.*

Romanians have what may be called "philosophical luck": their language comes equipped with a full-fledged philosophy of failure, a fluid ontology in which something's nonexistence is just as fine as its existence. The ultimate state of detachment, so hard to reach in any spiritual tradition, comes naturally to Romanians, just by speaking their language. Cioran never stopped admiring his fellow Romanians' resourcefulness when it came to failing. Years later, when a communist dictatorship was installed there under the close supervision of yet another foreign army, he wrote to a friend, "After so many pathetic failures, this country finally has the opportunity to experience the ultimate, the utter failure. An *improvement* on Orwell."[27]

Cioran was famously a misanthrope, yet there was one human type for which he had boundless understanding: the failure (*le raté, ratatul*). In 1941, already in Paris, he confessed to a Romanian friend, "I would like to write a *Philosophy of Failure,* with the subtitle *For the Exclusive Use of the Romanian People,* but I don't think I will be able to do it."[28] Whenever Cioran looked back to his youth, he would always remember, with a mix of tenderness and fascination, the great losers and the endless spectacle of failure he contemplated in Romania. He would never forget the village drunkard of his native Rășinari: while everybody else was working hard to make a living, the fellow was doing nothing but drinking himself to death. Cioran thought that a fine metaphysical protest: the drunkard was no ordinary loser, he was a practicing nihilist. In time, he would befriend many drunkards and losers, and never found them boring. As an emerging writer, Cioran was surely attracted by the country's literary scene, but not nearly as much as by its failure scene: "My best friends in Romania were not at all writers, but failures," he confessed later.[29]

One Romanian failure who particularly impressed Cioran was a star philosophy professor, Nae Ionescu. Cioran took his classes at the University of Bucharest, and along with Mircea Eliade, Mihail Sebastian, Constantin Noica, and a handful of others, was one of Ionescu's protégés. Even by Romanian standards, Ionescu was an outstanding failure. His lectures—charming, mesmerizing, giving off a distinct sense of authenticity—were often plagiarized. Sometimes Ionescu didn't show up to classes because he "didn't have anything to say," as he would excuse himself later. When he did show up, he would occasionally ask the audience to give him a topic to lecture on, only to improvise on the spot.

Once he singled out Cioran and asked for a prompt. The future religion basher ventured, "Angels." Perhaps Cioran meant to tease him: Ionescu's influence was deemed "demonic" in some intelligentsia circles, and he had recently appeared in cameo as an ugly devil in a Last Judgment scene on the wall of a newly renovated cathedral in Bucharest. The master was unfazed by this impertinent request and, over the next couple of hours, improvised a lecture, allegedly one of his most memorable, on the ontology of angels.

Ionescu's laziness was legendary. "He is an idler of genius," Mihail Sebastian observed.[30] Yet, if we are to believe Ionescu himself, it wasn't laziness that prevented him from writing and publishing anything in the field: he didn't publish as a matter of principle. An odd notion had entered his mind that doing so would corrupt him. He thought he could remain an honest person only "as long as he didn't publish any philosophy books." His theory was that it was preferable to be "an honest, self-aware, and respected loser than a scoundrel."[31]

According to many who knew him, Ionescu was in fact a first-class scoundrel. He was a man of many masks and countless trades: philosophy professor and intellectual guru, courtier and journalist, socialite and Casanova, political intriguer and occasional kingmaker. He came to have plenty of money, and it was never clear where it came from; some suggested embezzlement, others worse.

To call Ionescu "mercurial" would be an understatement. Just as, intellectually, he moved freely between the Jewish Kabbalah, the ascetic writings of the church fathers, Machiavelli's *Prince*, Ignatius of Loyola's *Spiritual Exercises*, and Goethe's *Faust*, so in practical matters he could do the most incompatible things. He could accept money from a generous Jewish banker one day, only to become the ideologue-in-chief of an anti-Semitic far-right movement the next. In the morning he could lose himself completely in prayer, only to cheat on his wife that afternoon. Many saw Nae Ionescu as a God-fearing Christian and one of the most brilliant minds of his generation—a "genius," by some accounts.

Always the philosopher, Ionescu developed a little theory of failure—which, appropriately, he preferred not to publish.

Losers in the Land of Success

Calvin's reprobate, then, is the ultimate loser—the archetype of our social failures. How we think about losers and failures today seems to be a late echo of the Calvinist doctrine of predestination—weak perhaps, but still an echo. To an extent, the connection is genealogical. Max Weber, for one, argued strongly for such a genealogy. His classic study on the relationship between the spirit of capitalism and Protestant ethics engendered by Calvin's theology remains persuasive.

Along with our economic type, Weber suggests, we seem to have inherited from the early Calvinists an understanding of what worldly success is, and implicitly a certain way of looking on the unsuccessful. Central to all this is a commitment to productive work—all-absorbing and all-absolving work, which translates into quantifiable wealth and visible social respectability. Since work and grace are tied together, a lack of commitment to the former can only mean the absence of the latter. "Unwillingness to work is symptomatic of the lack of grace," observes Weber.[32] The social response could be unforgiving. In Puritan New England, communities of the self-proclaimed elect ("visible saints," they called themselves) wanted nothing less than to expel the reprobate from their church. Since the "external church" contained both elect and reprobate, the former did not want to share even the same physical space with the latter. The presence of the reprobate could blemish the purity of the elect. For these people, writes Garry Wills, "the only religion recognized as authentic, as what God wills, was the Covenant of Grace, under which God's chosen were predestined to salvation." The others, those "not consciously saved in this way," could not be considered "communicating members of the church."[33]

More important, perhaps, than a detailed genealogy of our attitudes to failure is their morphology. Fundamentally, and despite the intervening historical distance, the early Calvinists and we late capitalists employ the same patterns of thinking. Save for some niceties of language, today's successful relate themselves to the losers of the social and economic game not very differently from how the communities of chosen believers treated the reprobates in their midst. The same assumption of ontological damnation defines both cases: it's who you are, and not what you do or say or think, that seals your fate.

The pattern exhibits several features: a primary need for differentiation, a good measure of self-righteousness, an obsession with purity and fear of contagion, a compulsion to exclude, a great anxiety over personal worth. Most important, in both cases there is the same postulation, through an act of societal fiat, of a group of people as "bad" human material, something the others single out and ostracize. Should our losers happen to meet Calvin's reprobates in the street one day, the meeting would be the least eventful of encounters. They might not even notice the other group, thinking it must be their own passing reflection in some shop window.

Elect and reprobate, successful and failure are thus chained together, like those doomed to remain in a marriage where love is absent and divorce out of the question. As Calvin showed with maddening rigor, the predestination is double: the successful need their failures as much as the elect need their reprobates. The successful despise the losers with a vengeance, and yet, if there is something they need more than anything else in the world, it is to have losers around. As the wise saying goes, It's not enough for me to succeed—others have to fail.[34] I am saved precisely because the other *is not*. Without the spectacle of others' misery, my success will never be complete. My salvation is accomplished only when I can contemplate, in all its dark splendor, others' concomitant damnation. Without their crushing, my victory is less victorious, and my success unfulfilling. Should the losers suddenly vanish one day, the successful would receive a mortal blow.

This pattern certainly preceded Calvin. His thinking about damnation is important not necessarily because the spirit of capitalism was born out of Calvinist ethics, but because Calvin, like few others, pushed the logic of predestination to its most extreme consequences, and in so doing revealed quite a bit about ourselves. Had he shown some compassion, it would have muddled things. Instead, thanks to his radicalism, we've been given full access to the mechanism's inner workings.

An Earnest Practice of Failure

Cioran did not content himself with being a distant observer of failure. Early on, he started practicing it himself, and he did so in style. In 1933, just out of college, he received a visiting fellowship at Friedrich Wilhelm University in Berlin. No sooner did he arrive there than he fell in love with the freshly installed Nazi regime. In November of that year, he wrote to his friend Mircea Eliade, "I am absolutely enthralled by the political order they've set up here."[35] Cioran had found in Hitler's Germany whatever he could not in the still relatively democratic Romania. The country was seized by political hysteria and mass mobilization, which Cioran thought to be an excellent thing. The Nazi regime had brought forth the sense of a historical mission that Romania's democracy would never be able to do.

While others (Simone Weil, for example) were seeing in the Nazi takeover of power in 1933 the debut of a historic catastrophe, Cioran could see only promise. What exactly made Hitler such a promising figure? His capacity to arouse the "irrational impulses" of the German people, answered Cioran, trying to sound like an expert. In another letter, in December 1933, he preached the virtues of dictatorship to a democratically minded friend from Romania and urged him to repent before it was too late: "Only a dictatorial regime is still worthy of attention. People do not deserve to be free. And I am somewhat saddened by the fact that you and others like you pointlessly praise a democracy which can't really do anything good for Romania."[36] Barely twenty-two years old, Cioran started practicing failure in earnest.

By the fall of 1933, Cioran was a rising star in Romanian letters, having as an undergraduate contributed a handful of strikingly original essays to some of the country's literary outlets. Now these periodicals wanted more from him; in particular, they wanted him to comment on the German political scene. Cioran gladly obliged. In a dispatch he sent to the weekly *Vremea* in December 1933, he wrote, pen firmly in hand, "If I like something about Hitlerism, it is the *cult of the irrational,* the exaltation of pure vitality, the virile expression of strength, without any critical spirit, restraint, or control."[37] Abusing a cliché much loved by the enemies of liberal democracy everywhere, Cioran pits a "decadent" and "effeminate" Europe against a proudly "masculine" Germany—all muscles, noise, and fury. Hitler is conspicuously the *man* in charge, and Cioran is appropriately impressed. Several months later, in July 1934, in another dispatch, he isn't shy about expressing his boundless admiration for the one with balls: "Of all politicians today, Hitler is the one I like and admire most."[38] And still the worst is yet to come.

Cioran is so smitten by the "virile" order established by Hitler in Germany that he wants a version of it transplanted into his home country. In a letter to another friend, he writes:

> I'm persuaded that our native good-for-nothingness could be stifled, if not eradicated, by a dictatorial regime. In Romania, only terror, brutality and infinite anxiety could still lead to some change. All Romanians should be arrested and beaten to a pulp; only after such a beating could a superficial people make history.

Issues of public interest are often mixed with matters of a more private nature. Right after this recipe for helping his fellow Romanians "make history," he drops a rather personal note: "It's awful to be Romanian," he writes. As a Romanian, "you never win the trust of any woman, and serious people smile at you dismissively; when they see that you are smart, they think you are a cheat."[39] We don't know the details of the affair, but we can guess.

The confession, oblique though it may be, takes us straight into young Cioran's drama. It unfolds in several layers. First, a peculiar notion seems to have hatched in his mind that he is not allowed to separate his personal worth from the historical merits of the ethnic community to which he happens to belong. Next, sizing up that community's worth, he finds it wanting. Historically, Cioran thinks, Romania has been a "failed nation," and its failure cannot but rub off on all Romanians. As if this was not bad enough, quitting

Romania is not an option either, since separating from one's country of birth leads to failure. There is failure in, and even more failure out. At a relatively young age, Cioran has managed to lock himself into a serious existential impasse; that this drama is largely one of his own making doesn't make it less painful.

It's this drama—"the drama of insignificance," he will call it later—that lies behind the book he publishes in 1936, soon after his return from Germany: *Romania's Transfiguration* (*Schimbarea la față a României*), which he has written, again, for therapeutic reasons. The book is meant, above all, to treat a wounded pride. That's what happens to those born in a "small culture": their pride is always wounded. "It is not at all comfortable to have been born in a second-rate country," Cioran writes. "Lucidity becomes tragedy." He feels so crushed by the minor cultural status of his country that, to ease the pain, he wouldn't hesitate to sell his soul: "I'd gladly give up half of my life if I could experience with the same intensity that which the most insignificant of Greeks, Romans or Frenchmen experienced even for a moment at the climax of their history."[40]

Reinventing himself, turning into *someone else* as a way to deal with *le désespoir d'être roumain,* is something Cioran will do all his life; self-alienation will be his second nature. In *The Trouble with Being Born,* one of the aphorisms reads, "In continual rebellion against my ancestry, I have spent my whole life wanting to be something else: Spanish, Russian, cannibal—anything, except what I was."[41] Cioran could forgive God for many things (even for bringing him into this world), but never for having made him Romanian. To be Romanian is not some biographical accident, but an unspeakable shame, a tragedy of cosmic proportions. "How can one be Romanian?" Cioran wonders exasperatedly. In *Romania's Transfiguration,* he describes his fellow Romanians as all too "mediocre, slow, resigned, understanding," and awfully well-behaved.[42] For the life of him, Cioran cannot accept such a people as his own. Impossibly passive and self-effacing, Romanians have missed their chance to leave a trace in the world. Romania has slept its way through history. If the country suddenly disappeared, nobody would miss it—indeed, few would notice.

But Cioran is nothing if not self-contradictory. Elsewhere in the book, he "loves Romania's past with a heavy hatred" and has big dreams for its future. He envisions nothing less than "a Romania with the population of China and the destiny of France." The country is fine—it just needs a bit of shaking up here and there; above all, it needs to be "pushed" into history. What that means exactly Cioran doesn't say, but he gives us a hint when he says that he can only "love a Romania in delirium." For such lofty ends anything is justified. All "means are legitimate," he writes, for "a people that opens a road for itself in the world. Terror, crime, bestiality, and perfidy are base and immoral only in decadence. . . . If they assist a people's ascension, they are virtues. All triumphs are moral."[43] Only a dictatorship of the irrational, the likes of which Cioran has seen at work in Germany, can save his country from itself.

In a few years, when Romania's own fascist movement, the violently anti-Semitic Iron Guard (for which Cioran's master, Nae Ionescu, served as chief ideologue for a while), would come to power for four long months, from September 1940 to January 1941, Cioran would endorse them, in his own ambiguous way.

A "Romania in delirium," of which he used to dream, was finally taking shape, and it was an ugly sight: Romanian Jews were hunted down and murdered in cold blood, their properties looted and burned to the ground, while the passive Gentile population was subjected to brutal Eastern Orthodox fundamentalist brainwashing. By then, Cioran was in France. During a brief trip back home, however, in a contribution dedicated to the memory of the movement's founding leader, Corneliu Zelea Codreanu (the so-called Captain), which he read on national radio, Cioran pontificated:

> Before Corneliu Codreanu, Romania was but an inhabited Sahara. . . . I had only a few conversations with Corneliu Codreanu. From the first moment I realized that I was talking

to a man in a country of human dregs. . . . The Captain was not "smart," the Captain was profound.[44]

This profound Captain had been, among other things, a political adventurer and rabid anti-Semite; he openly advocated political assassination and was a political assassin himself. Against the background of a precarious democratic culture in interwar Romania, aided by personal charisma and a singular lack of scruples, Codreanu almost singlehandedly pushed the country into political chaos in the late 1930s. And now Cioran was praising him.

When it comes to failing, a thinker—even one as unapologetically irresponsible as the young Cioran was—could hardly sink any lower. What was wrong with this man? you must be wondering, just as his democratically minded friends were at the time. In the coming years, Cioran himself would be visited by the question, with depressing urgency.

When he was first confronted with the enormity of his profascist political stance, soon after the end of the war, he almost didn't recognize himself in *Romania's Transfiguration* and in his political journalism. The horrors of the war and the Holocaust, in which some of his Jewish friends perished, woke him up abruptly. Then, the working of time made him see things a bit more clearly. "Every now and then, I wonder whether it was actually me who wrote those ramblings they keep quoting," he writes in 1973, in a letter to his brother. "Enthusiasm is a form of delirium. We did suffer from this disease, and no one wants to believe that we are now cured."[45] Elsewhere he writes, "My youth was desperate and *enthusiastic*; even today I suffer the consequences."[46] In a posthumous text, *My Country (Mon Pays)*, he refers to *Romania's Transfiguration* as "the ravings of a wild madman."[47] Someone else must have produced those rantings, not him, an older Cioran concluded.

This is sometimes the outcome of an intense practice of failure: before you know it, you bring another person into the world. One day you look for yourself in the mirror, only to discover someone else there looking at you, mocking you, and laughing at you like a madman.

It's never easy to pin Cioran down, but when it comes to his political past it's nearly impossible. It doesn't help that, beyond vague references to the "ravings" and "enthusiasm" of his youth, the later Cioran was reluctant to talk about "those years." And for good reason: he knew only too well what was there. Failure hates to travel alone: it usually enjoys shame's company. In another letter to his brother, he writes, "The writer who has done some stupid things in his youth, upon his debut, is like a woman with a shameful past. Never forgiven, never forgotten."[48] To the end of his days, Cioran's political involvement in interwar Romania would remain his biggest shame, his most shattering failure. Everything else paled by comparison. Always the nihilist, Cioran must have enjoyed a good failure, and was not someone to be easily shamed by his blunders, but this one appears to have been too much even for him.

A further glimpse into Cioran's peculiar manner of political thinking emerges in a letter he sent to Mircea Eliade in 1935: "My formula for all things political is the following: fight *wholeheartedly* for things in which you do not believe."[49] Not that the confession brings much clarity to Cioran's political involvement, but it places his "ravings" and "madness" in a certain psychological perspective. This split personality would also characterize the later Cioran. For a philosopher who sees the world as a failure of grand proportions, perhaps it makes some sense to mock the cosmic order (and himself in the process) by pretending that there is meaning where there is none. You know that everything is pointless, but by behaving *as if* it weren't, you articulate your dissent and undermine the designs of the "evil demiurge." You do that with much irony and humor, which is meant to counter the divine farce. He who laughs last laughs hardest.

Tramping as a Fine Art

In September 1927, while on leave in England, a young police officer working for the Indian Imperial Police in Burma resigned from his well-paid post rather than return to it. What he really wanted to be was a writer—a proper, full-time writer. Since he had no independent means, and his literary attempts hadn't shown much promise to date, he must have realized that, before he would know literary success (he was certain that he would), he would come to know poverty rather well.

The young man was right in both respects: Eric Blair did indeed become an important writer (one of the greatest, according to many), but not before he was impoverished. In the coming years, he somehow managed to connect the two—writing and poverty— intimately. At first, he was forced to be poor, but then he ended up making virtue of necessity and embraced poverty as a matter of professional duty. There was something fundamentally honest about him: he believed that to write about the destitute condition, he had to become, for shorter or longer periods, a destitute himself.

That destitution was to be one of the best things that ever happened to Blair—in any case, the best literary education he ever received. After graduating from elite Eton College, he didn't get much schooling; the Burma years certainly taught him something, but not enough. What Blair would learn now, in the streets of London and Paris, under bridges, in tramp hostels and in poorly paid jobs, would be decisive for his formation as a writer and thinker. Eventually, this "investigative tramping," and the attendant writing, would turn Eric Blair into George Orwell. His first book, *Down and Out in Paris and London,* published in 1933, documents his tramping years and remains one of the best first-hand accounts of how social failure works.

There is something odd about poverty, Orwell discovers as soon as he starts tramping: it's mostly the concern of those who are *not* genuinely poor. You typically obsess over poverty when you are on the bright side of the divide. It is the "thing you have feared all your life, the thing you knew would happen to you sooner or later." But when poverty does happen, Orwell finds, "it is so utterly and prosaically different." As with many things in life, poverty falls victim to romanticism and fantasizing: "You thought it would be terrible; it is merely squalid and boring. It is the peculiar *lowness* of poverty that you discover first; the shifts that it puts you to, the complicated meanness, the crust-wiping."[50] When the successful in a society malign the losers, they unwittingly make the latter a generous compliment; they find something glamorously terrifying in the latter's destitution. Orwell dispels the rumor: if there is anything terrifying about poverty, it is its utter banality.

Orwell had come from a comfortable background. Maybe when he was born, his family's wealth was no longer what it used to be, but still he grew up in relative affluence. Now, however, as he began climbing down the social ladder (a largely self-induced fall, but no less dramatic), he discovered things about poverty he had never imagined possible. Being poor brings a whole new dimension to how people see themselves, to how they engage in social intercourse and, in general, to how they operate in the world. Everything is different when you are penniless; the most insignificant of accidents can take on catastrophic proportions. And a new ingredient—shame—starts spicing up your life. Take the interaction with a sale assistant:

> You go to the greengrocer's to spend a franc on a kilogram of potatoes. But one of the pieces that make up the franc is a Belgian piece, and the shopman refuses it. You slink out of the shop, and can never go there again.[51]

Before the fall, you imagined poverty to be a clear-cut affair: you are penniless and that is that. Now you find that utterly naïve. Poverty comes in countless shades and gradations. Just like the society from which they've been excluded, the poor organize themselves hierarchically; there are the better-off among them, the average, the really poor, each category with its own subdivisions.

Having slid down through many shades of poverty in Paris, Orwell reaches one day a bottom of sorts, where he makes a new discovery: "life on six francs a day." He had never imagined such a life was even theoretically possible, let alone that he would embrace it. It turns out this shade of poverty was a crowded, lively place. "Thousands of people in Paris live it—struggling artists and students, prostitutes when their luck is out, out-of-work people of all kinds. It is the suburbs, as it were, of poverty."[52]

Just listen to him: the "suburbs of poverty"—poverty within poverty within poverty. Not even the finest universities of England could have taught Orwell such fine distinctions.

A Parasite's Life

When he returned from Germany, in 1936, Cioran worked a brief stint as a high school philosophy teacher in the city of Brașov, in central Romania. Another resounding failure. He didn't care much about the job's routines, and his teaching had neither structure nor method. He hated to give grades and could not stand the overachieving students. He was attracted instead to the lazy ones, to whom he gave, to make a mockery of the whole thing, consistently high grades. Unsurprisingly, Cioran's classes were in a perpetual state of chaos, and the students were as puzzled as his colleagues by this unlikeliest of teachers. During a logic class, for instance, Cioran would say that everything in the universe was irremediably sick, including the principle of identity. When a student once asked him, "What's ethics, sir?" Cioran told him he shouldn't worry, there was no such thing. When he quit eventually, the principal, to celebrate, drank himself into a stupor. Cioran's short-lived teaching stint was the last significant attempt he made to have a full-time job.

In 1937, realizing that he could never truly distinguish himself in that land of failure, Cioran decided to leave Romania for good, and to pursue elsewhere what he had by now come to see as his vocation: a full-time career in failure. He would always consider this decision to be "by far the most intelligent thing" he'd ever done. His first choice had been Spain—that most "spectacular example of failure," as you may recall—so he applied for a fellowship at the Spanish Embassy in Bucharest. But this was shortly before the start of the Spanish Civil War, and he never heard back. Paris was, he finally decided, the right place for someone with his aspirations: "Before the war," he remembers, "Paris was the ideal place to fail your life, and especially Romanians were famous for that." For a man with Cioran's life plans, Paris had the added benefit that it was "the only city in the world where you could be poor without being ashamed of it, without complications, without dramas."[53]

So he cut off his Romanian ties and adopted a new existence. For good measure, he gave himself a new name: E. M. Cioran. "After certain experiences," he reflected, we should "change names, since we ourselves are no longer the same."[54] At some point, he started writing and speaking almost exclusively in French. He would use Romanian only for cursing, for which French, he found, was poorly equipped. Changing languages so late in life was a painful experience, but he came to appreciate the sense of discipline that the new tongue brought not only to his writing, but to his life as well. French, he discovered, imposed limits upon its speakers— it "civilized" them. "I can't go crazy in French," Cioran said, puzzling generations of readers who had been attracted to him precisely by the stylistic perfection of his ravings in that language. In the long run, French may have saved Cioran from himself. "Setting limits for me, it saved me, it prevented me from exaggerating all the time," he said. "The acceptance of this linguistic discipline has moderated my delirium."[55]

This didn't mean that now Cioran became French—God forbid! He didn't quit one collective identity only to embrace another. His disastrous flirtation with fascism must have taught him how tricky such relationships are. After his failed affair with Romania, what he wanted was not another country, but a state of countrylessness: "*Je n'ai besoin de patrie, je ne veux appartenir à rien*" (I don't need a country, I don't want to belong to anything).[56] France gave Cioran not citizenship, but *la volupté de l'exil*. If there was one identity the reborn Cioran felt close to, it must have been that of the "wandering Jew." "*Metaphysically* speaking, I am a Jew," he writes.

In a letter he sent back home from Paris in 1946, Cioran almost bragged about his new situation: "I live in an attic, I eat in a student cafeteria, I have no profession—and, naturally, I make no money. I can't really complain about the fate that made it so that until the age of 35 I have been free to live on the fringes of society."[57] Things started to look up for the nihilist.

In theory, Cioran had come to Paris on a graduate scholarship. He was supposed to attend classes at the Sorbonne and produce a doctoral dissertation on some philosophical topic. But even as he applied for the scholarship, he knew perfectly well that he would never write such a thing. He had finally realized what he was after: *the life of a parasite*. All he needed to live securely in France was a student ID, which gave him access to cheap university cafeterias. He could live happily like that forever. And so he did, if only for a while:

> At forty I was still enrolled at the Sorbonne, I was eating at the student cafeteria, and I was hoping that this would last till the end of my days. And then a law was passed which forbade the enrollment of students older than twenty-seven, and which chased me away from this paradise.[58]

Expelled from the parasites' paradise, Cioran had to get inventive. He had always been a cynic in the modern sense of the word. Now he had the chance to practice the ancient variety as well; Paris was about to have its Diogenes. Just like the ancient Cynic, Cioran was not shy about asking for help. His slightly better-off Romanian friends came in handy. "In the 1940s and 1950s," notes a biographer, Cioran "used to wear hand-me-down clothes from luckier friends like Eliade and was introduced around Paris as 'Ionesco's friend.'"[59] At other times, Cioran had to rely on the kindness of strangers; he would befriend pretty much anyone who would offer him the prospect of a free dinner. That's how he got to know *les vieilles dames de Paris* so well. His rigorous training in philosophy must have helped; he would come with his exquisite conversation and sing for his supper.[60] There was, finally, the Paris church scene; whenever he had the chance, the God-basher would merrily show up at the Romanian Orthodox Church for free dining opportunities. In all this, Cioran proved himself admirably civil and flexible—if not hiding his misanthropy, at least making it a trifle more entertaining. No one is so misanthropic as to starve himself to death. Eventually, a good, selfless soul, Simone Boué, adopted the stray philosopher and helped him navigate the needs of his worldly existence to the end of his days.

But isn't this a form of intellectual prostitution? you might protest. If anything, Cioran would have found the question flattering. For "intellectual prostitution" brings together, so neatly, two worlds that were always dear to him. "When I was very young, I was only attracted by brothels and libraries," he remembered in old age.[61]

Some of his aphorisms reveal Cioran as a fine connoisseur of poverty. He writes, for example, "The poor, by thinking unceasingly of money, reach the point of losing the spiritual advantages of nonpossession, thereby sinking as low as the rich."[62] From entertaining old ladies to near-begging, Cioran would do anything to survive—except take up a job. Doing so would have been the failure of his life. "For me," an older Cioran recalls, "the main thing was to safeguard my freedom. Had I ever accepted to take up an office job, to make a living, I would have failed." In order not to fail, he chose a path most would consider failure embodied. Yet Cioran knew that failure is a complicated affair. "I avoided at any price the humiliation of a career. . . . I preferred to live like a parasite than to destroy myself by keeping a job."[63] As the great idlers and mystics

have always known (Cioran seems to have been both at once),
there is perfection in inaction—the less you act, the closer to the
absolute.

Cioran might have first got the notion from Nae Ionescu, but
he outdid his master, as good disciples always do. For all his
legendary laziness, Ionescu still had his shady business deals to
attend to, and his teaching, for which he had to plagiarize and
improvise, not to mention his womanizing, involvement in politics, and grooming of young fascists. But Cioran *did nothing* in
Paris. When an interviewer asked him about his working routines,
he answered, "Most of the time I don't do anything. I am the idlest
man in Paris. . . . The only one who does less than I do is a whore
without clients."[64]

He was not joking—or only half. It was his belief that, in a meaningless world, there is no reason to do anything whatsoever. "All
action is fundamentally useless," thought this modern pillar saint.
"I believe that the only right moment in history is the ancient period of India, when one would live a life of contemplation, when
one would be content just to look at things, without ever dealing
with them."[65] Cioran was a man of deep conviction: in a failed universe, a failure's life is the only life worth living.

In this respect, as in others, Cioran has his place in the great
contemplative tradition. What sets the contemplative apart from
other human types is a cultivated ability to dwell on the nonexistence of things: the rich virtuality that precedes their fall into
existence, the fundamental precariousness of their actualization,
and their inevitable return into the void.

Rather than get entangled in the cosmic mess, contemplatives
have a special ability to transport themselves to a moment when
the world has yet to happen. The exercise is worth doing for at least
three reasons. First, at a purely metaphysical level, the virtual not
only precedes the actual, it is worthier and more eminent. Why
waste your time on an imperfect copy when you have access to the
spotless original? Language itself sometimes privileges contempla-

tion over action. Take the Latin *negotium*. The word, among other things, implies business, active involvement in something. But it was originally a negative term: it was born out of the negation of *otium*—leisure time, withdrawing from the world, scholarly retreat, contemplation. Second, contemplation gives you a more accurate picture of existence. No sugarcoating, no deceptions, no spin. The great contemplatives have always been equally great realists. Finally, dwelling on the nothingness of things can be, at a more existential level, an enriching human experience, thanks to which we can live better—and more lucid—lives. Seeing the world from that vantage point makes for a jovial, relaxed, light-hearted relationship to it. Cioran's jokes were so good not despite his nihilistic outlook, but precisely because of it.

Practitioners of idleness have a bad reputation, but much of this comes from lazy thinking. When properly pursued, idleness can be a philosophical experience of the first order. Bertrand Russell wrote a long essay in praise of idleness. The great, consummate idlers of literature—Melville's Bartleby or Goncharov's Oblomov (who so fascinated Samuel Beckett, Cioran's friend and fellow idler)—are figures on a metaphysical quest: they illustrate alternative ways of being, to which "men of action" will never have access. Cioran had good reasons to brag about his idleness.

It's not that the idlers "do nothing": in the process, they attain an elevated form of existence—an accomplishment for which they rightly take pride. "It was with a certain quiet smugness," observes Goncharov, that Oblomov "contemplated his freedom to lie around on his divan from nine to three and from eight to nine and congratulated himself on not having to submit any reports or draft any document." That enabled him to free "his energies for giving the widest possible play to his feelings and his imagination."[66] Bartleby is similarly absorbed by his newly found idler's calling. He can't afford even the slightest change of schedule. He is too busy doing nothing to do anything else. Idleness is an all-absorbing, full-time occupation—indeed, a vocation. One can't do much else on the side.

The Dead Cat

Tramping puts Orwell in a position to look on everything—on other fellow humans and on society at large, on its hierarchies, values, rituals, and taboos—with new eyes. Having lived in Asia for several years, and crossed many a cultural border, Orwell had already developed a relatively broad view of society. His experiments with tramping, however, gave him access to social strata and groups he could not have reached otherwise. And great knowledge came with that. The insight, for instance, that social distinctions are insubstantial. Among the tramps, Orwell understands that, ultimately, regardless of their wealth, people are fundamentally the same. The notion that there is "some mysterious, fundamental difference between rich and poor" is flawed—a "superstition." In reality, he finds out, "there is no such difference."[67] Social distinctions, while seemingly unbridgeable, are an optical illusion. What causes such an illusion can be the simplest things in the world. Clothes, for instance.

Moving across dividing lines and shades of poverty, Orwell learns the vital importance of appearance. As a member of the British upper class, he must have taken clothes primarily as outward markers of membership in one class or another. A mere social convention. Now he finds otherwise. He learns what good actors and spies have always known: you are what you put on. You become your disguise. The others almost always see the mask, never the person; indeed, the person is the mask (*persona,* in Latin). As he puts on tramps' clothes, Orwell's first reaction is to cling to his old self: "Dressed as I was, I was half afraid that the police might arrest me as a vagabond, and I dared not speak to anyone, imagining that they must notice a disparity between my accent and my clothes."[68]

The assumption only shows how untrained Orwell still was in the ways of the world: in his naïveté, he assumed that he was something different from what his clothes showed him to be. In other words, that he had some deeper, substantial self, and that, upon encountering him, people would pay attention to that self and thus detect the real Eric Blair hiding behind this man of indigent appearance. "Later I discovered that this never happened," he writes. Socially, we are never what we think we are, but whatever others make us out to be. A man of means with the appearance of a tramp is a tramp. If you put on a tramp's clothes, for all intents and purposes, you become one. "Clothes are powerful things," Orwell concludes. "Dressed in a tramp's clothes it is very difficult . . . not to feel that you are genuinely degraded."[69]

Once Orwell receives his tramp's baptism, his sociological-literary exploration can begin in earnest. The discoveries he makes don't cease to amaze him; a whole new dimension of his social existence is revealed to him now. "My new clothes had put me instantly into a new world. Everyone's demeanor seemed to have changed abruptly," he realizes. "I helped a hawker pick up a barrow that he had upset. 'Thanks, mate,' he said with a grin. No one had called me mate before in my life—it was the clothes that had done it."[70] It's always the clothes. The hawker was not speaking to Orwell, but to the clothes he was wearing.

Not all his discoveries are as pleasant, though. Orwell realizes, not without shock, "how the attitude of women varies with a man's clothes. When a badly dressed man passes them they shudder away from him with a quite frank movement of disgust, as though he were a dead cat."[71] He shouldn't have been surprised: he *was* a dead cat.

The sight of the loser is as repulsive as that of a stinking carcass. The disgust is so compelling that it can undermine even the finest of manners. For that sight suddenly forces us, against our best intentions, to see through the whole masquerade, and face the deadly silence lurking behind the pleasant noise that normally accompanies our social interactions. The sight of the loser is unsettling because it reminds us of the worst things that can befall us: degradation, dissolution, destitution. Instinctively, if not consciously, we know that such things are always possible because the social order is always precarious. The abyss can poke at us at any time from the other side. Losers should certainly exist, we need them to be there somewhere, but this is just too close for comfort.

The Misfortune of Success

As someone who had such an absorbing relationship with idleness, it is no wonder that Cioran was suspicious of social success. To start with, he saw it as spiritually unhealthy: "Any success, in any realm, involves an inner impoverishment. It makes us forget what we are, it deprives us of the torment of our limits," he proclaimed.[72] Success makes us vain and superficial. Indeed, it is not just vulgar, but plainly fraudulent. Human existence is such a messy affair that, whenever someone finds their way too easily in it, we should suspect fraud.

"There is something of the charlatan in anyone who triumphs in any realm whatever," Cioran wrote.[73] Literary "triumphs" didn't impress him, and France's literary scene filled him with horror. With one early exception, he rejected all the awards that the country's literary establishment bestowed on him, even though some were financially significant and would have come in handy. When, relatively late in life, his work started to have an impact, he gave few interviews and kept a low profile. *"Je suis un ennemi de la gloire,"* he said emphatically, an act which, in itself, betrayed a certain anxiety. For what would happen to him and his integrity if, God forbid, he became successful?

Cioran had seen the damage that success had done to Jorge Luis Borges and pitied him for it. "The misfortune of being recognized has befallen him," Cioran writes. "He deserved better. He deserved to remain in obscurity, in the Imperceptible, to remain as ineffable and unpopular as nuance itself. . . . Consecration is the worst of punishments." Most unforgivable of all, Borges became popular with academics. Famous universities were vying to have him as a guest lecturer, giving him star treatment and fancy titles. What buffoonery, what a sad fate! "What is the use of celebrating him when the universities themselves are doing so?" Cioran wonders.[74]

He found the university as an institution not just bad, but positively evil—the "death of the spirit," something from which you need to run away if you care about your inner life. Even the best teaching done there was toxic. "One of the best things I've ever done in my life," he said in an interview, late in life, is to have "cut myself off completely from the university."[75] In this respect, as in others, he remained faithful to the only church to which he ever belonged: that of the unbelonging. "My only religion has been my freedom, my independence, the fact that I haven't had to rely primarily on a career."[76]

In *The Trouble with Being Born,* Cioran speaks of "an existence constantly transfigured by failure" as an enviable life project.[77] Such a life would be wisdom in flesh. Failure is Cioran's close companion and loyal muse. He looks at the world—at people, events, situations—through its unflinching eyes. He can measure, for example, the depth of someone's inner life by the way they approach failure: "This is how we recognize the man who has tendencies toward an inner quest: he will set failure above any success." How so? "Because failure, always *essential,* reveals us to ourselves, permits us to see ourselves as God sees us, whereas success distances us from what is most inward in ourselves and indeed in everything."[78] Show me how you deal with failure, and I will know who you are. For only in failure, "in the greatness of a catastrophe, can you know someone."[79]

Cioran developed a habit of reading success into failure and failure into every accomplishment. What he was most proud of was not his books, celebrated and translated all over the world as they became, nor his growing influence among people of philosophical taste. Not even his status as a master of the French language. "The big success of my life," he said, "is that I've managed to live without having a job. At the end of the day, I've lived my life well. I've pretended it has been a failure, but it hasn't."[80] To lead a good life is not to avoid failure, but to know how to make the most of your failing: "Only one thing matters: learning to be the loser."[81]

Here Cioran reveals one of the most important lessons of failure, and the most mysterious: when it's done well, and pursued to its natural end, failure is no longer tied to success as to an ugly twin. At this point failure is like perfectly transparent glass: you no longer see it, you see *through* it. The loser has transcended himself.

Little Tramp

Barely three years after the publication of *Down and Out in Paris and London* came another important moment in the history of tramping as a fine art: Charlie Chaplin's *Modern Times*. Unlike Orwell, Chaplin didn't have to learn how to be a tramp; he was born one—in a Gypsy caravan. He came from that London of ultimate destitution into which the upper-class Orwell would have to insinuate himself to complete his education. While Orwell was sent to study at Eton, Chaplin was sent to work. At seven, he was already sustaining his family. He never came of age because he had always been old enough. "You discover what it is like to be hungry," Orwell observed with some amazement at the beginning of his tramping experiment.[82] Chaplin never made that discovery—he was born hungry.

Given the circumstances of his birth and childhood, Chaplin probably wanted to be anything but a tramp, and yet he ended up being the most famous of them all: Little Tramp. In countless movies, starting from about 1914, he used the tramp character to make people laugh. If *Modern Times* differs from the preceding incarnations, it's not just because the film is, artistically, such an exquisite work, but because of the compelling vision of modern society that it articulates. Chaplin's chief accomplishment was to stay away from narrow, militant politics, and be what he eminently was: an artist superiorly able to expose the whole social arrangement around him, and, as he did so, to cause people not just to laugh, but also to think. If *Modern Times* has had such a considerable political impact, it's not because of Chaplin's politics, whatever they may have been, but because of his artistic and philosophical force. "He presents, he doesn't offer political solutions," observed Graham Greene when the film came out.[83]

It was Mahatma Gandhi who, unwittingly, gave Chaplin the prompt for the film. The two men had met in London in 1931. While Chaplin knew everything about the Mahatma, and was not just eager to meet him, but as nervous and fidgety as a schoolboy, the latter didn't even seem to know who Chaplin was. He hadn't seen any of his films, or any others for that matter. Brief as the meeting was, it allowed Chaplin to learn Gandhi's critical views on modernity and technology, which changed his own.

Little Tramp is swallowed up and spat out whole by the machines, as we've seen, in the film's early scenes. From there, he is taken to a clinic to recover his wits, but eventually he loses his job. The film's early machine scene is one of the most memorable, yet the rest of the story is just as relevant. Simone Weil found the film to be the mirror in which the industrialized Western world could find itself, in its naked state. There is almost no static frame in *Modern Times;* every single one speaks eloquently to us about important things that we normally prefer to remain ignorant about or pass over in silence. Chaplin is as eager as Weil to bring up for observation and consideration issues that their societies (and ours) find to be unmentionable.

The film's subtitle is Chaplin's irony at its most corroding: "A story of industry, of individual enterprise—humanity crusading in the pursuit of happiness." The story may be about all that, but since it's told from the vantage point of the excluded, it becomes a sad tale of chronic unemployment, social degradation, and unhappiness. The pursuit we end up seeing on screen is that of one man doing his best to stay afloat and yet going under just the same.

Odd as this may seem, an unmistakable sense of serenity permeates the film, which may be a reflection of the "great consolation" that Orwell found in poverty. "It is a feeling of relief, almost of pleasure, at knowing yourself at last genuinely down and out," he writes. "You have talked so often of going to the dogs—and well, here are the dogs, and you have reached them, and you can stand it. It takes off a lot of anxiety."[84]

This serenity, we come to realize, also has something to do with Little Tramp's uncanny role of sacrificial victim. Wherever he finds himself—at the assembly line, in prison or in a café, taking a rest in a posh neighborhood or strolling down the street—Little Tramp, as the social portrait of the loser, performs the same function: he embodies his society's worst fears and anxieties. Nothing is more unsettling for a society addicted to work and the pursuit of wealth than the sight of slacking. Slackers, writes Tom Lutz, "represent our fondest fantasies and our deepest fears."[85] Unemployment, homelessness, starvation, insanity, criminality, dissolution, failure—Little Tramp is supposed to exorcise them all.

In a Jungian sense, Little Tramp is society's shadow. Chaplin's character personifies all that which we refuse to admit to ourselves, which we deem shameful and despicable, and won't recognize as our own. And since there is so much that a wealth-obsessed society would prefer not to admit about itself, Little Tramp has taken on quite a task. He may be jobless, but he has the hardest job of all: to prevent other members of society from losing their bearing. No wonder that, when informed of his early release from prison, he would rather remain locked up. "Can't I stay a little longer?" he asks. "I am so happy here."

Through whatever he is doing, Little Tramp reveals himself to be a decent fellow—caring, affectionate, gentlemanly, full of talent, energy, and imagination. He is everything his society would like to be but cannot afford to be. Indeed, the tramp finds himself on the wrong side of the success-failure divide not just because he is decent, but because he is fundamentally out of place: there is too much of an artist in him, which is at odds with what society wants from us. He is not enough of a conformist, his bodily movements are not sufficiently machine-like, and—worst of all—he has retained a measure of inner freedom in a world where such a thing is economically inconvenient. Reason enough for society to spit him out, even though, in so doing, it loses its soul.

When he embarked on his tramping project, George Orwell sought not just literary inspiration, but also some kind of social redemption. He knew that what he was doing was exceptional, and yet he had to do it. The trouble, he observed, is that "intelligent, cultivated people, the very people who might be expected to have liberal opinions, never do mix with the poor."[86] As good, liberal-minded citizens, we may worry about poverty, and even try to find solutions—all in good faith. But we will do this from the safety of our highmindedness. Our noble principles, advanced culture, and intellectual sophistication will usually act as a protective screen between us and the thing itself: we deal with "the problem of poverty" or "the crisis of homelessness," never with dirt-poor people or with the homeless in flesh and blood. That's how we, loftily and cowardly, wash our hands and leave the little tramps of this world both dirt-poor and homeless. And that renders Little Tramp not an accidental, but a *perpetual sacrificial victim*.

All of this makes Chaplin's comedy one of the saddest in the history of American cinema. "What's the point of trying?" asks the tramp's lady companion, when all their efforts to stay afloat end in failure. The answer, unuttered, is obvious: None. No matter how hard they try, their efforts end in failure. This should be the story's logical conclusion—the very line with which the film should have ended.

For a few long seconds, during which he muddles this obvious conclusion into an unlikely happy ending, Chaplin fails to stand up to the pressure of his society's expectations. Unlike Little Tramp.

A Modern Gnostic

There is something distinctly Gnostic about Cioran's thinking. Gnostic insights, images, and metaphors permeate his work, as scholars have noticed. *A Short History of Decay, The Temptation to Exist,* and *The New Gods,* writes Lacarrière, are "texts which match the loftiest flashes of Gnostic thought."[87] Like the Gnostics of old, Cioran sees the creation of the world as an act of divine failure. Human history and civilization are nothing but "the work of the devil." In *A Short History of Decay,* he deems the God of this world "incompetent."[88] The French title of one of his most influential works (which in English has been published as *The New Gods*) says it all—*Le Mauvais demiurge:* "the evil demiurge." With unconcealed sympathy, Cioran calls the Gnostics "fanatics of the divine nothingness," and praises them for having "grasped so well the essence of the fallen world."[89] His Romanian roots continued to trouble him late in life. To have come from the Balkans was a shame nothing could diminish—except perhaps the fact that it was there that Thracians and Bogomils also lived: "I cannot forget that I have haunted the same whereabouts as they, nor that the former wept over the newborn and the latter, in order to justify God, held Satan responsible for the infamy of Creation."[90]

One of Cioran's greatest obsessions is "the catastrophe of birth," to which much of *The Trouble with Being Born* is dedicated. He cannot stress enough the enormity of this disaster: "We have lost, being born, as much as we shall lose, dying: Everything." Like the Gnostics, he is convinced that "the world came about through a mistake." Yet for him our coming into existence is more than an error: it is a metaphysical *affront.* Not even in old age could he come to terms with "the affront of being born." True freedom is the freedom of the unborn. "I long to be free—desperately free. Free as the stillborn are free." Cioran's fascination with the unborn generates macabre aphorisms: "If I used to ask myself, over a coffin: 'What good did it do the occupant to be born?' I now put the same question about anyone alive."[91] This is the same man who, as a child, made friends with the village's gravedigger, who supplied him with freshly dug skulls. He liked to play soccer with them.

In good Gnostic tradition, the cosmos is for Cioran in a "fallen" state, but so is the social and political world. Perhaps to transcend the political failures of his youth, the later Cioran sought to understand their deeper meaning, and to incorporate this understanding into the texture of his thinking. The result was a more nuanced philosophizing and a more humane thinker. His personal experiments with failure brought Cioran closer to a province of humanity to which he could not otherwise have had access: that of the ashamed and the humbled. In his French books you come across passages on failure of an inspired, drunken wisdom:

> At the climax of failure, at the moment when shame is about to do us in, suddenly we are swept away by a frenzy of pride which lasts only long enough to drain us, to leave us without energy, to lower, with our powers, the intensity of our shame.[92]

A lifelong contemplation of his own limitations eventually changed Cioran. As he grew older, he seems to have become more tolerant, more accepting of other people's flaws, follies, and oddities. Not, God forbid, that he ever ended up a "positive thinker." He would remain, to the end, a prophet of decadence, a thinker of dark, apocalyptic apprehensions. In *History and Utopia* (*Histoire et Utopie*, published in 1960), he writes:

> Whenever I happen to be in a city of any size, I marvel that riots do not break out every day: massacres, unspeakable carnage, a doomsday chaos. How can so many human beings

coexist in a space so confined without destroying each other, without hating each other *to death?* As a matter of fact, they do hate each other, but they are not equal to their hatred. And it is this mediocrity, this impotence, that saves society, that assures its continuance, its stability.[93]

No, Cioran never became a defender of liberal democracy. But he may have learned to enjoy the comedy of the world—indeed, to take part in undermining the cosmic failure. His later thinking exhibits something that, for want of a better term, may be called *joyous desperation* (Cioran sees himself as *un pessimiste joyeux*). It's the same pattern, over and over again: existence is found to be outrageous, plain awful, and yet somehow in that very awfulness there lies a promise of redemption. Life is unbearable, insomnia a killer, *le cafard* is eating at you slowly, and yet this is something that you can handle through writing. "Everything that is expressed becomes more tolerable."[94] Writing is a magnificent witchcraft that acts upon its practitioners and renders their lives a touch more livable. A catastrophe, to the extent that it is narratable, carries within itself the seeds of its own redemption.

The Principle of Differentiation

One of the more intriguing notions (if a minority one) to have come down to us from early Christian theology is that of *apokatastasis tôn pantôn:* "universal salvation," or "the restitution of all things" (*restitutio omnium,* in Latin). It is, roughly, the idea that, in the end, everything and everybody will be saved, or "restored"—the good *and* the bad, the saints *and* the sinners. No matter what happens along the way, the end is all-redeeming.

Origen of Alexandria was the preeminent proponent of *apokatastasis;* he thought that, since "the end is similar to the beginning," everything would eventually return to the untainted state before the Fall. And he was far from alone in entertaining such an idea—the phrase itself (*apokatastasis tôn pantôn*) comes from the Acts of the Apostles (Acts 3:21). But history had other plans. Origen was condemned for heretical views and pushed aside. His main heretical thesis? The very notion of "universal salvation." For all his penetrating insights, theological brilliance, and immense learning, Origen has remained a marginal figure in Western theology.

Noble though it was, the notion of *apokatastasis* went against one of our most fundamental instincts: that of *differentiation*. The stronger animal always needs to assert itself against—and to differentiate itself from—the weaker one. It is the law of all life. Again, it's not enough for you to succeed; the other has to fail. Only when reflected in the lowered eyes of the defeated does your victory appear safe. One of the social functions of the other is precisely to mirror and enhance your own victories and resolve your insecurities. In turn, the other will need another, even lower (if only slightly) than him, and so on. The differentiation never stops; the mirroring process is reproduced endlessly. No matter how rigidly a society is stratified (and all societies are stratified), within each stratum there will be another, and then another, and another. *Homo sapiens* didn't have to invent the differentiation. Not only were humans born with it, they survived because of it. Differentiation is the principle that keeps society together and prevents its members from devouring one another. For, once established, as the primatologist Frans de Waal has observed, "a hierarchical structure eliminates the need for conflict."[95]

We may choose a vaguer language to conceal the differentiation, or make it less offensive, but we cannot do without it. In the traditional caste system of India, the four large castes were not enough: each caste was subdivided into innumerable *jātis* (subcastes). There are some twenty-five thousand subcastes in India. Forward-looking Indians today find the system not only antiquated but repugnant and would like it abolished. Yet, ironically, most of them remain oblivious to the new income- and status-based stratification and fail to see how much alike the two caste systems in fact are: under both arrangements, people live in separate quarters, do different jobs, speak differently, eat differently, behave differently, and consider themselves different.

It's admirable yet perfectly naïve to hope that, as society evolves, we will manage to get rid of differentiation. Every known human society has generated its own forms of differentiation: social hierarchies, power structures, prestige systems, economic stratification. Historical progress (whatever that means) does not remove differentiation; it only makes the markers more insidious. A modern society like ours, which at the rhetorical level never stops praising equality, will do anything to increase actual social differentiations. Speaking of the United States in particular, Paul Fussell observed, several decades ago, that *"because* the country's a democracy, class distinctions have developed with greater rigor than elsewhere."[96]

That's why not *apokatastasis,* but *praedestinatio* became historically victorious.[97] Theologically controversial and ethically unpalatable though it is, predestination has won by a large margin. There is something dynamic, if perfectly savage, about its implicit social vision: it allows people to differentiate themselves from others, and to define themselves favorably in relation to them ("elect" vs. "reprobate"), even as those others, in turn, will see themselves as "elect" in relation to yet other "reprobates." As long as you can identify someone in relation to whom you are better off, the system works. The end result is a complex social hierarchy and a vast web of power relations, which no society can do without as it secures its survival and perpetuation. "A stable hierarchy is a guarantee of peace and harmony in the group," observes Frans de Waal about chimpanzees, but this is rigorously true of their human relatives as well.[98]

Our current capitalist system (and the civilization that comes with it) offers a perfect illustration of this state of affairs. Its most important principle may not be "the free market," or "private initiative," or "the freedom to conduct a business," but something much humbler: *ranking.* For the essence of capitalism is not the sheer amassing of wealth. The "end sought by accumulation," observed Thorstein Veblen more than a century ago, is to "rank high in comparison with the rest of the community in point of pecuniary strength."[99] Everything in our world—individuals and corporations, cities and countries, schools and universities, teachers and doctors, books and ideas, songs and poems—is judged in relation to other entities in the same category, and ranked accordingly. If something is not ranked, it can't truly take part in the social game—therefore, it doesn't really exist.

There is hardly anything that cannot be ranked. Human abilities—not just one's ability to make money and spend it, to contract and pay off debts, but even to think, to express oneself, to understand how the world works—are not only rigorously quantified, but ranked in relation to others' abilities to do the same thing. We are not what we think we are, but what our *ranking numbers* (standardized test results, class rank upon graduation, the ranking of the university we attended, credit score, and so on) say we are. The elites, by definition, are those whose rankings are highest, and they know it only too well. "Growing up elite," William Dereziewicz observes, means "learning to value yourself in terms of the measures of success that mark your progress into and through the elite: the grades, the scores, the trophies."[100]

Thanks to the brutal honesty of his theology, Calvin came to play an important role in the history of our thinking about differentiation. In no uncertain terms, he told his followers that they are *either* elect *or* reprobates. They will receive *either* God's grace *or* eternal damnation. Theologically, that was a harsh way to think about salvation, but Calvin knew better. He sensed, however obscurely, that his radical proposal would work in practice. The issue became central to the life of every single Calvinist believer, and transformed it inside out. "Am I one of the elect?" This crucial question, observes Weber, must "sooner or later have arisen for every believer and have forced all other interests in the background."[101] And that question called for another: "How can I be sure of my election?"

Calvin's own election was out of the question—he was sure of it because he trusted the "testimony of the expectant faith resulting from grace."[102] For ordinary Calvinist believers, however, unversed as they were in the subtleties of religious anxiety, such testimony was flimsy, and they needed something firmer. They hoped they could find some tangible signs of their election in the world around them, not in psychological nuances. And since those people were ardent believers, they eventually found them: industriousness and success in business, resulting in measurable personal prosperity, were deemed such signs. If one was augmenting God's glory through one's actions, these "good works" amounted to a "sign of election." Such works would be, in Weber's words, "the technical means, not of purchasing salvation, but of getting rid of the fear of damnation."[103] And ridding yourself of the fear of damnation is just as good as salvation itself. As part of the same hermeneutic effort, these blessed people decided that an unwillingness to work was the sign of the lack of grace. There is no place for idlers in Heaven. Contemplatives should go elsewhere.

People sought salvation, then, and they found money. And since they were desperate to be saved, they made increasingly large amounts of money. When they became rich enough, they must have stopped, looked around, and realized that, while they were making it big, others were going under. The signs were clear, Calvin had been right: some people are elect, while others are doomed. That's how godless capitalism was born: out of a great urge to find God's grace.

Over time the pattern has mutated into a purely secular one. The impulse it received from Calvinism certainly helped, but now it has become an autonomous system, with a mind all of its own. It no longer needs a specific religious context to function—it works wherever there is human nature. Which makes it so easily exportable. In Asia, for example, capitalism performs so well (including in nominally communist China) not just because it fits like a glove into its heavily hierarchical societies (testimony to Confucianism's endurance), but also because it has come there already fully developed. Modern Asian capitalism hasn't had to make the same mistakes as the West made. It could go straight to the winning formulas.

Failing Better

One of the most refreshing things about Cioran's later writings is his voice as a social critic. In *History and Utopia,* there is a chapter called "Letter to a Faraway Friend." The open letter was published originally in *La Nouvelle revue française* in 1957. The "faraway friend," living behind the Iron Curtain, was the Romanian philosopher Constantin Noica. Like Cioran, Noica had been a protégé of Nae Ionescu, and that must have brought them close. In this text, Cioran harpoons the political regime imposed on Eastern Europe by the Red Army for making a mockery of an important philosophical idea. "The capital reproach one can address to your regime is that it has ruined Utopia, a principle of renewal in both institutions and peoples."[104] A good Gnostic, Cioran believed that all power was evil, and he had no sympathy for any political regime; but one that needed Soviet tanks and secret police for its foundation and perpetuation was beyond the pale.

In his letter, Cioran subjects the West to an almost equally severe critique. "We find ourselves dealing with two types of society—both intolerable," he writes. "And the worst of it is that the abuses in yours permit this one to persevere in its own, to offer its own horrors as a counterpoise to those cultivated *chez vous.*"[105] The West shouldn't congratulate itself for "saving" civilization. The decline is already so advanced, Cioran believes, that nothing can be saved any more—except perhaps for appearances. The two types of society are not that different from one another. In the final analysis, it's only a matter of nuance:

> The difference between regimes is less important than it appears; you are alone by force, we without constraint. Is the

gap so wide between an inferno and a ravaging paradise? All societies are bad; but there are degrees, I admit, and if I have chosen this one, it is because I can distinguish among the nuances of trumpery.[106]

For all its analytical and stylistic merits, Cioran's open letter turned out to be a major gaffe. The addressee, who was trying to keep a low profile in the Romanian countryside, was an exceedingly well-mannered man, and in the habit of answering all letters, closed or open, regardless of where they came from. A superbly naïve man as well, Noica, upon completing his essay-response, addressed it to his friend in Paris and duly dropped the envelope in a mailbox. The Romanian secret police, which had its fingers everywhere, including in all the country's mailboxes, didn't miss it and didn't like the exchange, and Noica had to pay with several years of political prison.

The Dishwasher and the Millionaire

Humans are fundamentally the same, but they would do anything to distinguish themselves from one another—if only outwardly. Their instinct for differentiation compels them to. While busily tramping in London, Orwell made a surprising discovery: "The mass of the rich and the poor are differentiated by their incomes and nothing else, and the average millionaire is only the average dishwasher dressed in a new suit."[107] Orwell's intuition is important for understanding how differentiation works in a modern capitalist context. You can only distinguish yourself from others by making more money and showing it. Since others will do the same, you will have to earn even more than they do. The more you earn, the more you can spend and, therefore, the better your chances of securing a higher degree of differentiation. But since those from whom you seek to differentiate yourself are doing just the same, you cannot afford to stop.

The Calvinists of old earned money because they wanted to be among God's elect—what better differentiation than salvation? Today we make money to be among society's select. And since our thirst for social salvation is bottomless, no amount will be large enough to quench it. That there is no limit as to how much money can be made and spent, on the one hand, and that, for all our efforts at differentiation, we remain fundamentally the same, on the other hand, is what keeps the system in perpetual motion. We will always try to differentiate ourselves from others, even if we have to work ourselves to death. The "desire for wealth," observes Veblen, "can scarcely be satiated in any individual instance, and evidently a satiation of the average or general desire for wealth is out of the question."[108]

The fact that, as part of this game, we in today's liberal West have to adopt the pretense of an egalitarian ethos makes the game both more sophisticated and more vicious. "Despite our political embrace of political and judicial equality," writes Fussell, "in individual perception and understanding—much of which we refrain from publicizing—we arrange things vertically and insist on crucial differences in value."[109] In previous societies, social differentiation was always in the open: amply displayed, rigorously imposed, and properly internalized. And so it is still in many parts of the world today. In the civilized West, however, the higher one is on the social and economic ladder, the humbler one is supposed to *appear*. This must be one of the most unexpected victories of Western Christianity, if a posthumous one. Fussell, in the footsteps of Veblen, speaks of "the understatement principle": you have class to the extent that you know how *not* to show it. Only the "status insecure" show off. "Both women's and men's elite looks," writes Fussell, are achieved "by a process of rejection—of the current, the showy, the superfluous."[110]

The mask of humble simplicity is meant to help its wearer move up in the game, be it politics, business, or anything else. This mask performs a paradoxical function: it conceals the wearer's differentiation to the same extent that it reveals it. The wearer's humble outfit looks like that of others, but should you make inquiries, you will find out that it's ten times more expensive, is made of a different material, and can only be found in exclusive stores. Competitors will do anything to find one that looks at least as humble but is even more expensive. What they *cannot* do is exit the game and wear genuinely inexpensive items. Status signals constantly need to be sent out so that, at any given moment, everyone knows their place. That's an unspoken rule of the game. "The frequent exchange of status signals," writes Frans de Waal, "reassures bosses that they need not underline their position by force, which gives respite to everyone."[111]

This is, in a nutshell, the social essence of capitalism—the biggest game in town, and pretty much the only one. While most would say that capitalism is an arms race for success, it could also be called the "failure game." For it is failure that lies at the core of the capitalist idea: regardless of my actual wealth, I can differentiate myself from others only to the extent that they fail to amass as much wealth as I do. I may be very poor, but I can still differentiate myself from someone who is poorer than me. And that keeps me going. As well as the whole system.

The system, as it is set up, presupposes that anyone will be able to find someone else to look at and think, "That person makes less than I do, and is worse off than I am. What a loser!" "The invidious comparison can never become so favourable to the individual making it," writes Veblen, "that he would not gladly rate himself still higher relatively to his competitors in the struggle for pecuniary reputability."[112] No matter how unvisited by success you may be, there is always someone out there who is even less successful than you are. Even the most insignificant differences, real or imagined, matter. Recall the countless shades of destitution that Orwell discovered in Paris and London, those crowded "suburbs of poverty."

Henry David Thoreau, for one, seems to have understood this early on and realized what was at stake. In *Walden,* he asks rhetorically, "Why should we be in such desperate haste to succeed, and in such desperate enterprises? If a man does not keep pace with his companions, perhaps it is because he hears a different drummer."[113] But Thoreau was a dissenter, and so are those few who have stopped to listen to his drumming. What has prevailed instead is a world in which the "desperate haste to succeed," and the attendant anxiety of failure, has come to shape everything—from government offices to private chambers, from the life of a daily laborer to that of the head of a large corporation, from literary masterpieces to suicide notes.

What has fueled every capitalist success has been not joy, but dread—the dread of failure. There is no greater tragedy than status slippage, and we would do anything to avoid it. We would work ourselves to death. And if that doesn't kill us, we would outspend ourselves to death. Which is exactly what the system wants us to do.

"I Used to Be Cioran"

E. M. Cioran died on June 20, 1995. In a sense, though, he had left well before then. For the last several years he suffered from Alzheimer's disease and had been interned at the Broca Hospital in Paris. Fearing precisely such an ending, he had planned to commit suicide with his longtime partner, Simone Boué. They were to die together, like the Koestlers. But the disease progressed faster than he had anticipated, and the plan failed. Cioran had to die the most humiliating of deaths, one that took several slow years to do its work.

At first, there were just some worrying signs: one day he could not find his way back home from the city, which he—a consummate walker—knew as if he had been born there. Then he started losing his memory. His fabulous sense of humor, apparently, he lost last. One day, a passerby asked him in the street, "Are you Cioran by any chance?" His answer: "I used to be."[114] When someone brought to him—and read from—the newly published English translation of *The Trouble with Being Born*, he listened carefully and then exclaimed, *"Ce type écrit mieux que moi!"* (This guy writes better than I do!).[115] But the signs became too many and too serious to ignore: he started to forget at such an alarming rate that he had to be interned. Eventually, even words failed him: he could no longer name the most basic things. Then, it was the mind's turn. In the end, he forgot who he was altogether.

At one point during his long, final suffering, in a brief moment of lucidity, Cioran whispered to himself, *"C'est la démission totale!"*[116] It was the grand, ultimate failure, and he didn't fail to recognize it for what it was.

Doing Nothing

Scott Sandage has studied how the anxiety of failure was born in nineteenth-century America. "Failure" and "loser" had humble beginnings, he observes. They originally meant specific occurrences and situations. According to a children's book from 1852, for example, to fail was simply "to be unable to pay one's debts," and a "loser" was nothing more dramatic than someone who lost something. "Loser" was at the time "a neutral word for anybody who lost property, often by theft or natural disaster," Sandage writes. To illustrate the point, he quotes from a newspaper article in the aftermath of the 1820 Boston fire: "the keeper of the hotel, is a great loser, particularly in furniture and liquors."[117]

Everything changed quickly. Within a few decades, "failure" came to signify something much larger and deeper than a mere biographical accident, its meaning shifting from "the lost capital of a bankruptcy" to the "lost chances of a wasted life."[118] Having remade the business world, failure then stole into society at large, and into people's minds and hearts, shaping the way they saw and judged themselves. The word retained a Calvinist echo, but for the most part failure was now a godless affair.

All that was more than one hundred years ago. Since then, things have only got worse. Failure has been normalized and internalized. We have become not just used to it, but positively addicted to it—to the failure of others, that is. Our own we don't normally see, busy as we are at keeping an eye on theirs.

And yet our own failure is the most serious, if not the only real failure in this story. It consists, quite simply, of having fallen for the game in the first place, and then persisting in playing it. We play it ruthlessly, as if our own life depended on it. And, strangely enough, it does. It depends on it in much the same way the life of the addicted person depends on finding yet another dose: it saves us for the moment. As Rudolf, the hero of Thomas Bernhard's *Concrete*, notices, "we immediately use someone who is *still more* unfortunate than we are in order to get ourselves back on our feet."[119] Till we fall again.

And that is our undoing. For our unquenchable thirst for social success, our obsession with rankings and ratings, our compulsion to make ever more money only to be able to spend more will bankrupt us in the end—morally, spiritually, and even materially. Outwardly, we may look successful, prosperous, and happy, but we are empty inside. Walking shells. Our lives are as glamorous as they are hollow. We are seriously sick, and we are in bad need of a cure.

In theory, the cure should be a relatively simple affair: we don't have to do much. To be more exact, we have to *do nothing*. And yet that's precisely what renders it so exceptional. As Oscar Wilde observed, "to do nothing at all is the most difficult thing in the world, the most difficult and the most intellectual."[120] No wonder it took Cioran a lifetime, and a long series of failures, to master it.

At one level, Cioran, Oblomov, Bartley, and other great idlers look like exceedingly colorful figures, easier to find in fiction (or in Romania) than in real life. Yet they are not as eccentric as they seem. Every spiritual tradition worth its name recommends inaction, in some form or another, for shorter or longer periods, as a path to enlightenment. If we are to make any progress, we need to make a full stop first. We will never discover—let alone realize—ourselves while caught up in the maelstrom. As long as we keep ourselves compulsively busy, we cannot understand much—least of all where we are going.

Doing nothing would allow us to take a decisive step back, stand still, and have a good look at ourselves. Thanks to our stillness and detachment, we would be able to see our condition in a more truthful light. When we manage to make out the deadly emptiness we carry within, we will know we have started our recovery.

4

THE ULTIMATE FAILURE

No matter how far we run away from people, or how carefully we wrap ourselves up in our own solitude, society will always catch up. Not only because solitude is conceived in relation to others, but because we are compelled to use language—an eminently social product—to think or speak even to ourselves. Being a loser, a social outcast or nonentity, is an intimate experience indeed, yet there is a form of failure that is more intimate still—something so profoundly "ours" that we cannot share it with anybody else. Nothing in the world compares to what we experience when we face the ultimate failure: our own death.

The final circle of failure is so tight and personalized—"custom-made," you may call it—that it fits only one person in the world, and that's you. Others (family, friends, doctors) may accompany you, but when it comes to life's final moments, you are as alone as you will ever be. As you reach out for the door knob, you may be tempted to turn your head for one final look, but no one is there.

Truth be told, this type of failure takes place continuously, from the moment we are born, in the intimacy of our cells, till the moment of death. What we commonly call a "natural death"—as a well-defined event—is, at the cellular level, only the end of a life-long process. That doesn't make our exit any less significant. If anything, it is, in many respects, the most important moment of our lives. Across time and culture, how we die says a lot about how we live and what we make of our lives.

We Are Designed to Fail

When they seek to determine someone's cause of death, doctors often speak of "organ failure"—the failure of an essential system in the body (cardiovascular, renal, etc.)—or even of "multiple organ failure"—the loss of function of two or more such systems. No matter how old one is, one never dies of old age (technically, age cannot by itself be the cause of death), but because of some failure that takes place within the body. Such language is revealing. It suggests an unspoken, perhaps unconscious belief that our organs are meant to work indefinitely, and, by implication, that we are supposed to last indefinitely as well. We—this line of thinking goes—are not "exhaustible" (meant to burn for a while and then flicker away), but designed to live forever. Should we somehow manage to find better parts, or more expert maintenance, our mortality problem would be all but solved. It is largely such a belief that lies behind the transhumanism project.

What this belief betrays, more deeply, is that we are not properly equipped to think about death. In an important sense, we *don't get death*. We can certainly train ourselves to think of it, and some of us may succeed, but it doesn't come naturally. For the most part, nature has programmed us to ignore our own demise. Thrust into existence as we are, our main business here is to survive and reproduce, and not to ponder such unsettling issues as death, nothingness, or annihilation. Life knows how to take care of itself. This is what Goethe must have had in mind when he said, "It is entirely impossible for a thinking being to think of its own non-existence, of the termination of its thinking and life."[1] For Vladimir Jankélévitch, to think death is "to think the unthinkable" (*penser l'impensable*). "There is utterly nothing to think about death," writes Jean Améry, in a similar vein. The genius and the simpleton are "equally thwarted in confronting this subject."[2] To think of death in an adequate manner—to fully take it in—goes against our fundamental instincts as living creatures.

Yet death never fails to take *us* in. No matter how fulfilled our lives turn out to be, the same destination awaits us all: ultimate, biological failure. The existential threat of that failure has been with us all along, but to live in a state of relative contentment, most of us remain blissfully unaware of it—or at least manage to pretend. This pretense, however, has never prevented us from moving toward our destination, faster and faster, "in inverse ratio to the square of the distance from death," as Tolstoy's Ivan Ilyich expertly describes the process.[3]

When it came to death and dying, Leo Tolstoy was more than a distant observer: he was a consummate insider. The big question that ate at him all the time was, as he puts it in *Confession:* "Is there any meaning in my life that wouldn't be destroyed by the death that inevitably awaits me?"[4] To find an answer, Tolstoy never took his eyes off death; he observed it unceasingly, from multiple angles and in different circumstances, as his writing—and perhaps especially *The Death of Ivan Ilyich*—attests. All his life Tolstoy sought to understand the extraordinary power that death holds on our existence: how our fear of death, the anxiety or even terror caused in us by the thought of our mortality, shape the way we live and conduct ourselves. This was, for him, not navel-gazing, but a shattering, immersive experience, which he hoped would cure him of his own fear of death. Tolstoy prepared himself for the ultimate failure by dying, again and again, with every one of his characters that perished. He feared their fears, felt their pain, and was paralyzed by their anxieties. Long before his own end at some obscure railway station in 1910, he had experienced his own exquisitely portrayed deaths as Prince Andrei Bolkonsky, Anna Karenina, Hadji Murat, and Ivan Ilyich.

Life may be hard, the cliché goes, but death is even harder. *The Death of Ivan Ilyich* gives us some insight into the difficulty.

Suffering from an unspecified terminal disease, Ivan Ilyich eventually admits to himself, after much self-deception, that "something new and dreadful was happening to him, something of such vast importance that nothing in his life could compare with it."[5] Even at this late hour he was afraid to call death by its name. Naming it, he must have feared, would have somehow conjured it up and brought it to life, as if death hadn't been there all along. At one point, he refers to it as "that horrid, appalling, unheard-of something that had been set in motion within him and was gnawing away at him day and night, ineluctably dragging him off somewhere."[6]

Firmly rooted in life, as any living creature is, Ivan Ilyich just could not accept his nonexistence, imminent and inevitable though it was. "In the depth of his heart he knew he was dying," observes Tolstoy, "but not only was he unaccustomed to such an idea, he simply could not grasp it. . . . It simply was not possible that he should have to die."[7] Ivan was neither equipped nor prepared to accept his mortality. That he should do such a thing remained, to the very end, alien to him.

Ivan Ilyich died alone, as we all do. Tolstoy is too good a writer to insinuate himself into his hero's death—that narrow, custom-made space that was meant for him, and him alone. "He drew in a breath, broke off in the middle of it, stretched himself out, and died."[8] For all the indignities Ivan Ilyich had to suffer before he died, his end has a quiet solemnity about it. There is something of a professional undertaker's velvet-like courtesy in the way Tolstoy scribes his passing.

The Death of Ivan Ilyich is an account of one man's desperate struggle to stick to life, even as death is snatching him away. Much of the book is about death, but if you want to learn *how* to approach this last great failure—how to face it, how to own it—poor Ivan doesn't have much to tell you. A slightly better model is Antonius Block, from Ingmar Bergman's *The Seventh Seal.* A Swedish knight returning from the Crusades and plunged into a crisis of faith, Block is faced with the grand failure in the form of a man in black, which is how Death chooses to appear to him. The valiant knight does not hesitate to engage Death head-on. He doesn't flee, doesn't cry, doesn't beg for mercy—he challenges Death to a game of chess. "The condition is that I may live as long as I hold out against you. If I win, you will release me. Is it agreed?" the knight asks boldly. Taken aback, Death agrees.

Block cannot succeed in his game with Death—no one can—but victory is not the point. You play against the grand failure not to win, but to learn how to lose. Bergman teaches us a great lesson here: We will all die, but that's not the most important thing. What really matters is how we die and what we gain in the process. During his brief engagement with Death, Block must have experienced more than he did all his eventful life. He examines his life and his conscience and touches the limits of his earthly existence, and in so doing he gets to know himself a little better. He keeps searching for meaning even as he knows that the quest is largely in vain. He makes new friends, and befriends Death himself, which is no small feat. Without that final game of chess, the knight's existence would have been significantly poorer. In the end, even as he loses, Block accomplishes something rare: he turns failure into a fine art and manages to make the art of failing an intimate part of the art of living.

Yet, just as in the case of Ivan Ilyich, Antonius Block's encounter with the grand failure only shows how difficult it is to go against our survival instinct and come to terms with our mortality. Block is defiant, philosophical, and a joy to watch, but it is not at all clear that he exits this world at peace with himself. What he wants to find out from Death is above all an answer to some burning existential questions. When Death finally comes to take him away, he goes reluctantly, giving no sign that his questions have been answered. His final prayer says it all: "From our darkness, we call out to Thee, Lord. Have mercy on us because we are small and frightened and ignorant." For all we know, the prayer is addressed to a God in whose existence Block is unable, or unready, to believe.

But who says that dying is easy? Managing to extricate yourself from existence—with ease and grace, and without regret and agony—may be the most difficult thing to accomplish in life. It takes a long time and hard work and punishing self-discipline. It's not for nothing that such training—learning how to die, to get ready, to exit—is central to virtually all religions and to any spiritual tradition worthy of the name.

Bakayarō! Bakayarō!

The parade grounds of the Ichigaya Camp—the Tokyo headquarters of the Eastern Command of the Japan Self-Defense Forces (Jieitai)—looked like a rehearsal for Doomsday on that November morning. Ambulances and police cars arrived at high speed—lights flashing, sirens blaring. The camp's soldiers, summoned abruptly, gathered in confusion. No one had told them what exactly had happened, and the wildest rumors were circulating. Apparently, someone was to make a speech, to which they were supposed to listen. As more police cars and motorcycles arrived, people kept running in all directions, without anyone knowing for sure what was going on. For good measure, TV helicopters circled above, noisily filming the chaos and making it complete.

At last, the speaker made his appearance on the balcony. He stepped out of the commander's office, through a window, and seemed determined to address the soldiers gathered below. A smallish man, in his forties, athletic looking, yet with a strangely proportioned body, he sported some kind of military uniform (though not *their* uniform) and a headband featuring, in black Chinese ink, the ancient samurai motto *Shichishō hōkoku*—Serve the nation for seven lives. That made people slightly nervous: it was one of the slogans that the right-wing militarists had used during the war, from which the Jieitai had over the last two decades done its best to steer clear.

Be that as it may, the man looked like he knew what he was doing. In fact, he was the only one who seemed to have a notion of what was happening there. It soon became clear to the soldiers that the peculiarly uniformed, short-legged figure was the reason they were gathered there. His movements were precise and economical, in sharp contrast with the chaos all around him. The man had obviously come with a plan, and he was sticking to it. As soon as he started to speak, he revealed himself to be a skilled rhetorician— indeed, an experienced performer. For all the noise, if one happened to be under the balcony, one could make out what he was saying.

"It is a wretched affair to have to speak to Jieitai men in circumstances like these," he started. The noise from the helicopters above showed no signs of abating, but the speaker pressed on just the same: "I thought that the Jieitai was the last hope of Nippon, the last stronghold of the Japanese soul. . . . Japanese people today think of money, just money. Where is our national spirit today? . . . The Jieitai must be the soul of Nippon."[9]

At first, the soldiers listened with a mixture of curiosity and disbelief. It was not every day that one could witness such things in Nippon. But soon they started to show hostility. "Cut it out now!" some shouted. "Come down from there!" The speaker would have none of it. He demanded their attention ("Listen! Hear me out! Listen! Listen to me!") and continued: "We thought that the Jieitai was the soul of national honor. . . . The nation has no spiritual foundation. This is why you don't agree with me."[10]

If, initially, the soldiers' hostility, though manifest, was kept under control, now the men exploded. *Bakayarō! Bakayarō!* started to be heard. *Bakayarō* is a particularly offensive Japanese insult; its kindest (and blandest) translation would be "you moron!" The soldiers had good reason to be upset. For what the speaker was offering them was an invitation to a coup d'état—an undertaking in which he would be their leader and they would have to follow him loyally. The goal of the whole enterprise was lofty: "To protect Japan!

You must protect Japan! . . . Japanese tradition! Our history! Our culture! The Emperor!"[11]

The Japanese Constitution, imposed by the occupying American forces after the country's defeat in 1945, is explicitly pacifist. "Aspiring sincerely to an international peace based on justice and order," reads Article 9, "the Japanese people forever renounce war as a sovereign right of the nation and the threat or use of force as a means of settling international disputes." What that meant in practice was that Japan had denied itself the right to have a national army, relying instead for its protection on American forces. Anything having to do with the "army" was removed from official language. That's why these soldiers belonged to Japan's Self-Defense Forces, not to the Japanese Army, which was a constitutional impossibility. For a country whose history, culture, and collective identity had been shaped by a strong martial ethos, such a legal provision was too much, the speaker thought. There had been a campaign to amend the constitution, but all efforts had so far been in vain. The speaker was obviously angry that the Jieitai refused to be involved in the campaign. By so doing, he suggested, they consented to their own insignificance: "A man appeals to you! . . . Do you follow me? If you do not rise with me, if the Jieitai will not rise, the Constitution will never be amended! . . . You will be just American mercenaries."[12]

What he was proposing, quite simply, was overthrowing the democratically elected government, restoring all power to the emperor (*Tennō*), and returning to the old Japanese warrior ethos (*Bushidō*): "Are you *bushi*? Are you men? You *are* soldiers! Then why do you stand by the Constitution? You back the Constitution that denies your very existence! . . . Then you have no future! . . . You are unconstitutional!"[13]

The soldiers, all born years after the end of the war, who knew only vaguely what the speaker was talking about, were unmoved. The prospect of being led into battle—or into anything, for that matter—by the buffoonish figure gesticulating before them wasn't exactly enticing. But the buffoon would not give up so easily: "Don't you understand that it is you who defend the Constitution? . . . Why don't you wake up? There you are in your tiny world. You do nothing for Nippon!"[14] The soldiers remained unmoved. He gave them one last chance, asking, "Will any of you rise with me?" and waited for several long seconds. Nothing. All he got was repeated salvos of *Bakayarō!* "You moron!" He had planned to speak for thirty minutes but had to stop after just seven. It became obvious that he would not persuade anyone. *Bakayarō! Bakayarō!*

Some may have seen his picture in the newspapers. Just a few weeks before, the Tōbu Department Store, a fancy establishment in central Tokyo, had made him the object of an ample exhibition, which thousands of people had flocked to see. To say that he was famous would be an understatement: the *bakayarō* was a widely acclaimed genius. Many considered Yukio Mishima to be the best Japanese writer of his generation.[15] Uncommonly gifted and versatile, he could take up virtually any genre and do superlative work, penning novels, short stories, plays (both traditional and modern), philosophical essays, even articles on sports. By the age of forty, he had written around forty novels, eighteen plays, twenty volumes of short stories, and many essays. His work had been translated all over the world, and his plays were performed, to great acclaim, both in Japan and abroad. He was also a bodybuilder, a boxer, and a model. He acted in movies (with mixed results) and even directed some of them. He once directed an orchestra. He was an accomplished practitioner of traditional Japanese swordsmanship (kendo). He set up a small private army. One wonders what Mishima did *not* do.

By ordinary standards, Mishima was more successful than any other Japanese writer of his time. Lately, however, he had decided to court failure—indeed, to marry it. When the soldiers booed him off that platform, he wasn't surprised—neither upset nor offended.

He had been preparing for this outcome for a full year now. He may have been a complete idealist, but he never lost his sense of the real.

The grand act Mishima had been planning, as he saw it, was part of a very Japanese tradition of "noble failures." In this tradition, the heroes are meant to fail from the outset, but that's not the point: it is the process—the sheer performance of failure—that matters. That these people are fully aware that they are doomed and yet keep fighting just the same makes their failure particularly "noble." In succumbing, they transcend themselves and thus reveal something important about what it means to be human. The fact that "all their efforts are crowned with failure," observes Ivan Morris in his book *The Nobility of Failure*, "lends them a pathos which characterizes the general vanity of human endeavor and makes them the most loved and evocative of heroes."[16]

Mishima knew this tradition better than anyone else and was fascinated by it. Indeed, as his translator, Morris may have got the idea of his book from Mishima himself; *The Nobility of Failure* is dedicated to his memory. About one such instance of noble failure (the 1874 uprising against the Meiji government's policies of dramatic Westernization), Mishima observed that "it was an experiment bound to fail, but not before it revealed purity and orthodoxy and the substance, call it the core, of what we mean when we speak of Japan and the Japanese."[17]

Such a noble failure in Japan typically ends with the hero performing ritual suicide by belly-cutting (*hara-kiri*). Which is exactly what Mishima himself was about to do as he stepped back into the commander's office. He failed to persuade the soldiers, just as he had anticipated. Everything was going according to plan.

"A Life as One Long History of Failures"

If we come into the world equipped with an instinct to avoid death at all costs, then suicide, as a voluntary act of termination, should be impossible to put into practice. The decision to take one's own life is totally out of the ordinary course of things: we are not de-signed even to contemplate death properly, let alone to cause our own death voluntarily. Our entire biological setup should prevent us from doing so. Life cannot rise against itself. That's why, from a philosophical standpoint, suicide has always raised some fasci-nating questions.

Above all, the sheer fact that we can dispose of our own being marks us out decisively as humans. No other species does that. The capacity to kill oneself is "one of man's distinctive characteristics," writes Cioran. "No animal is capable of it, and the angels have scarcely guessed its existence."[18] Not that we should feel particularly flattered; if anything, this capacity is part of the human drama, and makes our condition even more complicated. *Homo sapiens,* writes Simon Critchley, is "distinguished by the capacity for self-slaughter, which is perhaps the price we pay for self-consciousness."[19]

Suicide doesn't just make us human; it makes us free agents in situations where freedom seems almost impossible to obtain. Finding ourselves in an existential cul de sac (suffering from an incurable and degenerative disease, or facing immediate arrest and a humiliating death after the failure of a plot to remove a tyrant, for example), where we seem to have run out of options, suicide can still offer us an honorable exit. "It will generally be found that as soon as the terrors of life reach the point at which they outweigh the terrors of death, a man will put an end to his life," Arthur Schopenhauer observed two centuries ago.[20] That's how one can still "die with dignity," in situations where dignity seems to be in short supply.

Killing oneself is often associated with failure, with the suicide seen as a big loser. In a penetrating study, *The Savage God,* inspired in part by the suicide of his friend Sylvia Plath, Al Alvarez deepens the relationship between suicide and failure. "Suicide may be a dec-laration of bankruptcy which passes judgement on a life as one long history of failures," he writes. And yet by deciding to kill your-self, you show that you still have a certain degree of control over your life. Such a decision, "by its very finality, is not wholly a failure." Through your act, you bring a sense of closure to a situation that seems to have none. Alvarez observes that there is "a whole class of suicides . . . who take their own lives not in order to die but to escape confusion, to clear their heads." Not to take revenge on society or make others feel guilty, but to put their own lives in order. Clarity by rope. The suicide's biography as "one long history of failures" is thus redeemed by the act itself. Defeat has been turned into something else. Which is not exactly failure. "Perhaps this is why totalitarian states feel cheated when their victims take their own lives," adds Alvarez.[21]

In such cases, suicide, while a free act, is shaped by external circumstances. If you suffer from terminal cancer, you can choose to die a slow, degrading death later, or take your life now. In the case of the latter, it is your cancer that determines your choice. If you are involved in a plot to kill a tyrant, and you come under suspicion, you can choose to wait for the tyrant's henchmen or kill yourself before they arrive. Should you choose the latter, you have been pushed there by your whole situation. Your suicide comes at the end of a series of steps, each of which you've taken freely, and all of which have brought you where you are now. You choose freely, but your circumstances dictate the parameters of your freedom.

Whoever has reached this point in life usually has serious reasons for doing so, futile as they may seem to others. That's why these people deserve their society's understanding. What they usually get instead is a silent condemnation. In our secularized societies, those who decide to take their own lives may no longer be considered unforgivable sinners destined to burn in hell, or criminals ("self-murderers"), but the collective imagination has its ways of punishing them. We tend to regard suicides and suicidal individuals as intrinsically pathological, people of whom other members of society should stay clear.

And there is good reason for that: thousands of years of evolutionary history have instilled in us the notion that we need to stick together to survive. Outside the group, life is, in Hobbes's memorable wording, "solitary, poor, nasty, brutish, and short." When a person decides to turn their back on the group and dispose of their life, we are programmed to feel unsettled; if others were to start imitating such behavior, the group's existence would be imperiled. If the group is to survive, such acts need to be suppressed. Hence the stigmatization. *Homo sapiens* learned this long before any religion or legal system explicitly banned suicide; that was only a late act of ratification.

The decision to take one's life, however, is too serious an act to be left to the discretion of a society's instinctive reaction. As the psychiatrist Thomas Szasz observed, rather than a sin, a crime, or an antisocial act, suicide should be considered "a fundamental human right." This is not to say that it is desirable. "It only means that society does not have the moral right to interfere, by force, with a person's decision to commit this act."[22] And talking sympathetically about suicide, as Szasz does, is not an apology for suicide. It's an attempt to understand, from within, one of the most difficult decisions a human being has ever had to make. If we can't do more to help these people, at the very least we owe them this understanding.

The Pleasures of Dying

As a child, Kimitake Hiraoka (Mishima's real name) did not seem meant for acts of martial bravery. He was weak and sickly, and spent most of his early years indoors, under the close supervision of his overprotective paternal grandmother, Natsuko Hiraoka. When allowed outside, he had to wear a breathing mask, and his movements were severely restricted. Under the pretext that it was too dangerous to raise a child on the second floor of a house, where the boy's parents lived, Natsuko "snatched" him from his mother's arms just weeks after his birth. "My bed," he would recall in his highly autobiographical novel *Confessions of a Mask* (*Kamen no*

Kokuhaku), "was placed in my grandmother's sickroom, perpetually closed and stifling with odors of sickness and old age, and I was raised there beside her sickbed."[23]

Natsuko adduced his poor health as an excuse, but it was *hers* that would play an important role in the whole affair. She was suffering from multiple ailments, and young Mishima became her primary caregiver, administering medication, dressing her sores, accompanying her to the bathroom, and in general putting up with her insufferable personality. Domineering and arbitrary, Natsuko had always been a difficult woman, and old age didn't make things any easier. On a whim, she could ask Mishima to put on girls' dresses, which he dutifully did. At other times, concerned for his health, and to keep him from learning "bad things," she forbade him to play with the neighborhood boys. "My only playmates," he wrote, "excepting maids and nurses, were three girls whom my grandmother had selected from the girls in the neighborhood."[24] Natsuko was prone to crises of hysteria, losing her temper easily, and even hitting those around her under the smallest pretext. Mishima put up with all this because he loved her. "At the age of eight I had a sixty-year-old lover," he would quip later. "Much time is saved by such a start," observed Marguerite Yourcenar, in her book on Mishima.[25]

Spending his infancy and much of his childhood in such unusual proximity could not but have a serious impact on the formation of Mishima's character. It was Natsuko's "fey spirit," Yourcenar thought, that planted in him "the seeds of madness once deemed necessary for genius."[26] Coming from an aristocratic background, Natsuko was educated and refined, in both Western and Eastern ways. She had endless stories to tell about Japan's past, and had developed a passion for Japanese theater, both Noh and Kabuki, which she passed on profitably to her grandson. It must have been during those early years that Kimitake became Mishima: the writer with an unusual grasp of the Japanese language and its many

historical layers, the connoisseur of all things refined and aristocratic, the unfailing gentleman, the perfect mask.

When Donald Ritchie met him in the late 1940s, his "invariable
courtesy" was the first thing he noticed. Mishima had "the finest
social manners of anyone I had ever met."[27] That was all Natsuko's doing. This chronically sick and not entirely sane old lady
embodied Mishima's intense emotional attachment to Japan's
past, just as her deteriorating condition came to instill in him a revulsion toward illness, infirmity, and old age.[28] Both feelings would
accompany Mishima for the rest of his life and merge in his final,
deadly performance.

No sooner did he become aware of himself as a person than he
began thinking about death. He recalls how, at a very young age,
he discovered his "heart's leaning toward Death and Night and
Blood." This was rarely the blood of others—usually it was his own.
He would find intense pleasure in imagining "situations in which
I myself was dying in battle or being murdered." Once, while
playing war with some girls, as he sometimes did, he collapsed
limply, pretending he had been killed in battle. The pleasure was
overpowering. "I was enraptured with the vision of my own form
lying there, twisted and fallen," he recalls. "There was an unspeakable delight in having been shot and being on the point of death."[29]
Being mown down by bullets, pierced by arrows, cut to pieces by
sword, limbs severed, flesh torn, blood spilling all over—such seem
to have been his favorite fantasies.

When Kimitake reached puberty, a new ingredient was added
into the mix: sex. From now on sex and death would be inextricably
linked in his life. One doesn't need to be Freudian to suspect a link
between Eros and Thanatos, but he pushed the connection to its
breaking point, and put himself on the line as he did so. At twelve
he discovered that he had a "curious toy" in his possession, one
that "increased in volume at every opportunity," indicating that,
"rightly used, it would be quite a delightful thing." He also noticed

that what set the toy in motion was not anything associated with the opposite sex, but sights of "naked bodies of young men on a summer's seashore," or the male "swimming teams seen at Meiji Pool," or "the swarthy young man a cousin of mine married." Such sights, appetizing though they may have been, weren't the most stimulating, though. What absolutely compelled his toy to "raise its head," as he put it, was the promise of death in the shape of "pools of blood and muscular flesh." Only that would arouse the young man properly:

> Gory dueling scenes on the frontispieces of adventure-story magazines . . . pictures of young samurai cutting open their bellies, or of soldiers struck by bullets, clenching their teeth and dripping blood from between hands that clutched at khaki-clad breasts . . . at the sight of such things the toy would promptly lift its inquisitive head.[30]

In *Confessions of a Mask* Mishima describes, in much detail, the experience of his first ejaculation. The book promised to be a tell-all, and he more than delivers. He tells everything—perhaps a bit more than everything, but the leaps of fantasy are telling. For when it comes to what makes a self, it is immaterial whether one has experienced something or invented it, whether one has actually done a deed or would only like to have done so. Everything, actual or only imagined, becomes real in the telling. The self we eventually weave is not just the sum total of what we have done, but also of a long series of *absences:* all that we've longed for but never got, the love that was not reciprocated, the unkept promises, the missed opportunities, the unfulfilled desires, all that we have only imagined or fantasized about, or have not even dared to dream. The missing parts may be more important than the real ones.

Back to Mishima's ejaculation. The experience was triggered by his pubescent encounter with a reproduction of Guido Reni's *Saint Sebastian*. In Reni's rendition, the saint is dying what Mishima would later consider a "beautiful death": he is being martyred. Young and handsome, completely naked save for a loincloth (and a malfunctioning one at that), Sebastian is offering himself as sacrificial victim. The saint's body is conspicuously in full bloom, but it is going to waste just the same. For all the fullness of life on display, death is drawing near. In Japan, the contemplation of cherry blossoms every spring is meant to acknowledge and celebrate precisely this link between life and death, as Mishima knew only too well.

Mishima's encounter with Reni's painting is a complex, layered experience. On one level, he contemplates the saint's bodily presence in purely aesthetic terms:

> His white and matchless nudity gleams against a background of dusk. His muscular arms, the arms of a praetorian guard accustomed to bending of bow and wielding of sword, are raised at a graceful angle, and his bound wrists are crossed directly over his head. His face is turned slightly upward and his eyes are open wide, gazing with profound tranquility upon the glory of heaven. It is not pain that hovers about his straining chest, his tense abdomen, his slightly contorted hips, but some flicker of melancholy pleasure like music.[31]

Yet Mishima doesn't remain a mere spectator for too long. Thanks to his outstanding artistic gifts, he can identify empathically with the figure in the painting. He is now writing *from within,* as though inhabiting the saint's body, feeling its warmth, smelling its smell, suffering its pain. He details knowingly—as if speaking of his own body—how the arrows have already "eaten into" the saint's "tense, fragrant, youthful flesh" and are about to "consume his body from within with flames of supreme agony and ecstasy."[32] Mishima's hand seems to be shaking as he writes this, as befitting one caught in such joyous agony.

There is then another layer, several shades darker, and not exactly contemplative. Here Mishima is no longer the disinterested aesthetic observer of an artwork, but a man aroused—properly, sexually aroused. Reni's painting is now triggering in him a raw, primitive reaction. His "entire being," he writes, "trembled with some pagan joy" upon its intimate encounter with the naked body in the painting:

> My blood soared up; my loins swelled as though in wrath. The monstrous part of me that was on the point of bursting awaited my use of it with unprecedented ardor, upbraiding me for my ignorance, panting indignantly. My hands, completely unconsciously, began a motion they had never been taught. I felt a secret, radiant something rise swift-footed to the attack from inside me. Suddenly it burst forth, bringing with it a blinding intoxication.[33]

To dispel any possible confusion, Mishima adds helpfully, "This was my first ejaculation."[34] The saint has now become a porn star. The blasphemous intention may have been lost on many readers in Japan, where Christians were then, as now, an insignificant minority, but the desire to shock was hard to ignore.[35] Yet to say that Mishima, while looking at the saint, fantasized about him as a potential sexual partner would be to miss the point. Saint Sebastian was not his imagined partner: he was Mishima himself. The identification was now complete, and it was more than just a writer's empathy. Mishima had managed to steal into the martyr's handsome body and become Sebastian himself. And, as Sebastian, he was now dying a violent death, and was finding that the experience gave him unspeakable erotic pleasure.

The experience was understandably brief, yet long enough to transform him. In a sense, his whole life afterward was nothing but a long, sustained effort to reach that orgasmic moment again, and make it permanent. The sickly boy Kimitake would in time become the famous writer Mishima—the genius, the provocateur, the cultural phenomenon. Yet much of what he would do in the coming decades would aim to re-enact Saint Sebastian's "beautiful death," translating it into Japanese, and making it his own *for good*. It was worth spending a lifetime, he must have reckoned, to die such an orgasmic death.

The Fundamental Problem of Philosophy

The *Lotus Sutra* tells the story of the Bodhisattva Medicine King who chooses to extricate himself from the world by way of fire: he sets himself ablaze and disappears in the smoke. The strategy Simone Weil used for her exit also had a clear spiritual dimension. Through her "decreation" she hoped to give back to God what was properly his. In Dostoevsky's *Demons*, Kirillov commits what has been called "philosophical suicide." As he approaches the decisive moment, the joy is intoxicating. By killing himself—the sheer performance of it—he will transcend his humanity and share in the divine nature. That he can turn his back on existence makes him feel like God himself: "I will proclaim self-will. . . . The attribute of my divinity is—Self-will! That is all, by which I can show in the main point my insubordination and my new fearsome freedom."[36] Through such an act, Kirillov can confront the grand failure on its own terms, and defeat it.

In all these cases, suicide is pushed to its breaking point—the point where the human being encounters the radically other. Not that many of us would or could do that, but the self-transcending dimension of the gesture is undeniable. For all the seeming pride or even arrogance involved, there is something radically humble about this philosophical suicide: one literally wants *nothing* from the world. When we want to be left alone, we say, "Let me be!" Someone who performs philosophical suicide takes a more radical step: "Let me *not* be!"

"There is but one truly serious philosophical problem, and that is suicide," writes Camus in *The Myth of Sisyphus*. "Judging whether life is or is not worth living amounts to answering the fundamental question of philosophy."[37] The statement has shocked, as it meant to, more than one generation of readers. Respectable scholars have dismissed it as the exaggeration of a philosophical *enfant terrible*. Yet Camus touched on one of the most agonizing issues a human mind can ponder. And he was not the first to give suicide such prominence. Before him, Schopenhauer regarded the decision to take one's life as a philosophical "experiment" of sorts, a "question which man puts to Nature," trying to "force" an answer from it:

> What change will death produce in man's existence and in his insight into the nature of things? It is a clumsy experiment to make, for it involves the destruction of the very consciousness which puts the question and awaits its answer.[38]

Schopenhauer's philosophical experiment is no ordinary human attempt. It is an experiment in radical humility.

Tough Guy

As he was stepping back into the commander's office, Mishima must have thought, however briefly, of the reason he was there in the first place, and of what had backed him into that corner. He may have recalled how his literary career kicked off, how successful it came to be, and how it then started to shrink on him. *Confessions of a Mask* was published to great acclaim in 1949, when Mishima was only twenty-four. The book established his reputation not only as one of Japan's premier young writers, but as a unique cultural phenomenon. When, soon after the end of the war, Utarō Noda, the editor of the literary magazine *Bungei,* asked him "if he wanted to be an original novelist or a well-known popular writer," Mishima replied, "categorically," that he wanted to be the latter.[39] That should be no surprise. Mishima was a born performer, and what he wanted above all was a stage. The spectacular success of *Confessions* brought him just that.

Along with the chance to practice his histrionics on a large scale, celebrity offered Mishima a massive readership and a good source of income. He had given up his fancy bureaucrat's job at the Ministry of Finance to become a full-time writer, and from now on he would have to live by his wit. In practice this meant that, apart from his serious literature (novels, essays, plays), he would have to generate a regular flow of serialized pulp fiction for low-brow, but high-paying, large-circulation magazines. This twofold literary career involved a rigorous daily schedule, which Mishima, thanks to his self-discipline and strict punctuality, managed rather well.

Punctuality was for Mishima as defining as his compulsion to plan and control everything in his life. He finished work on the last page of his last book on the morning of the last day of his life—just as he had planned. He wrote down the final line, signed the manuscript, and placed it in an envelope to be delivered to his editor. And then he moved on to the next item on the day's schedule—his appointment with death. Rarely has anyone met a deadline more literally.

For a while, this ambitious program worked and paid off. In the decade after the publication of *Confessions*, Mishima would bring forth, in quick succession, book after successful book, some of which, such as *The Sound of Waves* (*Shiosai*) and *The Temple of the Golden Pavilion* (*Kinkaku-ji*), were promptly translated around the world. In Japan they became instant classics and were turned into equally successful films. Mishima was as stylistically versatile as he was intellectually bold, coming up with new storytelling techniques and sources of inspiration with every new project. *The Sound of Waves* is a brilliant adaptation of Longus's *Daphnis and Chloe* (Mishima had recently visited Greece and become infatuated with all things "classical" and "Mediterranean"), while *The Temple of the Golden Pavilion* was based on the burning, in 1950, of a famous Buddhist temple in Kyoto by a young Buddhist acolyte.

Despite Mishima's considerable success, even as his writing was filling up his days and nights, he didn't find his literary career fulfilling. Something important was still missing in his life. He came to think he was living too much inside his mind and neglecting his body, and he wanted to fix that. When it came to performing physical tasks, however, Mishima was rather clumsy. Perhaps not as clumsy as Simone Weil, but sufficiently so to embarrass himself. When he took up swimming, he would sink "to the bottom of the pool like a stone," a friend recalled. When he started boxing, he was so "hopeless," and so "roundly beaten," that his worried friends begged him to give up.[40] For all his clumsiness, however, he would will himself into whatever he was doing with such determination that he would eventually attain a measure of success. That was typical Mishima; with him, everything was a matter of willpower.

That's how in 1955 he came to take up bodybuilding, which he would practice religiously for the rest of his life. The result was a muscular body, which he liked to exhibit whenever he had the chance. Yet since he put all his effort in his upper body, and neglected to work on his legs, the overall picture was unsettling: a heavy mass of muscles perilously supported by a pair of matchsticks. Some people, especially women, thought there was something disgusting about his physical appearance.

Eventually, not even bodybuilding gave Mishima the sense of fulfilment he needed. So in 1960 he chose to act in a yakuza movie. By now people in Japan were accustomed to his eccentricities, but this time he exceeded all expectations. The movie was tasteless and poorly made. Mishima played a small-time gangster—the film's title is *Tough Guy* (*Karakkaze Yarō*)—who, unsurprisingly, is gunned down in the end, and dies a long, tacky death. Much as Mishima enjoyed playing the role, the consensus was that his performance was mediocre. Fellow writers and artists, friends, and admirers felt disappointed. It was as though Mishima deliberately wanted to blemish his reputation—to degrade, if not destroy himself. What has happened to him? they started asking.

It was Mishima's first brush with failure. His biographer Henry Scott-Stokes, who knew him well, found Mishima's decision to appear in *Tough Guy* "indicative of his parlous state of mind at this time" and a "sign that he was losing control," and attributed it to the poor reception of his novel *Kyoko's House* (*Kyōko no Ie*), which he had published in 1959. A polyphonic work recording the interactions of four characters—a quartet of sorts—each representing a facet of Mishima's personality, the novel was particularly dear to the author. He reveals himself in it not just as one *persona*, but as a long, laborious masquerade. One mask is pulled off, only to reveal another, and then another, until you come to wonder, Which one is the real Mishima? One character, a boxer, represents his athletic side; another, an actor by profession, captures his exhibitionism; then a painter stands for Mishima the artist; and finally a businessman—the most intriguing of all, perhaps—is the face of Mishima the nihilist. Ten years after *Confessions*, Mishima decided to reveal himself once again, this time even more thoroughly, if slightly obliquely.

In hindsight, *Kyoko's House* is, as one critic put it, "an unsettling, even a terrifying, book."[41] The novel offered glimpses into the workings of Mishima's mind at the time, and ominous signs of things to come. Much of his evolution (or involution, as some would see it) over the next decade—the right-wing politics, nationalism, nihilism, even his violent death—is "prophesied" in this book. Yet the critics' verdict was almost unanimous: failure.[42] "One has to remember," Scott-Stokes writes, "that he had almost no experience of failure—and, at the same time, he set an enormous premium on success."[43] Mishima had exposed himself, and most people didn't even stop to look. Failure couldn't cut any deeper.

It was perhaps time for him to reconsider what he was doing with his life. As he did so, Mishima went back to one of his favorite obsessions: death. His whole worldview was colored by death—"there is no beautiful thing that does not contain death," he writes.[44]

His artistic vision had death at its core: "Unless I feel death somewhere, I cannot engage in artistic work."[45] But all that had been rather abstract. From now on, Mishima seems to have started to think of death in more practical terms. What would be *the best exit?* Then there was Dazai.

The Experiment

Schopenhauer's philosophical experiment may sound simple, but putting it into practice is a different matter. He himself was against suicide, and so was Camus. Cioran berated the universe all his life, and sang lavish praises to self-annihilation, but he forgot to kill himself when the time came. There is someone, however, who set up the experiment and went through it. He even left us a report. Significantly, this was part of a larger, lifelong experiment with failure.

Jean Améry knew failure like few others. Socially, for most of his life, he was (and considered himself to be) a *raté*. In his mid-fifties, having survived the Holocaust (including torture by the Gestapo), and written thousands of newspaper articles without much of an impact, he jokingly described himself as "a promising beginner." Failure had obviously taken an interest in Améry, and he reciprocated. He developed a fascination with all things failure-related: unhappiness, misfortune, bad luck, suffering, physical degradation, death. He was tenderly attracted to losers, marginals, and other unfortunates, and wrote about them at length. *Charles Bovary, Landarzt* (*Charles Bovary, Country Doctor*), published in 1978, is dedicated to one of the most famous *ratés* of European literature: Emma Bovary's husband. The novel-essay *Lefeu, oder der Abbruch* (*Lefeu, or the Demolition*) recounts the life and misfortunes of a failed Parisian painter—*Unglücksvogel* (unlucky bird), Améry calls him. Appropriately enough, when the book came out, it was poorly received and judged to be a failure.

In 1974, Améry tried to kill himself, but failed. He then wrote *On Suicide: A Discourse on Voluntary Death*. In 1978 he tried again and was successful. Produced between two suicide attempts, *On Suicide* has the brutal matter-of-factness of an insider's report. "Instead of viewing voluntary death from the outside," the author explains in the preface, "I have tried to view it from the interior of those who call themselves suicidal or suicides."[46] These people go against the grain and say no where everybody else says yes. "In the long run, you've got to live," pronounces the popular wisdom. "But *do you have to live?*" retorts Améry. "Do you always have to be there just because you were there once? In the moment before the leap, suicides tear to pieces a prescription of nature and throw it at the feet of the invisible prescriber."[47] While society labels their deaths "unnatural," the suicides insist on their natural right to quit an existence they find oppressive. Theirs is a declaration of independence of the most radical kind. They want to separate themselves not from this or that thing in the world, but from existence in the world as such, which they find to be a failed experience. "What is suicide as a natural death? A resounding no to the crushing, shattering *échec* of existence."[48] Through what they are doing, they throw a formidable challenge in the face of the grand failure itself: "Look, I am doing it myself. What else can you do to me?"

Améry's *On Suicide* is the raw, living testimony of a soul that had "had enough" of this world. Someone who experienced the "disgust with life" and "the inclination toward death" to a sufficient degree to want to embrace the void. We say that we "*flee* into death," Améry writes. "Where do we flee? Nowhere. We begin a trip in order to arrive at a point we can't imagine." And yet the urge is so overpowering that the unimaginable is preferable to a degrading existence. For the suicidal person's life is worse than death: it is a heavy burden, and so is everything that comes with it. "Our own body is a weight, a body that certainly carries us but one that we also have to carry. . . . Work is a burden, leisure is burdensome."[49] Everything weighs heavily on him.

On Suicide is not an autobiographical work in any conventional sense, and yet behind every statement, we sense an intimate, intensely lived experience. At one point, the writing becomes overtly personal. It is when Améry recounts his first, failed suicide attempt:

> Fettered, drilled through with tubes, fitted on both wrists with painful devices for my artificial nourishment. Delivered and surrendered to a couple of nurses who came and went, washed me, cleaned my bed, put thermometers in my mouth, and did everything quite matter-of-factly, as if I were already a thing, *une chose*. The earth did not have me yet: the world had me again and I had a world in which I was to project myself in order that I would once again be all world myself. I was full of a deep bitterness against all those who meant well who had done this disgrace to me.[50]

There must have been a moment, as he tried the second time, when he felt he *was* at his fullest: *"I die, therefore, I am,"* he had written expectantly in *On Suicide*.[51] That concluded the peculiar philosophical experiment at the end of which "the very consciousness which puts the question and awaits its answer" was destroyed.

A Man Born to Die

When Mishima was still an obscure writer, dreaming of making a splash on the postwar Japanese literary scene, the uncrowned king was Osamu Dazai. Dazai became a sensation in July 1947, at thirty-eight, when he published *The Setting Sun* (*Shayo*). The book, with an unsettling novelty and shocking directness, was the crowning achievement of his literary career, a more accomplished work than anyone would have imagined or expected. Just one year later, however, Dazai published *No Longer Human* (*Ningen Shikkaku*), which in every respect was even more shocking. With this book, Dazai had outdone himself, and many people thought that, after the new feat, he could not possibly come up with anything more startling. And yet he did. No sooner did Dazai put the final touches to *No Longer Human* than he drowned himself in a canal in Tokyo, along with one of his mistresses, Tomie Yamazaki. They had moved in together not long before, after he had abandoned both his wife, with whom he had three children, and another mistress, pregnant with his child. Dazai and Tomie had made a suicide pact. While most of us need someone to live with, Tomie wanted a partner to die with, and Dazai struck her as the ideal candidate.

For Osamu Dazai was a man born to die if there ever was one. It was as though extricating himself from the entanglement of existence was his life's mission. And he recorded everything as he went. Dazai's writing is the shattering testimony of someone fated to observe life from its outer edges, one foot always hanging perilously over the abyss. With an inhuman honesty and maddening precision, he wrote down everything he saw and felt from that vantage point. His writing is raw, visceral, almost physiological. He never speaks from imagination or hearsay, but from the position of someone who all his life felt he had come into existence by mistake, and was trying to find his way back.

One of the phrases most frequently used in Japan is *sumimasen*. It can mean different things, depending on the context, but typically conveys a polite apology, and involves a good measure of humility. You say *sumimasen* when you think you *may* be in someone's way or *may* have caused someone an inconvenience, however small. You say it even if none of that happened, to apologize preemptively. In one of his most intense pieces, "Standard-Bearer for the Twentieth Century," Dazai uses the form *umarete sumimasen*— "forgive me for having been born."[52] He didn't think he was in the way of someone in particular: he was in *everyone's* way. No matter what he did, even if he didn't do anything, Dazai believed he was an imposition—his sheer existence an inconvenience. All he wanted was to make his exit as quietly as possible. It would take him a long time, and considerable effort, to do that.

Fittingly, Dazai's misfortunes started with a suicide—not his own, but that of his literary idol, Ryūnosuke Akutagawa, in 1927. For some reason, that suicide triggered in the teenage Dazai a propensity toward a life of dissipation and dissolution, self-debasement and self-destruction, which would mark out his biography from then on. He first attempted to kill himself two years later, in 1929, but failed: the sleeping pills were not strong enough. The next year he went to Tokyo Imperial University to study French literature. Why French literature? Why not! He didn't know a word of French at the time, nor did he plan to learn the language. No sooner did he start his undergraduate studies than he had to quit them. Due to his involvement with a geisha from back home, his family had disinherited him. That pushed him off his precarious balance, and he attempted suicide for the second time.

This time, Dazai had company: a nineteen-year-old bar hostess who had fallen in love with him as he was making the tour of the bars in Ginza, Tokyo's fashionable shopping street. He would write later, "I persuaded the woman to leap into the sea with me at Kamakura. When you're defeated, I thought, it's time to die."[53] She died, but he didn't. He failed again, and lived not only to tell the tale, but also to face prosecution (as an accomplice to the young woman's suicide). Meanwhile, his family, taken aback by the new suicide attempt, allowed him to marry the geisha, and reinstated his allowance on condition that he attend classes and stay clear of politics (he was in the habit of donating to illegal communist groups).

Dazai found politics easy enough to quit, but attending classes was harder. To keep the allowance, he lied to his family, assuring everybody that he was on track to graduate, and felt appropriately guilty. To "deceive someone who trusts you," he would write, "is to enter a hell that can take you to the brink of madness."[54] Guilt didn't prevent Dazai from writing, though. If anything, it made him more creative. He kept developing his style—the first-person, self-flagellating autobiographical prose for which he would become famous.

As guilt doesn't like to travel alone, the thought of death never quite left Dazai. In the fall of his twenty-fourth year, he entertained it particularly intensely. "I hadn't a single thing to live for," he would recall. "I resolved that I, as one of the fools, one of the doomed, would faithfully play out the role in which fate had cast me, the sad, servile role of one who must inevitably lose."[55] In 1935, he applied for a journalist's job with a newspaper in Tokyo, but was rejected for lack of a degree. High time for another suicide attempt. "In mid-March, I went to Kamakura alone," he writes. "I planned to hang myself in the mountains there."[56] Kamakura, a seaside town just south of Tokyo, was the place where, some five years before, Dazai had tried to drown himself with the bar hostess. He had been improving his skills with every new attempt, but success was slow in coming:

> Being able to swim, it wasn't easy for me to drown myself, so I chose hanging, which I'd heard was infallible. Humiliatingly enough, however, I botched it. I revived and found myself breathing. Perhaps my neck was thicker than most. . . . I'd tried to prescribe my own fate and failed.[57]

Things would not get any better from here. While in the hospital for an unrelated health issue, Dazai was given a heroin-based painkiller, and he developed a serious drug addiction. First, he used the drug to get rid of the pain, then, gradually, "to blot out my shame and ease my distress." Predictably, addiction made his life even more miserable, and his economic situation ever more desperate, turning him into a near beggar:

> I presented the figure of a ragged and half-mad derelict. . . .
> I was the basest, most reptilian young man in Japan. My

reason for going to Tokyo was always to borrow ten or twenty
yen. I once wept at a meeting with a magazine editor. I had
editors shout me down.[58]

For all his troubled state of mind, Dazai recorded everything, his
extreme lucidity making his predicament all the more devastating.
He never stopped taking note of the outside world and of how
people reacted to his presence. When he hit rock bottom, he recorded the encounter in all its brutality: "I was already twenty-nine,
and I had nothing. One *dotera* to wear."[59] Eventually, Dazai had to
be interned in a mental institution, where he underwent the cruelest of treatments: he was locked up in a room and left to his own
devices. It was one of the most traumatic events in his trauma-filled
life, but the cold turkey cure worked: the addiction was gone.

Once released, Dazai discovered that, in his absence, his wife
had cheated on him with one of his friends. That put him in the
mood for yet another suicide attempt, in March 1937. He and his
unfaithful wife were to "die together," he recalls. "Surely even God
would forgive us. In a spirit of camaraderie, like brother and sister,
we set out on a journey. Minakami Hot Springs. That night, amid
the mountains there, we attempted suicide."[60] Another failed attempt, defective sleeping pills this time. Having survived, the
couple parted ways, never to see each other again.

The next several years, as Japan was going through a series of
calamities—militarism, war, extensive destruction, and finally utter
defeat—were not that bad for Dazai. For once, disasters were
happening not to him directly, but to the world around him. He
remarried and, for a while, had the semblance of a normal life.
He kept writing and could publish at a time when most Japanese writers could not.

When the war ended, the ruined country recognized itself in
Dazai, who for most of his life had been a ruin himself. The vast
landscapes of devastation, the endless anxiety, the soul-eating hu-

miliation, which Dazai had been depicting in his work, were now the staples of so many Japanese. The new Japan, having barely survived a collective suicide attempt, found its prophet. And just as the country was starting to listen to him properly, the prophet embarked on another suicide attempt. This time he succeeded.

Osamu Dazai and Tomie Yamazaki drowned themselves in the Tamagawa Canal on June 13, 1948. It was the rainy season in Tokyo, and the two corpses were fished out only days later, on June 19. It would have been his thirty-ninth birthday. It looked as though death had finally brought a sense of order to Dazai's anarchic life.

How to Die a "Good Death"

The philosophers' interest in death as a purely theoretical issue (death as cessation of one's being, as an act of radical self-transcendence, or as an experiment) has been overshadowed by their concern with death as a rather practical matter: how to live our lives without letting fear of death ruin them, how to cope with our precariousness and finitude, how to die a "good death."

In the *Phaedo*, Plato has Socrates say that philosophy is nothing but "rehearsal" or "preparation for death" (*meletē thanatou*). To philosophize is to rehearse your exit; the more you contemplate, the better you become at coming to terms with your mortality. It is worth considering Socrates's circumstances at the time he said this: he was in his prison cell, surrounded by friends and disciples, just hours shy of his execution. He may have intended the definition as a *bon mot* more than anything else. The punchline was somewhat inevitable: the master of the examined life had ended up where he was now *because* of his philosophy. The strong connection between philosophizing and dying was there, in that narrow prison cell, for all to see. For good measure, later in the dialogue, Socrates offers a live demonstration of how his definition works in practice: he walks to his death as naturally as others would go out for a stroll—with no fear, no hesitation, no second thoughts. If philosophy is "preparation for death," judging by the way he died, Socrates was indeed a great philosopher.

Ever since Socrates's famous last drink, his ending has never ceased to be admired as a model of the consistency that a philosopher should achieve between his ideas, his life, and his death. From Seneca to Boethius to Montaigne to Simone Weil, Western thought has acquired a distinctly *therapeutic* function (in the East it had it for a long time): any philosophizing worth its salt, this line goes, should be able not only to help us make sense of the world, but to teach us how to live better lives, and how to face death more serenely. In so doing, philosophy has sometimes turned into a series of "spiritual exercises," to use Pierre Hadot's term.

If we look for some groundbreaking theoretical propositions in Stoicism, for instance, we will be disappointed. As therapy, however, Stoicism is unmatched. The Stoics explicitly referred to philosophy as an "exercise" (*askēsis*) to be practiced daily and embodied in one's life, and not a set of theoretical statements to adhere to on a strictly intellectual plane. For the Stoics, observes Hadot, "philosophy did not consist in teaching an abstract theory," but rather in "the art of living." Philosophy "causes us to *be* more fully, and makes us better." It is above all about causing a transformation in the one who practices it. Properly practiced, Hadot suggests, philosophy leads to nothing less than

> a conversion which turns our entire life upside down, changing the life of the person who goes through it. It raises the individual from an inauthentic condition of life, darkened by unconsciousness and harassed by worry, to an authentic state of life, in which he attains self-consciousness, an exact vision of the world, inner peace, and freedom.[61]

An "authentic state of life" is one that has the recognition of our mortal condition at its core. The "art of living" involves an art of dying, too. To live well is to know how to accept our finitude, how to conquer our fear of death, and, in general, given our fundamental next-to-nothingness, how to dwell on the edge of the abyss without losing our bearings. In this tradition, to philosophize is to act upon the frightened flesh, to instill firmness in a wavering soul, to kill off our fear of annihilation. To have mastery over our life is above all to be master over our death: "We are in no one's power when death is in our power," writes one of the premier therapist philosophers, the Stoic Seneca.[62]

The case of Lucius Annaeus Seneca deserves closer attention, for rarely has a philosopher given himself more fully to the pondering of death. A sickly constitution, and some unpleasant episodes in his eventful life, helped Seneca become a "death-driven philosopher," as Emily Wilson dubs him.[63] From an early age, Seneca suffered from intense asthma attacks—"little deaths," he called them. As he grew older, his respiratory troubles grew worse. To cure what may have been a form of tuberculosis, he spent some ten years in Alexandria. The prolonged Egyptian vacation may have helped, but not much. Seneca would go on living, but with the shadow of death always near. Later in life, in a letter to his friend Lucilius, Seneca would describe in detail what happened to him, and what went on in his mind, during those states of near-asphyxiation, which the Roman doctors called *meditatio mortis*, "rehearsal for death."

With such a unique medical record, Seneca found himself at the center of philosophy as therapy, if in a brutally naturalistic manner. While Plato, in the *Phaedo*, recommended "preparation for death" as a philosophical aspiration, Seneca had to go through his *meditatio mortis*, over and over again, because of his poor health. When he said, in another letter, "we die every day" (*cotidie morimur*), he was not advancing some wild philosophical notion, but uttering an intimate truth: something he felt painfully, with every new attempt to breathe. For him, to live was to snatch as many moments of life as possible from the claws of death. Given his health troubles, it is almost ironic that Seneca lived into his sixties—a long life by ancient standards—and that when he died, it wasn't his poor health that did him in.

Seneca dedicated some of his works exclusively to death (*Ad Marciam* and *De Consolatione,* for instance), but the topic also shows up in the most unexpected places. He could be writing on weather, politics, history, or the latest fashion in Rome, and death could stick its head out—just like that. The *Moral Letters to Lucilius* (*Epistulae Morales ad Lucilium*) are exemplary in this regard. Although the letters are written in the form of private communications addressed to a close friend, they are left conspicuously open—not just courting the gaze of others, but actively encouraging it.

Like the rest of Seneca's work, his "moral letters" are a sophisticated exercise in self-branding: they are meant to fashion a certain image (*imago*) of the sage, and to surreptitiously project it upon the public mind. The reader finds out what his daily life was like to the last detail: he shares his routines and travels, his habits, his likes and dislikes, and a thousand other trifles dropped as if in passing. Yet everything, even the most insignificant item, is carefully filtered and arranged to induce a certain public perception. Seneca wanted above all to be seen as a total, head-in-the-clouds philosopher, uninterested in and unaffected by the ways of the world, no matter how worldly his daily life happened to be. If he had social success and money and power, those were just accidents. Had he had none of these, he would have been exactly the same person— or so he wanted us to believe. Among the philosopher's many creations (and he was a prolific author), this *imago*—Seneca as a literary character in his own work—is one of his finest and most accomplished.[64]

Concern with mortality (thinking about death, overcoming fear of it, achieving mastery over it) played an important role in Seneca's self-fashioning project; the practice of philosophy as "preparation for death" was essential to his self-representation. Death shows up early in the *Letters*. In the very first epistle, Seneca articulates an idea around which much of his philosophizing revolves: death is not something that will happen at the end of our life; we start dying as soon as we are born. "We are wrong to think that death lies ahead," he writes. "Much of it has passed us by already, for all our past life is in the grip of death."[65] By the time we die, we've died so much already that it doesn't make much of a difference. Elsewhere, in letter 24, he draws an explicit connection between our being in the world and the passage of time:

> We die every day, for every day some part of life is taken from us. Even when we are still growing, our life is shrinking. We lost our infancy, then childhood, then youth. All our time was lost in the moment of passage, right up to yesterday, and even today is divided with death as it goes by.[66]

Centuries later, Heidegger would do spectacular things with this insight. He loved to quote a dark medieval adage: "As soon as a man comes to life, he is at once old enough to die."[67] Taking it as a springboard for his own thinking, Heidegger pushed the notion to its breaking point, weaving a theory of human existence as fundamentally "Being-toward-death" (*Sein-zum-Tode*). But Seneca wasn't interested in theories. In line with the tradition of philosophy as *therapeia,* his aim was to teach himself and others how to live a good life—one unspoiled by the fear of death. For "the worst thing about death is what precedes it—the fear."[68] What he meant to do was to persuade people to see their mortality in a new light—and change their life as a result. He urged them to get used to being no more—and to overcome their instinctive tendency to stick tenaciously to life.

"Mr. Dazai, I Dislike Your Literature"

As Mishima was stepping back into the commander's office, he may also have recalled, however fleetingly, the great lengths to which he had gone—and the painful efforts he had made—to distance himself from Dazai.[69] When he started plotting his literary career, Dazai was casting a long shadow in Japan, and Mishima wasn't one to live in someone else's shadow. They met only once. Mustering all the courage he could, the only thing Mishima said to the famous writer was, "Mr. Dazai, I dislike your literature."[70] Dazai, drunk as a skunk, barely took notice.

Mishima's remark was disingenuous. His feelings for Dazai were more complicated. For starters, he could not comprehend the extent to which Dazai neglected to take care of himself. Obsessed with his own physical weakness in childhood, Mishima came to regard the body as the true site of the self: you are what you look like. If only Dazai had been in better physical shape, he thought, his mind and soul would have worked differently. In 1955, he writes of Dazai in his diary, "The defects in his character, a goodly half of them, could have been cured by cold-water massage, mechanical workouts, and a regularized life." This implicit rebuke gradually evolved into disgust: "I know of no other writer who from my very first contact with him filled me with so violent a physiological revulsion." Mishima was repelled by Dazai's "shameless self-caricature" and "glorification of despair."[71]

And yet he had to admit that this revulsion was "due to my immediate sense that Dazai was a writer at pains to expose precisely that which I most wanted to conceal in myself."[72] What Mishima found in Dazai was the same irrepressible attraction to the abyss that he had detected in himself from an early age. While to him the abyss promised the ultimate ecstasy, Dazai, more humbly, must have seen in it a promise of rest. Mishima recognized in Dazai a fellow traveler—and was embarrassed. You just don't show up at such an important meeting on your knees, in rags and in such poor shape.[73] Always his grandmother's dutiful servant, Mishima believed that there had to be ceremony in everything, including death. Especially death.

The Philosopher as Charmer

A philosophy like Seneca's is performative to the highest degree: it is primarily meant to *do*, rather than to state, describe, or explain. Its target is not just the readers' minds, but their entire being: it *acts* upon their emotions, imagination, and intimate beliefs, even upon their bodies. A philosophical work of this kind, observes Hadot, is written "not so much to inform the reader of a doctrinal content but to form him, to make him traverse a certain itinerary in the course of which he will make spiritual progress."[74] For this to happen, philosophy needs rhetoric—in the broadest sense of the word. That Seneca was such a gifted writer certainly helped. There is no knowing how many of his contemporaries he persuaded to be less fearful of dying; what we do know is that Seneca's work has been persuasive enough to last twenty centuries.

The *Moral Letters* show us why. No sooner do you start reading them than your attention is arrested. The prose is consistently good and engaging, limpid and wit-driven, but Seneca is too intelligent a writer to rely on glib fireworks. "Despite his clarity," remarks Paul Veyne, Seneca "still must be taken seriously as a philosopher."[75] There is depth and substance and real thinking beneath the seductive style. The chief reason Seneca writes so captivatingly, you realize, is that, more than passing some intellectual content on to you, he is acting upon you. His text is actively enchanting and mesmerizing you so that you drop your guard and he can take you captive. If philosophy is to have an effect on us, we need to spend some time in its custody.

What Seneca seeks to achieve through such a technique is to teach us to "die well." Should we learn this, paradoxical as it may sound, we would be living better lives: "Whether one dies sooner or later is not the issue; the issue is whether one dies well or badly. And dying well means that one escapes the risk of living badly."[76]

A good life is not a life "lived to the fullest," or one spent in blissful ignorance of all things unpleasant or depressing, as pop culture wants us to think. We live a genuinely good life when we place our fragility and mortality firmly at its core, when we acknowledge and accept our limits, and remain fully aware that we spend all our existence, precariously, on the edge of the abyss. "There's no way to know the point where death lies waiting for you, so you must wait for death at every point," Seneca writes in letter 26.[77] The best way to deal with the grand failure is not to pretend it does not exist, but to embrace it. Nothing will "do as much to help you toward self-control in all things," he writes in letter 114, "as the reflection that life is short, and the little we have of it is uncertain. In every act, keep your eyes on death."[78] And the more you look at it, the less strange it becomes. Allow death into your routines, give it a smile from time to time, and you will feel increasingly at ease around it. Show it goodwill, for "dying well is dying willingly."[79] A death befriended is a death tamed, one in whose hands you can place yourself in confidence. And that will have been a life well lived.

In case this argument is not persuasive, Seneca tries another. If we adopt the "view from above" and look at our existential predicament from a certain distance, we can understand it much better. Seneca's health troubles came in handy here. He recalls one of his near-asphyxiation experiences. "Even as I was suffocating," he reports in letter 54, "I did not fail to find peace in cheerful and brave reflections." Realizing that he is being tested by death, the philosopher—pushed dangerously close to the edges of existence—has the revelation that he has known this state already. When exactly?

> Before I was born. Death is just nonexistence. I know already what that is like: what will exist after me is the same as existed before me. If there is any torment in this thing, then there must have been torment also before we saw the light of day. Yet we did not feel any discomfort at that time.[80]

Like many things in life, death is a matter of perspective. Change your angle and frame of reference, and you will not only see things differently; sometimes you will discover completely different things.

When one thinks of death as intensely as Seneca did, sooner or later one arrives at the notion that to be a master of your life is to master your death, and not just to accept it willingly, but, if necessary, even to choose and administer it. "The great man is not the one who merely commands his own death but the one who actually finds a death for himself," he writes, in his 70th letter.[81]

What Seneca himself did when he reached the hour of his own death is another matter. The circumstances and manner of his end were not his choice. This points to one of the more dramatic aspects of Seneca's biography—or of anyone's, for that matter: regardless of how hard we try to master our lives, there will always be something beyond our control. And we have to make provisions for that.

Mishima's Samuraization Project

Mishima was not a humble man, which he was well aware of. At the same time, he knew that humility was central to any spiritual tradition, including the Japanese one, with its peculiar combination of Buddhism, Shinto, and *Bushidō*, to which he was so much attracted. To be able to partake in this spirituality Mishima had to humble himself, and he believed that the experience of death would offer him just that. He had always found death attractive, and now he had a chance to combine utility and pleasure. He must have thought that this, too, was a matter of willpower, which was "the Mishima method" he applied to everything in life. He wanted to *will himself into humility,* an act which in itself betrays significant pride, and he thought he could get away with that.

Mishima dismissed Dazai's death as a "man-of-letters' suicide," which, in his parlance, was meant to be offensive. "There are two kinds of suicide," he said in an interview. "One is suicide from weakness and defeat. One is suicide from strength and courage. I despise the former and praise the latter."[82] He regarded Dazai's ending as representative of a failed death. While celebrating his thirtieth birthday, on January 14, 1955, Mishima told a couple of friends that he was considering taking his own life, but suicide after thirty would be "as unseemly as Dazai's."[83] At such an age, he informed his shocked guests, he was already too old to die a "beautiful death." Or was he?

It was Mishima's conviction that to die beautifully was to die young and healthy, the body in its prime, just like Saint Sebastian's. "Beautiful people ought to die young," he decreed.[84] At some point he found—or made up—a loophole in his own rule: you can be older and still die beautifully if you die a samurai's death. Such an end, the exact opposite of a man-of-letters' death, was a redeeming one, regardless of the person's actual age. Once this distinction had been made, Mishima set out to pursue a samurai's death, saying, "I do not recognize anything other than a samurai's killing himself with his own sword."[85]

There was a small inconvenience: to die a samurai's death one had to be a samurai, which Mishima was not.[86] It didn't help matters that the samurai class had been abolished in Japan almost a century before. But he was not to be dissuaded by technicalities. He invented a samurai legend for himself (the early years he spent with his grandmother must have helped), took up kendo, instilled more traditional Japanese ceremony into his life, and sought to live the way he thought the samurais of old did.

A book Mishima had been reading regularly since he was a teenager was to play a crucial role in his samuraization project: Yamamoto Tsunetomo's *Hagakure,* an eighteenth-century collection of commentaries on samurai life covering everything from spiritual guidance and the art of war to simple practicalities.[87] It is not difficult to see why *Hagakure* fascinated Mishima. For someone who had placed violent death at the core of his life project, the book is nothing short of a recipe for good living. One can only imagine the joy Mishima must have experienced when he came across a passage like this:

The Way of the Warrior (*bushido*) is to be found in dying. If one is faced with two options of life or death, simply settle for death. It is not an especially difficult choice; just go forth and meet it confidently. . . . Rehearse your death every morning and night. Only when you constantly live as though already a corpse (*jōjū shinimi*) will you be able to find freedom in the martial way, and fulfill your duties without fault throughout your life.[88]

Taking such a path would allow Mishima to die a beautiful death even though he was past cherry blossom age. He was pleased to discover that there had been a precedent: Saigō Takamori, who had played a decisive role in overthrowing the Shogunate in 1868, only to rebel, less than a decade later, against the very government he used to serve. Given the superiority of government forces, Takamori's rebellion was doomed to fail—his defeat was a mathematical certainty—and yet he fought valiantly to the bitter end. His death was worthy precisely because Takamori didn't do anything to prevent it. He was thus a prime example of the Japanese tradition of noble failures. For all his eventual defeat, Takamori is revered in Japan as one of the country's greatest samurais—some call him "the last samurai." As you walk into Tokyo's Ueno Park today, you can't miss his slightly incongruous appearance. The dog at his feet, part of the statue, surreptitiously calls to mind those samurais dying a "dog's death" mentioned in *Hagakure*. If Takamori "died at age fifty as a hero," Mishima observed with relief, there was still hope for him. If he could only pull off something similarly daring, he too "would be able to do it before reaching the final age to be a hero."[89]

Through imagination, determination, and sheer willpower, Mishima managed to reinvent himself as a samurai at a time when samurais were only a remote memory. All he needed now was to invent a cause to die for. *Invent* a cause? You don't know Mishima.

The Two Senecas

The image of himself that Seneca crafted throughout his written work, and which he assiduously sought to project upon the public mind, lies in dramatic contrast with the picture that we get from his contemporaries and historians. On the one hand, there is the humble lover of wisdom from Cordoba; the perpetual outsider; the man who praises poverty and lives the simple life; the ascetic figure who somehow manages to feed on air; the accidental courtier who never feels at ease at the court, preferring instead the peace and quiet of his library; the sick and otherworldly Seneca. On the other hand, we find the mercurial Seneca, the versatile intellectual ready to sell his pen to the highest bidder; the consummate insider and shameless careerist; the brownnose and the tyrant-teacher (*tyrannodidaskalos*, in Cassius Dio's stinging formulation); the schemer and plotter; the money lender who was "filthy rich"— *Seneca Praedives*, as Martial called him. Seneca's is a Jekyll and Hyde story, the likes of which Western philosophy has hardly seen before or since. Many philosophers, seemingly taking an oath of nonconformism, end up with startling biographies, yet few are more stunning than Seneca's.

Given his place at the Roman court, Seneca was often the target of gossip and slander. That's all understandable; envy has always been in abundant supply. Yet the facts are damning. For almost a decade (from AD 54 to 62), Seneca served as Nero's private tutor, speechwriter, and advisor. His position was that of *amicus principis* (friend of the princeps). Especially during the first part of Nero's rule, his influence was significant. It was Seneca who wrote the accession speech Nero gave before the Roman Senate, as well as the emperor's eulogy for Claudius, presented at the latter's funeral. He also devised the letters justifying Nero's political murders before the Senate. As Nero became increasingly more unhinged, Seneca became more entangled in his master's political mess. Even if he was not directly involved in the execution of Nero's worst deeds, Seneca must have been aware of their planning. And he didn't do much to stop them. Since one of his functions at Nero's court was to manage public relations, Seneca did everything he could to justify them after the fact—to the Senate, to the Romans, to posterity.

And he was embarrassingly good at that. The Stoic philosopher made a fabulous spin doctor. After Nero killed his stepbrother Britannicus, for example, Seneca produced this gem, in *De Clementia*:

> You, Caesar, have given us the gift of a state unstained by blood. This proud boast of yours, that you have spilt not a drop of human blood in the whole world, is all the more remarkable and amazing, because nobody ever had the sword entrusted to him at an earlier age.[90]

The statement about Nero not spilling "a drop of human blood" is literally—but only literally—true: Britannicus was killed by poison. Seneca's pen could work wonders of make-believe, whether he was writing "moral letters" to friends or whitewashing Nero's bloody deeds. Unhappy is the tyrant who doesn't have a skilled philosopher in his service!

Cutting the Apple

Sun and Steel (*Taiyō to Tetsu*), which Mishima published in 1968, is an unusual writing. For one thing, it is a book in which Mishima takes on book-writing itself—it can be read as his anti-literary manifesto. More importantly, it explains not only what had happened to its author over the previous several years, but what he was about to do next. His own bloody ending is foretold—and you don't even have to read between the lines. It was as though, after the failure of *Kyoko's House,* he wanted to give his readers one last chance.

Central to *Sun and Steel* is Mishima's notion that "he who dabbles in words can create tragedy, but cannot participate in it."[91]

Writing was no longer enough for him now: he craved action in the real world, which would take his histrionism to a new realm altogether. Masterful as his use of the Japanese language was, Mishima found it wanting. A higher mastery would be that of the "language of the body." As with any language, achieving such proficiency takes practice, time, and work—workouts, more exactly. It takes, in other words, "sun and steel": sunbathing and weightlifting. Just as Mishima's ambition as a writer was to become one of the greatest stylists of the Japanese language, now he wanted nothing less than superlative performance as a master of the "language of the flesh."

Using a terminology borrowed from European aesthetics, Mishima distinguishes two chief impulses in his life. There is, first, an impulse toward "classical" perfection. He observes how his muscles "have gradually become something akin to classical Greek." Mishima had lately taken lessons in classical Greek, and he would have known that the ancient Greeks used the word *meletē* to describe the process whereby—through constant effort and concentration— we become increasingly better at a given task, be it playing a musical instrument, practicing a sport, or even dying (*meletē thanatou*), according to Plato. This "classical" moment is all about *paideia* and enlightenment—about constructive outcomes. "Bulging muscles, a taut stomach, and a tough skin," he thought, would correspond to an "intrepid fighting spirit, the power of dispassionate intellectual judgement, and a robust disposition."[92]

The second impulse is "romantic" and involves an opposite spirit: "The romantic impulse that had formed an undercurrent in me from boyhood on, and that made sense only as the *destruction* of classical perfection, lay waiting inside me." This destructive drive would eventually come to define Mishima: "Like a theme in an operatic overture that is later destined to occur throughout the whole work," the romantic impulse "laid down a definitive pattern for me before I had achieved anything in practice." Whatever was "classical" and "luminous" in Mishima will now have to submit to the stronger, darker drive. Whereas the "classical" impulse demanded of him to build a beautiful body, the "romantic" one issued the opposite commandment: "You shall sacrifice all that beauty to me!" Mishima explains:

> I cherished a romantic impulse towards death, yet at the same time I required a strictly classical body as its vehicle; a peculiar sense of destiny made me believe that the reason why my romantic impulse towards death remained unfulfilled in reality was the immensely simple fact that I lacked the necessary physical qualifications. A powerful, tragic frame and sculpturesque muscle were indispensable in a romantically noble death.[93]

Mishima had been attracted to the abyss for a long time now, but it was a largely irrational impulse. In *Sun and Steel*, he rationalizes his death drive, gives it philosophical respectability, and explains why he finds it worth pursuing. It is not supreme jouissance that he is after, he tells us now, but something else: *ultimate knowledge and understanding*. Here Mishima the unhumble may be at his closest to humility. Let's imagine, he writes, a beautiful, "healthy apple":

> The inside of the apple is naturally quite invisible. Thus at the heart of the apple, shut up within the flesh of the fruit, the core lurks in its wan darkness, tremblingly anxious to find some way to reassure itself that it is a perfect apple. The apple certainly exists, but to the core this existence as yet seems inadequate. . . . For the core the only sure mode of existence is to exist and to see at the same time.[94]

As long as something remains unseen, it doesn't truly exist; for that to happen, it needs the encounter with a penetrating gaze. Only such penetration would bring it into existence, even though this means destroying it at the same time. There is only one means of "solving this contradiction": the knife. A knife is to be plunged "deep into the apple so that it is split open and the core is exposed to the light." At that point, "the existence of the cut apple falls into fragments; the core of the apple sacrifices existence for the sake of seeing."[95]

Once he is done comparing apples and samurais, Mishima moves on to discuss his own death. Just like the apple in his parable, he too needs a brutal act of penetration to give him access to the ultimate significance of what he is. Without that he would never become an authentic being:

> Admittedly, I could see my muscles in the mirror. Yet seeing alone was not enough to bring me into contact with the basic roots of my sense of existence, and an immeasurable distance remained between me and the euphoric sense of pure being. Unless I rapidly closed that distance, there was little hope of bringing that sense of existence to life again.[96]

What Mishima is doing here is not just eloquent—it's also telling. It is eloquent because these are aesthetically superior passages in a book of otherwise uneven literary quality (Marguerite Yourcenar calls it "almost delirious"). And it is telling because, for all its fancy philosophical dress, Mishima's insight is about the same link between Eros and Thanatos that he discovered when he had his first, Saint-Sebastian-induced ejaculation. The imagery and symbolism are profoundly sexual: knife, penetration, "cutting into the flesh of the apple—or rather, the body." To penetrate and be penetrated at once, that is the ultimate erotic experience. For good measure, Mishima adds into the mixture the shattering of the senses and blood, which has always been erotically charged for him. "Blood flows, existence is destroyed, and the shattered senses give existence . . . its first endorsement, closing the logical gap between seeing and existing. . . . And this is death."[97]

"There has never been a death more foretold," you tell yourself as you finish reading *Sun and Steel*. And if that was not enough,

Mishima even makes a teasing reference to "some incident" whereby a number of things would conspire to bring his life to a successful completion: "I could not help feeling that if there were some incident in which violent death pangs and well-developed muscles were skillfully combined, it could only occur in response to the aesthetic demands of destiny."[98]

The "incident" will take place in due course because, as Yourcenar observed, Mishima was an excellent plotter, not only of his stories, but also of his own life—"I want to make a poem of my life," he wrote once.[99] It will be known in Japan as *Mishima jiken*—the "Mishima incident." As it happened, Mishima plotted the "incident" just as he was working on the plot of his most ambitious literary project, the tetralogy *The Sea of Fertility*—a "world-explaining novel," he called it. The whole point of Mishima's larger, existential plot was to finish the tetralogy and his life at the same time. "I think I have said everything I can," he told Donald Ritchie just as he was about to finish the last novel in the tetralogy.[100] Once the writing was done, the living was over as well.

The Filthy-Rich Moral Philosopher

Seneca's job came with its rewards. When Britannicus was killed, Nero seized his estate and distributed it generously among friends and associates. Seneca was one of the beneficiaries. The philosopher had come from an affluent family, but it was his work for Nero that made him super-rich. The emperor gifted him with land, gardens, vines, villas, estates. The poverty-praising philosopher came to own so much land, in so many places, that he could hardly keep track of it. He had estates, in different parts of the empire, that he had never seen. "By today's standards," concludes Emily Wilson, he was "at least a multimillionaire."[101] Seneca, observes another biographer, had "one of the greatest fortunes of his age, seventy-five million denarii . . . , a sum equivalent to one-tenth, or even one-fifth, of the annual revenue of the Roman state."[102]

So much money comes with its own difficulties: what is one to do with it? To solve the problem, Seneca decided to give it to others—with interest. That's how he went into moneylending. Apparently, he was quite good at it. Contemporary sources describe him as a smart, even aggressive operator. Cassius Dio goes so far as to point to Seneca's reckless money lending as one of the causes of the Boudica uprising in Britannia: when Seneca called in his loans to British tribal leaders, abruptly and on unreasonable terms, many in Britannia went bankrupt. In response, this line goes, the province rebelled against Rome.

Serious inconsistencies between what one professes and how one acts would be damning for any moral philosopher, but for someone who professed that "philosophy teaches us how to act, not how to talk," and for whom an idea was nothing unless it was embodied, such shortcomings should be catastrophic. Why should anyone listen to Seneca or follow his teachings if he was the first to ignore them? How could he sermonize, so grandly, *Concordet sermo cum vita* ("Let our speech be in harmony with our life!") only to disregard it, so blatantly, in his own life? Is Seneca's whole philosophical program some elaborate joke on his readers and on posterity? Such questions troubled his admirers then as they do now. That we still speak of Seneca today, more than two thousand years after his death, goes to show that they haven't been properly answered—or, indeed, properly asked.

Meanwhile, the philosopher's life followed its course—if not for very long. Sooner or later, Seneca was bound to enter on a collision course with Nero, and he knew that only too well. Twice he asked the emperor to allow him to retire, and he was turned down twice. Eventually, he tried to take a de facto retirement, leading an increasingly withdrawn life and spending as much time away from the court as he could. But his absence became conspicuous; the famous spin doctor's silence invited gossip. When, in AD 65, a plot to kill Nero was exposed, Seneca's name was mentioned. It's unlikely that he had much to do with the plot, but Nero was only too happy to disregard that.

There Was Method to His Madness

Once Mishima had made up his mind and decided that the time had come for the knife to cut into the apple, "some incident" was relatively easy to concoct. As his biographers have observed, before the mid-1960s Mishima had been distinctly apolitical. Now, as he was actively plotting the "incident," he thought he needed a political ingredient to pepper it with. Politically, he placed himself on the far right, but it was as though he had flipped a coin; he could almost as easily have ended up a communist martyr.[103] In a debate with Waseda University students, in October 1968, Mishima offered the rationale for his choice of such a position. He spoke to the students of his frustration with the writerly profession, which he now tended to dismiss as disembodied and unmanly, as well as of a new vision of himself. To assert his newfound spirit, he felt he had to act upon the world somehow, and for that an opponent was needed. "Without an opponent, there's no point to action." And here things become interesting:

> I was very much in need of an opponent and I settled on communism. It is not as if Communists had attacked my children or set my house on fire. I have very little reason really. I simply chose communism as an opponent, because I needed an opponent to provoke me to action.[104]

So much for strongly held and well-defined political views. Mishima certainly entertained sincere beliefs regarding the emperor, the samurai spirit, and the nobility of self-sacrifice, but they had almost nothing to do with his politics, and everything to do with his aesthetics and philosophy of culture.[105]

As it happened, it was in defense of the emperor that Mishima established the Shield Society (Tatenokai) in October 1968. This was his private militia ("Captain Mishima's toy army," the Japanese media dubbed it), made up of fewer than one hundred students. Toy army though it may have been, the Tatenokai needed funding, which Mishima did out of his own pocket—a rather expensive hobby. He commissioned fancy uniforms for his toy soldiers, and arranged their training with the Jieitai. As with everything Mishima, there was much ceremony and ritual involved in the Tatenokai: pompous oath taking, flashy parades, and not a little showing off. The launch ceremony was held on the roof of the National Theater (an appropriate location, some promptly observed), just across from the Imperial Palace. The *Sankei* reporter described the soldiers' uniforms as being in a "loud style that at first glance made you think of the doormen of a first-class hotel."[106] Mishima cut a strange figure. Some of his friends felt "embarrassed" for him. Not that he cared.

The Tatenokai was to play a key role in Mishima's "incident." The society's stated purpose was left conveniently vague: to "shield" the emperor from the "threat of communism," which could mean anything and nothing. Mishima toyed with several possible assignments for the soldiers in his toy army, one more fantastic than the next: engaging in bloody skirmishes with left-wing student organizations, aiding the riot police during student protests, fighting to the death against "communists" in case of civil war. An equally insane plan was to storm into the Imperial Palace and defend it with their blood. It's not entirely clear who the palace was to be defended from, and it doesn't help matters that at one point, as Mishima himself confessed to a friend, "what he truly wanted to do was to kill the *Tennō* [the emperor] in the Imperial Palace."[107] In some convoluted way, in Mishima's mind, such an act would have strengthened the imperial institution.

During those final years, as Mishima was plotting the "incident," many of his close friends became increasingly worried about his sanity. "It required no special powers of observation," writes Scott-Stokes, "to realize that Mishima was in grave trouble; his pranks and capers had gradually assumed a more and more grotesque form, culminating in the Tatenokai."[108] Mishima may have been losing his mind, but there was method to his madness. One of the *Bushidō* commandments was for the warrior to enter the "death frenzy" (*shini-gurui*), which outwardly might look like madness pure and simple. Such "derangement" is essential because, as the *Hagakure* puts it, one "cannot accomplish great exploits in a normal frame of mind. Just become insane and desperate to die."[109] Mishima seemed to be doing just that.

As he entered his final year, Mishima came up with increasingly specific plans that involved only a handful of trusted Tatenokai members. After several options were discussed and dismissed, on September 9, 1970, they settled on the plan they eventually followed on November 25: under the excuse of wanting to show a venerable Japanese sword to the commander of Camp Ichigaya, General Kanetoshi Mashita, Mishima, along with four Tatenokai members, would visit the general in his office and take him prisoner. The commander would not be hurt, but he would not be released until the troops had assembled in front of his office's balcony, so that Mishima could address them and talk them into rebellion. Mishima was perfectly aware that he would not be able to persuade the soldiers to rebel.[110] But the point was not to persuade anybody.

Mishima's followers now realized, to their dismay, that there was no plan A. Mishima planned the "incident" for a long time, in much secrecy and in maddening detail, but he only planned for failure—he didn't make any preparations in the event he was successful. He did *not* really want to convince the soldiers to overthrow the government. All he wanted was to die a samurai's "beautiful" death. And for that he had to fail first.[111] In this he followed literally the *Hagakure* admonition: "Just become insane and desperate to die."

Along with Mishima, only one disciple, Masakatsu Morita, was allowed to take his life. Mishima was to commit *hara-kiri,* and

Morita would do the *kaishaku* for him—that is, he would behead Mishima to end his agony. Then Morita would commit *hara-kiri* himself, with another member of the team, Hiroyasu Koga, doing the *kaishaku* for him. And that would be it. The others would live to tell the tale. Mishima correctly anticipated that there would be a trial, and a highly publicized one at that, during which the whole affair would be revealed. Apart from his own death, what he wanted most was that his story be told—with as much fanfare as possible.

Morita was particularly close to Mishima, and not just because he was the leader of the Tatenokai. Apparently, he was also Mishima's lover. Mishima was a "bearer of two swords," as the Japanese phrase would have it, but "he preferred men."[112] This made it possible for the Japanese media to frame the "incident" as a case of homosexual *shinjū* (lovers' suicide), a very Japanese tradition.[113] Which may have been the best way to miss, or to hide, the whole point.

Exitus

Rather than ordering the execution of his former tutor, Nero asked him to commit suicide, which, considering his general moral degradation of late, was quite generous. When the Praetorian Guard arrived to convey the emperor's orders, Seneca was dining with friends. Since the imperial messengers didn't give him time to prepare a will, he told his dinner companions that, instead of offering them expensive gifts, as he would have liked to, they would have to content themselves with *imago vitae suae* ("the image of his life"), as Tacitus reports. It was the same *imago* the philosopher had been tinkering with for decades: the carefully curated version of himself that, he hoped, would remain untainted by his obscene wealth, his aggressive moneylending, his association with Nero, and the many compromises he had made with the world. Indeed, in Seneca's mind, his suicide was to be the final chapter and the culmination of this self-fashioning project. One of his models was

Socrates, whose death Plato recounted in *Phaedo*. The other was Cato of Utica's particularly gruesome ending (self-stabbing-cum-self-disembowelment), which was held in high regard in Rome. Seneca ended with a combination of the two, to which he added some twists of his own.

His initial plan was to die by that venerable Roman method—vein-slashing. But he was old and skinny, and his body emaciated, and not enough blood would come out of his wrists. He persisted, though, and went on to cut behind his knees as well. The same result: still alive and kicking, though "exhausted by the savage rackings." Never one to give up, Seneca kept improvising. And sermonizing. Since, as Tacitus observes, "even at the very last moment his eloquence was in plentiful supply, he called his scribes and transmitted a very considerable amount."[114] You would die in vain if your death didn't become a story, or part of one—the scribes' job was to make that happen.

Realizing that the Roman method had failed him, Seneca went Greek and tried to imitate Socrates. After all, it had been his belief that "it was the hemlock that made Socrates great."[115] The philosopher had hemlock handy, but for some reason the poison refused to work: "when it was brought, he swallowed it in vain, being already cold in his joints, and his body blocked against the power of the poison." If one were to read this in a work of fiction, one would think it poorly done. But Seneca's dying was better than fiction, just as his life had been. Eventually, the philosopher was taken to a hot bath, where, because of his chronic respiratory troubles, he soon "was asphyxiated by the steam."[116] For all the methods he had tried, and all the detours he had made, Seneca died of asphyxiation—the same death for which he had been rehearsing all his life.

The saga of Seneca's death is quite a story: careful preparation and utter failure, perseverance and mishaps, humiliation and messiness aplenty. No method seemed to work. Death didn't seem to want him, much as he wanted to die. Given that he had prepared a lifetime for it, Seneca was pretty inept at dying. For all his study of the great men's endings, he eventually failed to imitate them. Compared with Socrates's death, Seneca's looks like a low-quality copy. And yet it's this botched ending—so clumsy and yet so touching—that endears Seneca to us. Far from diminishing his legacy, it complicates and enriches it. We are moved precisely by the clumsy, the error-prone, the inept-at-dying Seneca, which we gather from the story he left behind.

And that makes us realize something important: Seneca had been right to bet everything on the *imago vitae suae*. In the end, he won everything—and more. We know today a great deal about Seneca's personal shortcomings and of the unpalatable compromises he had to make as Nero's advisor and spin doctor. And yet all that doesn't diminish our attraction to the philosopher. We still read him and ponder his words and quote them. We take him seriously. What Seneca said on poverty we find both profound and worth following, even though we know so much about his personal wealth. What he taught about philosophical detachment goes straight to our heart, even if we know how dangerously attached he was to Nero and his court. How is that possible?

It is possible because we don't normally engage with the real, the historical Seneca, but with the fictionalized self he brought into existence in his work. We don't fall in love with Nero's occasional partner in crime when we read Seneca, but with a very persuasive piece of literature.

The Mishima Incident

As he rushed back into the commander's office, Mishima must have felt twice relieved. First, because he had failed to persuade the soldiers: now he *had to die*. And his was to be a "beautiful death" because that's how true samurais die when they fail. Second, because the exact manner of his dying, *hara-kiri,* was nothing new to him: he had done it before. He knew death inside out. He had performed it already.

For Mishima had been plotting to the last detail not only his fictions and his life, but also his death, by far the most important of all his works. In 1960, he published a short story, *Patriotism* (*Yūkoku*), about a young officer indirectly involved in a 1936 mutiny against the Imperial Army (the so-called "February 26 incident"). Caught between the loyalty he owed to his fellow officers and that which he owed to the emperor, the officer decides to commit *hara-kiri*, with his wife next to him, first serving as a ceremonial witness to his suicide and then committing suicide herself. In 1966, a film was made based on Mishima's short story: he both directed it and played the officer.

It turned out to be the performance of his life: there is nothing of the kitsch-loving, muscle-pumped show-off here. The presence of death, if only vicarious, transfigured him. "This is neither a comedy nor a tragedy," Mishima said. It is "simply a story of happiness."[117] The half-hour, black-and-white film—brimming with references to the Noh theater, set claustrophobically in one small room, static shot after haunting static shot—is like a preview of Mishima's own death. It is all there, almost more than we can take: the cutting of the apple, the penetration, the climax, the exhaustion.[118] The act is swift and decisive, and Mishima is at his most intense: the knife in his hand is being "plunged deep into the apple," which is now "split open" and its core "exposed to the light." For that to happen, the apple has to "fall into fragments" and be destroyed. That's the way of all apples and bodies in this world: you have to sacrifice your existence "for the sake of seeing." Seeing what? Nothing.

Once he was back in the general's office, Mishima did precisely that: he stripped himself of the uniform, took the required position on the floor, and cut his belly. All those years of bodybuilding came in handy. When asked once why he took up weightlifting, his response was frankness itself: "Because I am going to die committing seppuku. . . . I wish to be sure that my stomach will be pure muscle with no fat on it."[119] And no fat interfered with his work on that day: the cut was clean, swift, and expertly done. A Japanese biographer offers the details, with clinical, sickening precision: "The wound Mishima made by disembowelment started at 1.6 inches below his navel, 5.5 inches long from left to right, and 1.6 to 2 inches deep. Twenty inches of intestines came out." It was "a magnificent seppuku," he concludes.[120]

Except it wasn't. Mishima's assistant, Morita, for all their rehearsals over the previous days, failed to do his part and perform the *kaishaku*. Trembling badly, he cut into Mishima's shoulder and then into his neck, without actually beheading him, thus prolonging rather than reducing his agony. Hiroyasu Koga had to step in to clean up the mess and give Mishima the decisive blow, before doing the same thing for Morita.

Mishima's ending thus became an unsightly site of butchery and clumsiness. The rehearsal in the film was so much better than the real thing. That should have humbled him a bit.

The River and the Swimmer

In *Oedipus at Colonus,* Sophocles has the chorus say, "Not to be born is, beyond all estimation, best; but when a man has seen the light of day, this is next best by far, that with utmost speed he should go back from where he came."[121] Nihilists of all stripes have been much taken by this insight. *"Not to have been born,"* Cioran exclaims, "merely musing on that—what happiness, what freedom, what space."[122] He contemplates the vast unfolding of nothingness that precedes coming into existence—and is enchanted.

The insight is not just some eccentrics' philosophical fancy; it is deeply rooted in religion, and often comes with the gravity of a revelation. According to an ancient story, recounted by Nietzsche in *The Birth of Tragedy,* King Midas hunted in the forest for Dionysus's companion, the wise Silenus. When the king managed to capture Silenus, he asked him what is "the best and most desirable of all things for man." Silenus took some convincing, but eventually the demigod startled Midas with this answer:

Oh, wretched, ephemeral race, children of chance and misery, why do you compel me to tell you what it would be most expedient for you not to hear? What is best of all is utterly beyond your reach: not to be born, not to *be*, to be *nothing*. But the second best for you is—to die soon.[123]

Similarly, Gnostic theology always points to a privileged realm: the state of perfection that precedes existence. That which is yet to be born—the world, a person, a building, or a book—may be nothing, but at this stage it is at its utmost. Any actualization is a limitation, any coming into existence, an impoverishment. Walking in the Gnostics' footsteps, medieval Cathars managed to rediscover the insight and grafted new life on it. During an Inquisition investigation in late thirteenth-century France, a Cathar believer confessed his hope that sexual abstinence would bring us closer to a heavenly state: "For if people would hold on to barrenness, all God's creatures would soon be gathered together [in heaven]."[124]

We don't have an exact name for this place—before and beyond existence—for which we look in vain while we are caught up in the maelstrom. Human language is poorly equipped to express something so transcendent and so important, but one word has been employed more often than others. It is the one that Silenus uses: *nothingness.* "A nothingness that is everything," in Comte-Sponville's memorable formulation.[125] Or "divine nothingness," in Cioran's. Stoner, the hero of John Williams's eponymous novel, has at one point the vision of a great "nothingness" into which "all things" are "at last diminished."[126] No wonder some also refer to this primal abyss as God himself. Meister Eckhart found God easily associable with "emptiness," and so did the Gnostic Basilides, who thought that God's highest attribute was his nonexistence. Others call it "Nirvana," literally meaning "blown out," as when a flame flickers away, and nothing remains of it.

Eventually, words are not that important. What matters is what they gesture toward: our fundamental need for a larger frame of reference. We will never be able to see our situation with any clarity unless we manage to extricate ourselves from it and consider it, calmly and dispassionately, from a certain distance. As long as you're swimming in a river, you will not be able to understand the river itself. You certainly know what water is like, deeply immersed as you are in it, but your knowledge, while intense, will be limited. Entangled in the stream, you will be too affected by it and too busy staying afloat to engage in any real understanding. For that you will need to climb out of the water, find some elevated position, and contemplate from there. Not only will you be safer, but you will be more knowledgeable, and even wiser. All you need is something—a rope, or a branch, some tool—to help you out. Failure can be such a tool.

We can use the experience of failure to extricate ourselves from the entanglement of existence (physical, political, social, biological), with a view to gaining a better understanding of it, and in the hope of leading a more enlightened and wiser life. Failure seems particularly well suited for the job—better than a rope. Following its course, we learn whatever there is to learn about ourselves, the world, and our place in it, and especially about that which transcends us and the world: the abyss on the edge of which our existence happens.

Failure is an eye-opening experience like few others. Thanks to its occurrence in the physical world, we start to see the cracks in the fabric of existence, and within ourselves. As things fail to perform their function, they expose the fundamental precariousness of the world around us. That's how we get a first glimpse of the abyss. Failure also reveals human history to be nothing but a continual struggle for conquest and dominance and annihilation of others, and our political institutions (even the best of them) to be precarious and imperfect. Another glimpse. Thanks to failure, we also come to see how unreasonable a society's demands can be on its members, how whimsical its expectations, how shallow its judgments. Failure exposes the vanity and bareness of it all, in the process giving us an even better glimpse of the abyss. Finally, failure shows us just how close we are, biologically, to nonexistence, and how intimately involved with death we become with every passing day. This one is no longer a glimpse, but a proper, frontal view of the abyss. The abyss looks back and fixes us silently with bullfighter's eyes.

The silence we see in that gaze, should we pay enough attention, is no ordinary silence. It is the sound of ultimate stillness.

For as long as we live, consciously or unconsciously, we long for a realm of absolute calm. We have a promise—and a foretaste—of it whenever we manage to fall into deep sleep. No matter how much we act in the world, the amount of energy we spend, the detours we take, the destination is always the same—the place of ultimate stillness where we can at last find our peace. The more impatient of us sometimes do the utmost to reach it faster. Yukio Mishima, Osamu Dazai, and Jean Améry (as well as Simone Weil) are limit cases that show us how strong that longing can be. Their endings illustrate, to a painful degree, the extreme length to which a human being can go to find this realm. No matter how tumultuous their lives were, how stormy and noisy, they all hoped that the great stillness that awaited them would bring closure and relief.

Theirs are extraordinary stories of self-denial, self-destruction, and eventually self-transcendence. Such examples are not meant to be imitated, but we cannot afford to ignore them either. For the extreme cruelty of these stories—like the cruelty of myth and religion, like that of great art—is *the cruelty of life itself*. Dionysus and Prometheus, Oedipus and Antigone, Ivan Ilyich and Emma Bovary, not to mention the countless martyrs of religion, don't suffer because they are masochistic—or their chroniclers, sadistic. *We* need them to suffer—we've produced their stories, after all. We represent them in agony because, by absorbing their suffering, we hope to cure ourselves of our own ills. The greater their pain, the more complete our *katharsis*. We know instinctively that we will not be healed unless we learn how to face the unspeakable cruelty that lies at the core of life itself.

The serpent's venom is both poison and medicine.

Farewell

The peculiar thing about the circle of ultimate failure is that, as we proceed through it, we bring with us the failures we've experienced in previous circles. The failure of things (the near fatal car accident you were in as a teenager, the technical malfunction that almost killed you ten years later), the political disasters (the arbitrary arrest, the police beatings, the trauma of constant surveillance), the inevitable societal failure (your marginalization and ostracization, people's stopping talking to you)—they all show up when we are about to exit, as if for a party. A farewell party.

When the hour of our death comes, whether we realize it or not, everything that has been amiss in our lives, our failings and shortcomings and shameful deeds, the pain we have been through, the projects we have botched or left unfinished, they all turn up there too—to receive their absolution. An Origenian *apokatastasis* of sorts, only on a small personal scale.

The most original of farewell parties, this must be. For the guests are our own scars and wounds, big and small; our traumas and humiliations, shames and embarrassments, of which there are always plenty. They are all lined up there to say their farewell. As we meet each one of these guests and size them up, we know that we are faced with different parts of ourselves—provisional instantiations of our own self. Meeting them is like looking in the mirror and seeing not just our current state, but our previous states as well. As each millstone has cut deeper into our flesh, another, slightly more refined version of us has emerged, and now we meet them all in one place. Once we've seen them, we can leave at last, for there is nothing else for us to do there.

An odd party indeed, but when you think about it, a better arrangement is hard to imagine. For when we finally make it to the door, we know exactly what we leave behind—what we have been. We exit clean and unattached to anything, scar-covered and worn out, yet whole. With some luck, even cured.

EPILOGUE

Every morning, when we wake up, there is a moment—the briefest of moments—when our memory hasn't come back to us. We are not yet ourselves because we don't have a story to tell. We can be anyone at this stage, but right now we are no one. We are a blank sheet of paper waiting to be written on. As our memory gradually returns, we start recalling things: where we are, what happened before we fell asleep, what we need to do next, the tasks of the day ahead. We start becoming ourselves again as the memory of these things comes back and slowly forms a story. When everything has fallen into place, and the story is complete, we can be said to have come back to life. We now have a self. The sheet is covered with our story—we *are* our story.

This is the most significant moment of every day, and philosophically the most gripping: the process through which we come into existence, and our self comes back to us, every time we wake up. If, for some reason, things failed to fall into place and form a coherent narrative, we would never find ourselves. The sheet would remain blank. We would miss ourselves in the same way we would miss someone who didn't show up for a meeting.

Human beings are fundamentally narrative-driven creatures. Our lives take the shape of the stories we tell; they move this way or that as we change the plot. These stories are what gives our existence consistency, direction, and a unique physiognomy. We are irreducible individuals not because of, say, our DNA, but because no story can be told in exactly the same way twice. Even the slightest change of rhythm and diction produces a different story. Another person.

At our most intimate, then, *we are what we tell ourselves we are.* The German philosopher Wilhelm Dilthey called this process the "coming together of a life"—*Zusammenhang des Lebens.* The stories we tell about our life are sometimes more important than life itself. They are what brings that life together and makes it what it is: *our* life. Without them, we would remain only some insignificant occurrence in the planet's biosphere.

As storytelling animals, we need stories not just for coming into existence every morning, but for pretty much everything—for things big and small, important and trivial, ennobling and shameful. We need a good story to live by and to die for, to fall in love with someone and out of love with her, to help us fight for a cause or betray it.

We likewise need a story to cure ourselves of the *umbilicus mundi* syndrome. To achieve true humility it is not enough just to be humble. We also need to weave a story that structures our self-effacing efforts and gives them sustenance, continuity, and meaning. We have to *narrate our way into humility.* And that's what renders humility one of the most difficult stories to tell. For the self that narrates is the same one that longs for self-effacement and seeks to be lowered and subdued. The narrator's voice, so vital to storytelling, has to be silenced. But how are we going to tell a story with silence? How can we narrate ourselves and reduce ourselves to dust at the same time? Dust has never had any stories to tell. That puts humility and storytelling seriously at odds with each other.

For all her extraordinary self-effacement, Simone Weil left behind a "spiritual autobiography," to say nothing of her letters and notebooks. Eventually, she produced a remarkably well articulated

story of herself, if one built around a long series of absences: deprivation, self-denial, self-starvation, dematerialization, decreation.
For good measure, Weil also surrounded herself with friends who
were gifted narrators, as though she instinctively knew that one day,
when her uncommon biography was to be pieced together and
brought to public life, their storytelling skills would come in handy.

Unlike Weil, Mahatma Gandhi never hesitated to talk about
himself. He may have aspired to be "humbler than the dust," but
he found that aspiration compatible with an ambitious self-
narration project, which he pursued doggedly all his life. In mid-
career, Gandhi issued a voluminous *Autobiography*, to make sure
that there was an "authorized version" of his experiments with
failure. By bragging continuously about his pitfalls, shortcomings,
and "Himalayan blunders," he hoped to square the circle of humble
self-narration. For someone as opposed to modern civilization as
Gandhi was, his media savviness was a sight to behold. No matter
how busy his schedule, he would always make time to meet with
reporters and journalists, whom he rarely failed to entertain. He
badly needed them for his self-narration project.

E. M. Cioran was a misanthrope and a recluse who cherished
his self-imposed marginality. Yet he eventually made a deliberate
choice, late in life, to come out of his inner exile and give a series
of interviews to discerning journalists. These conversations reveal
Cioran as a great *causeur* and a first-class humorist. The famous
misanthrope did some serious smiling on camera. Indeed, Cioran's
own writing was markedly performative, meant to bring a certain
degree of narrative order into a highly anarchic inner life: "Had I
not written," he reflected, "the depressive moods I've had all my
life would have undoubtedly led me to madness or complete
failure."[1] All his life Cioran wrote his way out of the absyss, even
as he never stopped being fascinated by it.

Osamu Dazai didn't leave us an explicit autobiography, but he
didn't have to: his entire oeuvre is nothing else. He lived the life of
a failure and wrote unabashedly about it, but in his telling, both

"failure" and "life" changed their meanings. And so did "death." Dazai turned his own death into a narrative project of radical humility, on which he labored all his life, and as part of which he sought to write his way back into the abyss. The abyss kept pushing him back into life, till one rainy day in June it had to give in and admit him.

In spite of his intense political involvement and busy social existence, Seneca never stopped working on the story ("image") of his life. The result is that Seneca the literary character is more consistent and persuasive, more authentic and worth following than Seneca the person. This situation may have helped Seneca solve his "humility problem"—after a fashion. On the one hand, it is hard to expect humility in an *amicus principis* and the owner of large estates and vast sums. On the other, humility (intellectual, moral, existential) is central to Seneca the literary character, the one who so fascinates us. Few authors have written their way into humility more masterfully than Nero's former spin doctor.

Even though Yukio Mishima brought forth many great fictions, he came to believe that the best story he could ever put together was not a work of fiction, but his own death. That's why he plotted it in such maddening detail. As part of that plot, he ordered some of his closest followers not to follow him in death, so that they could live on and tell the tale—*his* tale. He thought that without that final story—the performance of his own death—his work, uncommonly voluminous though it was, would have remained unfinished and compromised. This is the story of Mishima's *willing himself into humility*, the most unhumble of projects—a rather complicated affair. But who says that narrating oneself into humility is simple? When it comes to achieving humility, nothing is.

"Telling stories is as basic to human beings as eating," writes Richard Kearney. "More so, in fact, for while food makes us live, stories are what make our lives worth living."[2] Or not worth living.

When one lives on the edge of the abyss, as we do, the answer to the fundamental question about the worthiness and meaning of existence depends heavily on the story one tells oneself. And since failure lies at the core of who we are, the most important stories we tell about ourselves, as well as those we read about others, are primarily tales of failing. Indeed, from the Greek tragedies to the latest news reports, there has never been a good story without some degree of failure in it. Such are the narratives that fascinate us. Why would we want to read about the inner life of robots? Failure and storytelling are intimate friends, always working in cahoots.

That's why the observation that our life has been "a complete failure," has "no meaning," or "is not worth the pain" is one many of us may make in the course of our existence. Yet few of us choose to end it right then and there in response. This is not because we lack courage (when one wants to die, one finds the courage), but because we feel that the story, failure-filled though it may be, has not run its course. We want to wait and see. And that is telling.

At any given moment, we may find our life to be empty and our existence meaningless, but we know, at some deeper level, that we are not done yet. Our story is just not over, and it's frustrating— profoundly, viscerally so—to quit a story before the end, whether it's a book, a film, or your own life. Once we have reached that point, we may decide that there is nothing left to tell, but quitting the story while it is still being told is a violation not just of narrative but of nature. The longed-for meaning may be revealed at the very end, and we will no longer be there to receive the revelation. It is written, after all, that the "pearl" we are supposed to retrieve can only be found at the story's end.

Can a story save my life, then? Yes, it can. The truth is, only a story can redeem our lives. And not just our lives, but life itself. That's the reason why, in case you've wondered, there are so many stories in this book, from beginning to end. Without stories, we would be nothing.

Notes

Prologue

1. Vladimir Nabokov, *Speak, Memory* (New York: G. P. Putnam's Sons, 1966), 19.
2. Quoted in David McLellan, *Utopian Pessimist: The Life and Thought of Simone Weil* (New York: Poseidon Press, 1990), 93.
3. Samuel Beckett, *Nohow On: Company, Ill Seen Ill Said, Worstward Ho. Three Novels* (New York: Grove Press, 1980), 102.
4. E. M. Cioran, *Cahiers: 1957–1972* (Paris: Gallimard, 1997), 715.
5. *The Acts of Thomas*, trans. Harold W. Attridge (Salem, OR: Polebridge, 2010).
6. E. M. Cioran, *The Trouble with Being Born*, trans. Richard Howard (New York: Seaver Books, 1976), 29.
7. E. M. Cioran, *Entretiens* (Paris: Gallimard, 1995), 29.

1. In a Fallen World

1. "The world is the product of a divine tragedy, a disharmony in the realm of God, a baleful destiny in which man is entangled and from which he must be set free" (Kurt Rudolph, *Gnosis: The Nature and History of Gnosticism* [San Francisco: Harper & Row, 1983], 66).
2. James M. Robinson, ed., *The Nag Hammadi Library in English* (San Francisco: Harper and Row, 1977), 145.
3. Jacques Lacarrière, *The Gnostics*, trans. Nina Rootes (New York: Dutton, 1977), 31.
4. William Smith and Henry Wave, *A Dictionary of Christian Biography, Literature, Sects and Doctrines*, 4 vols. (London: Little, Brown, 1877), 4:587.

5. Hans Jonas, *The Gnostic Religion: The Message of the Alien God and the Beginnings of Christianity* (Boston: Beacon Press, 2001), 49.

6. Jonathan Wright, *Heretics: The Creation of Christianity from the Gnostics to the Modern Church* (Boston: Houghton Mifflin Harcourt, 2011), 26.

7. Rudolph, *Gnosis*, 75.

8. Jonas, *The Gnostic Religion*, xxxi.

9. Lacarrière, *The Gnostics*, 25.

10. Lacarrière, *The Gnostics*, 10.

11. Lacarrière, *The Gnostics*, 31.

12. Emmanuel Le Roy Ladurie, *Montaillou: The Promised Land of Error*, trans. Barbara Bray (New York: Vintage, 1979), 157.

13. The bibliography on Simone Weil is enormous and growing every day. For my purposes here, I've found particularly helpful, apart from Weil's own writings (including her letters and notebooks), works cited in the notes by Simone Pétrement, Jacques Cabaud, Francine du Plessix Gray, Gabriella Fiori, Jean-Marie Perrin and Gustave Thibon, and Palle Yourgrau, and several works not directly cited: David McLellan, *Utopian Pessimist: The Life and Thought of Simone Weil* (New York: Poseidon Press, 1990); Sylvie Weil, *Chez les Weil: André et Simone* (Paris: Buchet / Chastel, 2009); Robert Zaretsky, *The Subversive Simone Weil: A Life in Five Ideas* (Chicago: University of Chicago Press: 2021).

14. Simone Pétrement, *Simone Weil: A Life*, trans. Raymond Rosenthal (New York: Pantheon Books, 1976), 8.

15. Jacques Cabaud, *Simone Weil: A Fellowship in Love* (New York: Channel Press, 1964), 17.

16. Francine du Plessix Gray, *Simone Weil* (New York: Penguin, 2001), 6–7.

17. Quoted in Pétrement, *Simone Weil*, 70.

18. Jean-Marie Perrin and Gustave Thibon, *Simone Weil as We Knew Her* (London: Routledge, 2003), 117.

19. Quoted in Gray, *Simone Weil*, 15.

20. Quoted in Gray, *Simone Weil*, 15.

21. Perrin and Thibon, *Simone Weil as We Knew Her*, 109.

22. Pétrement, *Simone Weil*, 29.

23. Gabriella Fiori, *Simone Weil: An Intellectual Biography*, trans. Joseph R. Berrigan (Athens: University of Georgia Press, 1989), 26.

24. Quoted in Pétrement, *Simone Weil*, 85.

25. Pétrement, *Simone Weil*, 420.

26. Quoted in Fiori, *Simone Weil*, 191.

27. Quoted in Gray, *Simone Weil*, 76.

28. Quoted in Fiori, *Simone Weil*, 63.

29. "Her gifts as a teacher were tremendous," writes Thibon, who took private Greek lessons from her (Perrin and Thibon, *Simone Weil as We Knew Her*, 117).

30. Pétrement, *Simone Weil*, 78.

31. Simone Weil, *Seventy Letters*, trans. R Rees (Oxford: Oxford University Press, 1965), 10.

32. Pétrement, *Simone Weil*, 227.

33. Weil, *Seventy Letters*, 11.

34. According to Weil, "only Chaplin understood the workers' condition in our epoch" (Pétrement, *Simone Weil*, 267).

35. Quoted in Pétrement, *Simone Weil*, 279.

36. Pétrement, *Simone Weil*, 274.

37. Pétrement, *Simone Weil*, 472 (quoted in), 29.

38. For a good discussion of the importance of failure in engineering, see, for example, Henry Petroski, *To Engineer Is Human: The Role of Failure in Successful Design* (New York: Vintage, 1992) and Charles Perrow, *Normal Accidents: Living with High-Risk Technologies* (Princeton, NJ: Princeton University Press, 2000).

39. Gray, *Simone Weil*, 8.

40. Pétrement, *Simone Weil*, 254.

41. Simone de Beauvoir, *Memoirs of a Dutiful Daughter*, trans. James Kirkup (New York: Harper, 2005), 239.

42. "The Russian Revolution," Weil writes, "has evolved rather like the French Revolution: the necessity to struggle with arms against an inner and outer enemy . . . resulted in the death of the best elements and forced the country to hand itself over to a bureaucratic, military, and police dictatorship that has nothing socialist or communist about it but the name" (quoted in Pétrement, *Simone Weil*, 201).

43. Quoted in Pétrement, *Simone Weil*, 201.

44. Quoted in Pétrement, *Simone Weil*, 246.

45. Pétrement, *Simone Weil*, 43.

46. Quoted in Fiori, *Simone Weil*, 58.

47. Weil, *Seventy Letters*, 15.

48. Weil, *Seventy Letters*, 15.

49. Weil, *Seventy Letters*, 18.

50. Weil, *Seventy Letters*, 18, 30.

51. Weil, *Seventy Letters*, 24.

52. Weil, *Seventy Letters*, 30.

53. Weil, *Seventy Letters*, 35.

54. E. M. Cioran, *The Trouble with Being Born*, trans. Richard Howard (New York: Seaver Books, 1976), 79.

55. Quoted in Pétrement, *Simone Weil*, 235.

56. Simone Weil, *Waiting for God*, trans. Emma Craufurd (New York: Harper, 1973), 117.

57. Quoted in Pétrement, *Simone Weil*, 242.

58. Weil, *Seventy Letters*, 19–20, 22.

59. Simone Weil, *First and Last Notebooks*, trans. Richard Rees (Oxford: Oxford University Press, 1970), 101.

60. "I am personally not a Catholic," she would admit, but "I consider the Christian idea, which has its roots in Greek thought and . . . has nourished all of our European civilization, as something that one cannot renounce without becoming degraded" (quoted in Pétrement, *Simone Weil*, 290).

61. Weil, *Waiting for God*, 66–67.

62. Weil, *Waiting for God*, 67

63. For a very good discussion of this topic, see Brett M. Frischmann and Evan Selinger, *Re-Engineering Humanity* (Cambridge: Cambridge University Press, 2018). For a different point of view, see Mark C. Taylor, *Intervolution: Smart Bodies Smart Things* (New York: Columbia University Press, 2020).

64. Quoted in Pétrement, *Simone Weil*, 394.

65. Simone Weil, *Letter to a Priest* (New York: Penguin, 2003), 19, 17, 36–37.

66. Weil, *Letter to a Priest*, 34. "In practice," she writes, "mystics belonging to nearly all the religious traditions coincide to the extent that they can hardly be distinguished. They represent the truth of each of these traditions" (Weil, *Letter to a Priest*, 47).

67. Weil, *Letter to a Priest*, 43–44.

68. Weil, *Letter to a Priest*, 14.

69. Weil, *First and Last Notebooks*, 100.

70. Weil, *Letter to a Priest*, 78.

71. Weil, *Letter to a Priest*, 39.

72. Weil, *Letter to a Priest*, 62.

73. Quoted in Gray, *Simone Weil*, 217.

74. Weil, *Letter to a Priest*, 55–56.

75. Weil, *Seventy Letters*, 130.

76. Weil, *Seventy Letters*, 130.

77. Weil, *Seventy Letters*, 130.

78. Iris Murdoch, *Existentialists and Mystics: Writings on Philosophy and Literature*, ed. Peter Conradi (New York: Penguin, 1997), 378.

79. Murdoch, *Existentialists and Mystics*, 378.

80. Murdoch, *Existentialists and Mystics*, 338.

81. Jane Foulcher, *Reclaiming Humility: Four Studies in the Monastic Tradition* (Collegeville, MN: Cistercian Publications, 2015), 115.

82. Quoted in Foulcher, *Reclaiming Humility*, 165.

83. André Comte-Sponville, *A Small Treatise on the Great Virtues: The Uses of Philosophy in Everyday Life*, trans. Catherine Temerson (London: Picador, 2002), 141.

84. Comte-Sponville, *A Small Treatise on the Great Virtues*, 147.

85. Quoted in Pétrement, *Simone Weil*, 537.

86. Weil, *Waiting for God*, 63.

87. Carl Sagan, *Pale Blue Dot: A Vision of the Human Future in Space* (New York: Random House, 1994), 7.

88. Murdoch, *Existentialists and Mystics*, 385.

89. Jonathan Sacks, "The Silence of the 'I': Humility as an Unfashionable Virtue," June 14, 2018, ABC Religion and Ethics (Australian Broadcasting Corporation), https://www.abc.net.au/religion/the-silence-of-the-i-humility-as-an-unfashionable-virtue/10094642.

90. There is a similar practice in Jainism: *sallekhana* (also known as *samlehna, santhara, samadhi-marana*, or *sanyasana-marana*).

91. Le Roy Ladurie, *Montaillou*, 225n1.

92. Palle Yourgrau, *Simone Weil* (London: Reaktion Books, 2011), 27, 30.

93. Weil's ideas did not simply duplicate the Gnostic doctrines, but her religiosity was penetrated by a Gnostic spirit. Thibon could say of her, "At the same time as she exalts God, she depreciates his handiwork: there is still a yawning chasm between the Creator and the creature. On the one hand, there is a God who is pure goodness and on the other a world which is governed *on all levels* by a Spinozistic necessity" (Perrin and Thibon, *Simone Weil as We Knew Her*, 137).

94. Weil, *First and Last Notebooks*, 103.

95. Weil, *First and Last Notebooks*, 103.

96. Weil, *First and Last Notebooks*, 218.

97. Weil, *Gravity and Grace*, 78.

98. Weil, *Gravity and Grace*, 79.
99. Weil, *Gravity and Grace*, 87.
100. Weil, *First and Last Notebooks*, 269.
101. Weil. *Gravity and Grace*, 81.
102. Weil. *Gravity and Grace*, 88.
103. Weil, *Gravity and Grace*, 79.
104. Weil, *First and Last Notebooks*, 243–244.
105. Weil, *Waiting for God*, 89, 135.
106. Weil, *Waiting for God*, 100
107. Quoted in Pétrement, *Simone Weil*, 531, 528.
108. Weil, *First and Last Notebooks*, 97–98.
109. Weil, *First and Last Notebooks*, 98.
110. Weil, *First and Last Notebooks*, 353.
111. Weil, *Gravity and Grace*, 56.
112. Weil, *Gravity and Grace*, 137.
113. Quoted in Fiori, *Simone Weil*, 7.
114. Pétrement, *Simone Weil*, 26.

2. The Ruins of Political Failure

1. Volker Ullrich, *Hitler: Ascent, 1889–1939* (New York: Knopf, 2016), 240.
2. Thomas Mann, *Death in Venice, Tonio Kroger, and Other Writings*, ed. Frederick A. Lubich (London: Continuum, 1999), 298.
3. Fyodor Dostoevsky, *The Brothers Karamazov*, trans. Richard Pevear and Larissa Volokhonsky (New York: Farrar, Straus and Giroux, 2002), 254.
4. John Gray, *Seven Types of Atheism* (New York: Farrar, Straus and Giroux, 2018), 3.
5. "Political religion is the sacralization of a political system founded on an unchallengeable monopoly of power, ideological monism, and the obligatory and unconditional subordination of the individual and the collectivity to its code of commandments. Consequently, a political religion is intolerant, invasive, and fundamentalist, and it wishes to permeate every aspect of an individual's life and of society's collective life" (Emilio Gentile, *Politics as Religion*, trans. George Staunton [Princeton, NJ: Princeton University Press, 2001], xv).
6. Quoted in Ullrich, *Hitler*, 385.
7. Milton Mayer, *They Thought They Were Free: The Germans, 1933–45* (Chicago: University of Chicago Press, 1917), 281.

8. For this reconstruction of Gandhi's life, personality, and public career I've relied significantly on works by Jad Adams, Louis Fischer, Ramachandra Guha, Arthur Herman, Pyarelal Nayar, Tridip Suhrud, Kathryn Tidrick, and Alex von Tunzelmann, cited in the notes, as well as others, including Douglas Allen, *Mahatma Gandhi* (London: Reaktion Books, 2011); Faisal Devji, *The Impossible Indian: Gandhi and the Temptation of Violence* (Cambridge, MA: Harvard University Press, 2012); Robert Payne, *The Life and Death of Mahatma Gandhi* (New Delhi: Rupa Publications, 1997); and Ananya Vajpeyi, *Righteous Republic: The Political Foundations of Modern India* (Cambridge, MA: Harvard University Press, 2012). I owe special thanks to Tridip Suhrud for an enlightening and unforgettable conversation on Gandhi's failures in Shimla.

9. Quoted in Arthur Herman, *Gandhi and Churchill: The Epic Rivalry That Destroyed an Empire and Forged Our Age* (New York: Bantam Dell, 2008), 558.

10. Quoted in Alex Von Tunzelmann, *Indian Summer: The Secret History of the End of an Empire* (New York: Henry Holt, 2007), 267.

11. Quoted in Herman, *Gandhi and Churchill,* 114.

12. *Times of India,* August 9, 1947.

13. Quoted in Herman, *Gandhi and Churchill,* 555.

14. Quoted in Herman, *Gandhi and Churchill,* 582.

15. "Between the masses and myself," said Gandhi, "there is a bond which defies description, but is nevertheless felt alike by them and me. I see in the fellowship with them the God I adore" (quoted in Rajmohan Gandhi, *Mohandas: A True Story of a Man, His People and an Empire* [New Delhi: Penguin India, 2007], 300).

16. Paul Woodruff, *First Democracy: The Challenge of an Ancient Idea* (London: Oxford University Press, 2005), 2.

17. Simone Weil, *The Iliad; or, The Poem of Force,* trans. Mary McCarthy (Wallingford, PA: Pendle Hill, 1991), 11.

18. Quoted in Bertrand M. Patenaude, *Stalin's Nemesis: The Exile and Murder of Leon Trotsky* (London: Faber and Faber, 2009), 231.

19. Frans de Waal, *Chimpanzee Politics: Power and Sex among Apes* (Baltimore, MD: Johns Hopkins University Press, 2007), 4.

20. Konrad Lorenz, *On Aggression* (London: Routledge, 2002), 228–229.

21. Albert Camus, "Democracy Is an Exercise in Modesty," trans. Adrian van den Hoven, *Sartre Studies International* 7, no. 2 (2001): 12–14.

22. Woodruff, *First Democracy,* 6.

23. "Democracy thrives on humility. Never to be confused with docile meekness or submission, humility is the cardinal democratic virtue, the antidote of arrogant pride: it is the quality of being aware of one's own and others' limits" (John Keane, *The Life and Death of Democracy* [New York: Norton, 2009], 855).

24. I focus here on Athenian democracy because it comes to us fully fledged, with a reasonably good description of how it worked in practice, and it is the version that inspired modern attempts at democracy. John Keane, however, puts democracy's birthplace "in the 'East,' in the lands that geographically correspond to contemporary Syria, Iran and Iraq" (Keane, *The Life and Death of Democracy*, xi).

25. David Stuttard, *Nemesis: Alcibiades and the Fall of Athens* (Cambridge, MA: Harvard University Press, 2018), 122.

26. Woodruff, *First Democracy*, 169.

27. Mohandas K. Gandhi, *The Collected Works of Mahatma Gandhi*, 100 vols. (New Delhi: Publications Divisions, Ministry of Information and Broadcasting, Government of India, 1958–1994), 90:38.

28. Quoted in Tridip Suhrud, "Editor's Introduction," in Mohandas K Gandhi, *An Autobiography; or, The Story of My Experiments with Truth*, trans. Mahadev Desai (New Haven, CT: Yale University Press, 2018), 21.

29. Gandhi, *An Autobiography*, 48.

30. Gandhi, *An Autobiography*, 49.

31. Gandhi, *An Autobiography*, 57, 58.

32. Gandhi, *An Autobiography*, 78.

33. Gandhi, *An Autobiography*, 186.

34. Gandhi, *An Autobiography*, 488.

35. George Orwell, "Reflections on Gandhi," in *A Collection of Essays* (New York: Harcourt, 1981), 171.

36. Gandhi, *An Autobiography*, 719–720.

37. Quoted in Ramachandra Guha, *Gandhi: The Years That Changed the World, 1914–1948* (New York: Knopf, 2018), 892 (italics in original).

38. Quoted in Andrew Delbanco, *College: What It Was, Is, and Should Be* (Princeton, NJ: Princeton University Press, 2012), 45.

39. Derek Bok, *Universities in the Marketplace: The Commercialization of Higher Education* (Princeton, NJ: Princeton University Press, 2003), 30n.

40. Umberto Eco, *Foucault's Pendulum*, trans. William Weaver (New York: Random House, 1997), 617.

41. Eco, *Foucault's Pendulum*, 618.

42. Gray, *Seven Types of Atheism*, 72.

43. Hannah Arendt, *The Origins of Totalitarianism* (Cleveland, OH: Meridian Books, 1961), 351.

44. Quoted in Herman, *Gandhi and Churchill*, 538.

45. Quoted in Guha, *Gandhi*, 777.

46. Orwell, "Reflections on Gandhi," 172.

47. Jad Adams speaks of Gandhi's "persistent, underlying failure to understand radical evil" (Jad Adams, *Gandhi: The True Man behind Modern India* [New York: Pegasus Books, 2011], 222).

48. Gandhi, *Collected Works*, 68:203–204.

49. Quoted in von Tunzelmann, *Indian Summer*, 94.

50. Quoted in Herman, *Gandhi and Churchill*, 446.

51. Gandhi, *Collected Works*, 75:177.

52. Quoted in Herman, *Gandhi and Churchill*, 445.

53. Quoted in Herman, *Gandhi and Churchill*, 406, 445.

54. Jean-Jacques Rousseau, *The Basic Political Writings*, trans. Donald A. Cress (Indianapolis, IN: Hackett, 2011), 200.

55. Quoted in Herman, *Gandhi and Churchill*, 492.

56. Gandhi, *Collected Works*, 49:15–18.

57. Herman, *Gandhi and Churchill*, 193.

58. Mohandas K. Gandhi, "Hind Swaraj," in Rudrangshu Mukherjee, ed., *The Penguin Gandhi Reader* (New York: Penguin 1996), 51.

59. Nathuram Godse, *Why I Assassinated Mahatma Gandhi* (New Delhi: Surya Bharti Parkashan, 1993), 40.

60. Pyarelal Nayar, *Mahatma Gandhi: The Early Phase* (Ahmedabad: Navajivan, 1965), 15.

61. Gandhi, *Collected Works*, 10:202.

62. That the revolution must be violent is unambiguous in Marx and Engels. In *The Communist Manifesto*, for example, they say that "the violent overthrow of the bourgeoisie lays the foundation for the sway of the proletariat." In *Das Kapital*, Marx writes, "Force is the midwife of every old society pregnant with a new one."

63. Karl Marx and Friedrich Engels, "The German Ideology," in Karl Marx and Friedrich Engels, *Collected Works*, vol. 5 (London: Lawrence and Wishart, 1989), 52–53 (italics in original).

64. Quoted in Jeremy D. Popkin, *A New World Begins: The History of the French Revolution* (New York: Basic Books, 2019), 304.

65. Quoted in Popkin, *A New World Begins*, 315.

66. Popkin, *A New World Begins*, 218.

67. Edmund Burke, *Reflections on the Revolution in France and Other Writings* (New York: Everyman's Library, 2015), 454.

68. Burke, *Reflections on the Revolution*, 500.

69. Arthur Koestler, *Darkness at Noon*, trans. Daphne Hardy (New York: Bantam, 1968), 81.

70. Quoted in Popkin, *A New World Begins*, 544.

71. Alexis de Tocqueville, *The Ancien Régime and the French Revolution*, ed. Jon Elster, trans. Arthur Goldhammer (Cambridge: Cambridge University Press, 2011), 19.

72. François Furet, *The French Revolution, 1770–1814*, trans. Antonio Nevill (Oxford: Blackwell, 1998), 137.

73. Quoted in Popkin, *A New World Begins*, 289–290

74. Quoted in Louis Fischer, *The Life of Mahatma Gandhi* (New York: Harper & Row, 1983), 92.

75. Quoted in Rajmohan Gandhi, *Mohandas*, 140.

76. Gandhi, *Collected Works*, 14:384.

77. Ruth Scurr, *Fatal Purity: Robespierre and the French Revolution* (London: Vintage, 2007), 6–7.

78. Scurr, *Fatal Purity*, 89.

79. Quoted in Scurr, *Fatal Purity*, 215.

80. Quoted in Scurr, *Fatal Purity*, 275.

81. Furet, *The French Revolution*, 146.

82. Graeme Fife, *The Terror: The Shadow of the Guillotine: France, 1792–1794* (New York: St. Martin's Press, 2004), 51–55.

83. Fife, *The Terror*, 56.

84. Furet, *The French Revolution*, 131.

85. Fife, *The Terror*, 66.

86. Quoted in Scurr, *Fatal Purity*, 134.

87. Orwell, "Reflections on Gandhi," 172.

88. Gandhi, *Collected Works*, 13:301.

89. Quoted in Rajmohan Gandhi, *Mohandas*, 36.

90. Gandhi, *Collected Works*, 47:119.

91. Rajmohan Gandhi, *Mohandas*, xi.

92. Quoted in Fischer, *The Life of Mahatma Gandhi*, 375.

93. *Indian Opinion*, December 1907.

94. Quoted in Adams, *Gandhi*, 91.

95. Gandhi, *Collected Works*, 70:236.

96. Furet, *The French Revolution*, 144.

97. Scurr, *Fatal Purity*, 10

98. Quoted in Sean McMeekin, *The Russian Revolution: A New History* (New York: Basic Books, 2017), 129.

99. Richard Pipes, *The Russian Revolution* (New York: Vintage, 1991), 387.

100. Orlando Figes, *Revolutionary Russia, 1891–1991: A History* (New York: Henry Holt, 2014), 96.

101. Quoted in Richard Pipes, *The Three "Whys" of the Russian Revolution* (New York: Vintage, 1995), 32.

102. Quoted in McMeekin, *The Russian Revolution*, 312. "It's a terrible misfortune that the honor of beginning the first Socialist revolution should have befallen the most backward people in Europe," Lenin complains elsewhere (quoted in Victor Serge, *Memoirs of a Revolutionary*, trans. Peter Sedgwick with George Paizis [New York: New York Review Books, 2012], 133).

103. Pipes, *The Three "Whys" of the Russian Revolution*, 32–33.

104. Quoted in Pipes, *The Three "Whys" of the Russian Revolution*, 7.

105. As Victor Serge observed, it was a "generally accepted thesis, which Lenin stated several times, that Russia, agricultural and backward (from an industrial standpoint) as it was, could not create a lasting Socialist system for itself by its own efforts, and that consequently we should be overcome sooner or later unless the European revolution . . . assured Socialism of a broader and more viable base" (Serge, *Memoirs of a Revolutionary*, 112).

106. Serge, *Memoirs of a Revolutionary*, 94.

107. Memorandum to N. N. Krestinsky, September 1918, in Richard Pipes, ed., *The Unknown Lenin: From the Secret Archive* (New Haven, CT: Yale University Press, 1996), 56 (italics in original).

108. Quoted in Joshua Rubenstein, *Leon Trotsky: A Revolutionary Life* (New Haven, CT: Yale University Press, 2011), 90.

109. Quoted in Figes, *Revolutionary Russia, 1891–1991*, 217.

110. McMeekin, *The Russian Revolution*, 267.

111. Quoted in Richard Pipes, ed., *The Unknown Lenin*, 183 (brackets in original).

112. Simone Weil, *Oppression and Liberty*, trans A. Wills and J. Petrie (London: Routledge and Kegan Paul, 1958), 74.

113. Quoted in Anne Applebaum, *Gulag: A History* (New York: Doubleday, 2003), 102.

114. Figes, *Revolutionary Russia, 1891–1991*, 199.

115. Figes, *Revolutionary Russia, 1891–1991*, 201.

116. Margarete Buber-Neumann, *Under Two Dictators*, trans. Edward Fitzgerald (New York: Dodd, Mead, 1950), 9.

117. Quoted in Adams, *Gandhi*, 210.

118. Quoted in Adams, *Gandhi*, 211.

119. "Mohandas Gandhi entered politics," writes Kathryn Tidrick, "not to liberate his country in the sense understood by other Indian leaders and the western public which followed his career with such fascinated attention, but to establish the Kingdom of Heaven on earth. The Indian masses, who revered him, grasped this, up to a point. They knew that a mahatma walked among them, poured out their devotion, and awaited results" (Kathryn Tidrick, *Gandhi: A Political and Spiritual Life* [London: Verso, 2013], xi).

120. Gandhi, *An Autobiography*, 272.

121. In her intriguing book Kathryn Tidrick follows this aspect of Gandhi's life and thought.

122. Gandhi, *Collected Works*, 29:408.

123. Quoted in Rajmohan Gandhi, *Mohandas*, 431.

124. Gandhi, *Collected Works*, 67:195.

125. Quoted in Adams, *Gandhi*, 137.

126. Applebaum, *Gulag*, 109.

127. Orlando Figes, *Just Send Me Word: A True Story of Love and Survival in the Gulag* (London: Penguin, 2012), 192–193.

128. Up to twenty million people, mostly men, are thought to have been imprisoned in the camps (Figes, *Just Send Me Word*, 5).

129. Alexander Solzhenitsyn, *One Day in the Life of Ivan Denisovich*, trans. Ralph Parker (London: Penguin, 1998), 14.

130. Quoted in Figes, *Just Send Me Word*, 86.

131. Eugenia Semyonovna Ginzburg, *Journey into the Whirlwind*, trans. Paul Stevenson and Max Hayward (New York: Harcourt, 1967), 63.

132. Buber-Neumann, *Under Two Dictators*, 27.

133. Similarly, in the Nazi camps the inmate was referred to as a "piece" (*Stück*). The first rollcall in the camp makes Primo Levi realize that he is no longer a person, but a *pezzo* (Primo Levi, *Se questo è un uomo* [Torino: Einaudi, 1986], 22).

134. Applebaum, *Gulag*, 102.

135. Varlam Shalamov, *Kolyma Tales*, trans. John Glad (New York: Penguin Books, 1994), 43.

136. Vasily Grossman, *Life and Fate*, trans. Robert Chandler (New York: Harper & Row, 1985), 845.

137. That Gandhi's fanciful ideas did not stand a chance was clear to many from the beginning. His "medievalist programme," writes Orwell, was "obviously not viable in a backward, starving, overpopulated country" (Orwell, "Reflections on Gandhi," 172).

138. Gandhi, "Hind Swaraj," 21.

139. Gandhi, "Hind Swaraj," 23–24.

140. Gandhi, "Hind Swaraj," 30–32.

141. Gandhi, "Hind Swaraj," 34.

142. Gandhi, "Hind Swaraj," 33.

143. Gandhi, *Collected Works*, 10:168–169.

144. Gandhi, "Hind Swaraj," 49.

145. Gandhi, "Hind Swaraj," 36–37.

146. Gandhi, "Hind Swaraj," 34.

147. Buber-Neumann, *Under Two Dictators*, 115.

148. Buber-Neumann, *Under Two Dictators*, 115.

149. Alexander Solzhenitsyn, *The Gulag Archipelago*, trans. Thomas P. Whitney (New York: Harper Perennial, 2007), 615.

150. Danusia Stok, ed., *Kieslowski on Kieslowski* (London: Faber and Faber, 1993), 125.

151. Gandhi, *Collected Works*, 23:45–47.

152. Quoted in Rajmohan Gandhi, *Mohandas*, 653.

153. Quoted in Rajmohan Gandhi, *Mohandas*, 300.

154. Gandhi, *Collected Works*, 93:227.

155. Quoted in Herman, *Gandhi and Churchill*, 578.

156. Here's Gandhi's detailed definition of a *brahmachari:* "One who never has intention, who by constant attendance upon God has become proof against conscious or unconscious emissions, who is capable of lying naked with naked women, however beautiful they may be, without being in any manner whatsoever sexually excited. Such a person should be incapable of lying, incapable of intending or doing harm to a single man or woman in the whole world, is free from anger and malice and detached in the sense of Bhagavadgita" (Gandhi, *Collected Works*, 87:107).

157. V. S. Naipaul, *The Indian Trilogy* (New Delhi: Picador India, 2016), 80.

158. Quoted in Fischer, *The Life of Mahatma Gandhi*, 379–380.

3. Winners and Losers

1. Quoted in Scott A. Sandage, *Born Losers: A History of Failure in America* (Cambridge, MA: Harvard University Press, 2005), 276–277.
2. Diogenes the Cynic, *Sayings and Anecdotes, with Other Popular Moralists*, trans. Robin Hard (Oxford: Oxford University Press, 2012), 15.
3. Diogenes the Cynic, *Sayings and Anecdotes*, 18.
4. Sandage, *Born Losers*, 2. "Failure" has different connotations in other languages. In Italian, for example, *fallimento* means both "failure" and "bankruptcy" (among other things).
5. For this portrait I've relied largely on Cioran's own writings (including letters, notebooks, journalism, and interviews), but also on the research done by Gabriel Liiceanu, Marta Petreu, Ion Vartic, and Ilinca Zarifopol-Johnson. Special thanks are due to Dan Petrescu for a very instructive conversation on Cioran.
6. E. M. Cioran, *Entretiens* (Paris: Gallimard, 1995), 17. Unless otherwise specified, all translations in this chapter are by the author.
7. E. M. Cioran, *The Trouble with Being Born*, trans. Richard Howard (New York: Seaver Books, 1976), 99. Elsewhere, Cioran says, "Everything . . . that is expressed, in terms of intensity, is degraded. This is the meaning of therapy through writing" (Gabriel Liiceanu, *Itinerariile unei vieți: E. M. Cioran; Apocalipsa după Cioran* [Bucharest: Humanitas, 2011], 94).
8. Quoted in Ilinca Zarifopol-Johnston, *Searching for Cioran*, ed. Kenneth R. Johnston (Bloomington: Indiana University Press, 2009), 47.
9. Cioran, *Entretiens*, 10.
10. Liiceanu, *Itinerariile unei vieți*, 124.
11. Cioran, *The Trouble with Being Born*, 168.
12. E. M. Cioran, *All Gall Is Divided*, trans. Richard Howard (New York: Arcade, 1999), 19.
13. Cioran, *The Trouble with Being Born*, 79 (italics in the original).
14. Scripture quotations are from Revised Standard Version of the Bible, copyright © 1946, 1952, and 1971, National Council of the Churches of Christ in the United States of America. Used by permission. All rights reserved worldwide.
15. Jean Calvin, *Institutes of the Christian Religion*, 2 vols., ed. John T. McNeill (Louisville, KY: Westminster John Knox Press, 1960), 1:469.
16. Calvin, *Institutes of the Christian Religion*, 2:923.
17. Calvin, *Institutes of the Christian Religion*, 2:926.

18. Calvin, *Institutes of the Christian Religion*, 2:978.

19. Calvin, *Institutes of the Christian Religion*, 2:978–979.

20. Max Weber, *The Protestant Ethic and the Spirit of Capitalism*, trans. Talcott Parsons (London: Routledge, 2005), 60, 59.

21. Calvin, *Institutes of the Christian Religion*, 2:952

22. Weber, *The Protestant Ethic*, 58–59.

23. Calvin, *Institutes of the Christian Religion*, 2:926, 956, 931.

24. Calvin, *Institutes of the Christian Religion*, 2:939, 947.

25. Quoted in Zarifopol-Johnston, *Searching for Cioran*, 61.

26. Liiceanu, *Itinerariile unei vieți*, 105.

27. Quoted in Marta Petreu, *An Infamous Past: E. M. Cioran and the Rise of Fascism in Romania*, trans. Bogdan Aldea (Chicago: Ivan R. Dee, 2005), 173 (italics in original).

28. Quoted in Marta Petreu, *An Infamous Past*, 197.

29. Quoted in Ion Vartic, *Cioran naiv și sentimental* (Cluj-Napoca: Biblioteca Apostrof, 2000), 54–55.

30. Mihail Sebastian, *For Two Thousand Years*, trans. Philip Ó Ceallaigh (London: Penguin, 2016), 149.

31. Tatiana Niculescu-Bran, *Seducătorul Domn Nae: Viața lui Nae Ionescu* (Bucharest: Humanitas, 2020), 60, 87.

32. Weber, *The Protestant Ethic*, 105.

33. Garry Wills, *Head and Heart: A History of Christianity in America* (New York: Penguin, 2008), 19.

34. That it is so difficult to establish the saying's exact source (candidates as different as La Rochefoucauld, Somerset Maugham, Gore Vidal, Iris Murdoch, and even Genghis Khan have been mentioned) only proves its depth and universal relevance.

35. Quoted in Petreu, *An Infamous Past*, 4.

36. Quoted in Petreu, *An Infamous Past*, 8.

37. Petreu, *An Infamous Past*, 9 (italics in original).

38. Quoted in Petreu, *An Infamous Past*, 11.

39. Quoted in Zarifopol-Johnston, *Searching for Cioran*, 99.

40. Emil Cioran, *Schimbarea la față a României* (Bucharest: Humanitas, 1990), 30, 34.

41. Cioran, *The Trouble with Being Born*, 69.

42. Cioran, *Schimbarea la față a României*, 53.

43. Cioran, *Schimbarea la față a României*, 42, 99, 91, 42.

44. Quoted in Petreu, *An Infamous Past*, 192.

45. Quoted in Petreu, *An Infamous Past*, 240.

46. Quoted in Zarifopol-Johnston, *Searching for Cioran*, 41 (italics in original).

47. Emil Cioran, *Mon Pays / Țara mea* (Bucharest: Humanitas, 1996), 10.

48. Quoted in Petreu, *An Infamous Past*, 4.

49. Petreu, *An Infamous Past*, 182 (italics in original).

50. George Orwell, *Down and Out in Paris and London* (New York: Harcourt, 1961), 16–17 (italics in original).

51. Orwell, *Down and Out*, 19.

52. Orwell, *Down and Out*, 19.

53. Liiceanu, *Itinerariile unei vieți*, 111, 67.

54. Cioran, *The Trouble with Being Born*, 78.

55. Liiceanu, *Itinerariile unei vieți*, 120.

56. Cioran, *Entretiens*, 34.

57. Quoted in Petreu, *An Infamous Past*, 191.

58. Cioran, *Entretiens*, 10–11.

59. Zarifopol-Johnston, *Searching for Cioran*, 160.

60. In those years, Cioran was "always on the edge of poverty, always on the lookout for a dinner invitation in exchange for his talents as a conversationalist" (Zarifopol-Johnston, *Searching for Cioran*, 119).

61. Liiceanu, *Itinerariile unei vieți*, 19.

62. Cioran, *The Trouble with Being Born*, 182.

63. Liiceanu, *Itinerariile unei vieți*, 111.

64. Cioran, *Entretiens*, 10–11.

65. Cioran, *Entretiens*, 35.

66. Ivan Goncharov, *Oblomov*, trans. Stephen Pearl (Richmond, UK: Alma Classics, 2015), 26–27.

67. Orwell, *Down and Out*, 120.

68. Orwell, *Down and Out*, 129.

69. Orwell, *Down and Out*, 129.

70. Orwell, *Down and Out*, 129.

71. Orwell, *Down and Out*, 129.

72. Cioran, *The Trouble with Being Born*, 175–176.

73. E. M. Cioran, *Anathemas and Admirations*, trans. Richard Howard (New York: Arcade, 1991), 12.

74. Cioran, *Anathemas and Admirations*, 223.

75. Cioran, *Entretiens*, 40.

76. Liiceanu, *Itinerariile unei vieți*, 111.

77. Cioran, *The Trouble with Being Born*, 48.

78. Cioran, *The Trouble with Being Born*, 17 (italics in original).

79. Liiceanu, *Itinerariile unei vieți*, 124.

80. Liiceanu, *Itinerariile unei vieți*, 78.

81. Cioran, *The Trouble with Being Born*, 121.

82. Orwell, *Down and Out*, 19.

83. Quoted in David Robinson, *Chaplin: The Mirror of Opinion* (Bloomington: Indiana University Press, 1983), 100.

84. Orwell, *Down and Out*, 20–21.

85. Tom Lutz, *Doing Nothing: A History of Loafers, Loungers, Slackers, and Bums in America* (New York: Farrar, Straus and Giroux, 2006), 102.

86. Orwell, *Down and Out*, 120.

87. Jacques Lacarrière, *The Gnostics* (New York: Dutton, 1977), 127.

88. E. M. Cioran, *A Short History of Decay*, trans. Richard Howard (Oxford: Basil Blackwell, 2012), 142.

89. E. M. Cioran, *The New Gods*, trans. Richard Howard (Chicago: University of Chicago Press, 2013), 8–9.

90. Cioran, *The Trouble with Being Born*, 20.

91. Cioran, *The Trouble with Being Born*, 56, 116, 9, 18.

92. Cioran, *The Trouble with Being Born*, 34.

93. E. M. Cioran, *History and Utopia*, trans. Richard Howard (New York: Arcade, 2015), 80 (italics in original).

94. Liiceanu, *Itinerariile unei vieți*, 94.

95. Frans de Waal, *Mama's Last Hug: Animal Emotions and What They Tell Us about Ourselves* (New York: Norton, 2019), 181.

96. Paul Fussell, *Class: A Guide through the American Status System* (New York: Simon and Schuster, 1992), 152 (italics in original).

97. A brilliant case for "universal salvation" has been made recently by David Bentley Hart in *That All Shall Be Saved: Heaven, Hell, and Universal Salvation* (New Haven, CT: Yale University Press, 2019).

98. Frans de Waal, *Chimpanzee Politics: Power and Sex among Apes* (Baltimore, MD: Johns Hopkins University Press, 2007), 111.

99. Thorstein Veblen, *The Theory of the Leisure Class* (New York: Penguin, 1994), 31.

100. William Deresiewicz, *Excellent Sheep: The Miseducation of the American Elite and the Way to a Meaningful Life* (New York: Free Press, 2014), 15.

101. Weber, *The Protestant Ethic*, 65.

102. Weber, *The Protestant Ethic*, 66.

103. Weber, *The Protestant Ethic*, 69.

104. Cioran, *History and Utopia*, 10.

105. Cioran, *History and Utopia*, 10.

106. Cioran, *History and Utopia*, 12.

107. Orwell, *Down and Out*, 120.

108. Veblen, *The Theory of the Leisure Class*, 32.

109. Fussell, *Class*, 21.

110. Fussell, *Class*, 54.

111. De Waal, *Mama's Last Hug*, 181.

112. Veblen, *The Theory of the Leisure Class*, 31–32.

113. Henry David Thoreau, *Walden and Civil Disobedience* (New York: Signet, 2012), 109.

114. Vartic, *Cioran naiv şi sentimental*, 334.

115. Zarifopol-Johnston, *Searching for Cioran*, 170–171.

116. For Cioran's final days, see Zarifopol-Johnston, *Searching for Cioran*, 169.

117. Sandage, *Born Losers*, 11, 130–131.

118. Sandage, *Born Losers*, 4.

119. Thomas Bernhard, *Concrete*, trans. David McLintock (London: Faber & Faber, 2013), 154 (italics in original).

120. Oscar Wilde, *The Complete Work of Oscar Wilde*, vol. 4, ed. Josephine M. Guy (Oxford: Oxford University Press, 2007), 174.

4. The Ultimate Failure

1. "Es se einem denkenden Wesen durchaus unmoeglich, sich ein Nichtsein, ein Aufhoeren des Denkens und Lebens zu denken." This important insight is not easy to find, in this formulation, in the body of Goethe's work, but it is traceable to C. A. H. Burkhardt's *Goethes Unterhaltungen mit dem Kanzler Friedrich v. Müller* (Stuttgart: J. G. Cotta, 1904). Thanks to Anthony Adler for helping me locate the quote's source.

2. Jean Améry, *On Aging: Revolt and Resignation*, trans. John D. Barlow (Bloomington: Indiana University Press, 1994), 104.

3. Leo Tolstoy, *The Death of Ivan Ilyich*, trans. Lynn Solotaroff (New York: Bantam Dell, 2004), 105.

4. Leo Tolstoy, *Confession*, in *The Death of Ivan Ilyich & Confession*, trans. Peter Carson (New York: Norton, 2013), 140.

5. Tolstoy, *The Death of Ivan Ilyich*, 69.

6. Tolstoy, *The Death of Ivan Ilyich*, 70.

7. Tolstoy, *The Death of Ivan Ilyich*, 79–80.

8. Tolstoy, *The Death of Ivan Ilyich*, 112.

9. Henry Scott-Stokes, *The Life and Death of Yukio Mishima* (New York: Moonday Press, 1995), 25.

10. Scott-Stokes, *The Life and Death of Yukio Mishima*, 25.

11. Scott-Stokes, *The Life and Death of Yukio Mishima*, 26.

12. Scott-Stokes, *The Life and Death of Yukio Mishima*, 27.

13. Scott-Stokes, *The Life and Death of Yukio Mishima*, 27.

14. Scott-Stokes, *The Life and Death of Yukio Mishima*, 27.

15. In sketching this portrait of Yukio Mishima I rely on the work done by a number of Mishima scholars: Damian Flanagan, John Nathan, Andrew Rankin, Henry Scott-Stokes, and Naoki Inose and Hiroaki Sato. For Dazai, I found Phyllis I. Lyons's work very helpful. Special thanks are due to William Brecher for helping me with this chapter. Peter Cheyne first introduced me to Dazai, for which I owe him thanks.

16. Ivan Morris, *The Nobility of Failure: Tragic Heroes in the History of Japan* (New York: Noonday, 1975), xxii.

17. Quoted in John Nathan, *Mishima: A Biography* (Cambridge, MA: Da Capo Press, 2000), 214.

18. E. M. Cioran, *A Short History of Decay*, trans. Richard Howard (Oxford: Basil Blackwell, 2012), 38.

19. Simon Critchley, *Notes on Suicide* (London: Fitzcarraldo Editions, 2020), 12.

20. Arthur Schopenhauer, *Studies in Pessimism*, trans. T. Bailey Saunders (Cosimo Classics, 2007), 28.

21. Al Alvarez, *The Savage God: A Study of Suicide* (London, Bloomsbury, 2013), 107, 154.

22. Quoted in Andrew Solomon, *The Noonday Demon: An Atlas of Depression* (New York: Scribner, 2001), 247.

23. Yukio Mishima, *Confessions of a Mask*, trans. Meredith Weatherby (New York: New Directions, 1958), 5–6.

24. Mishima, *Confessions of a Mask*, 25.

25. Marguerite Yourcenar, *Mishima: A Vision of the Void*, trans. Alberto Manguel (Chicago: University of Chicago Press, 2001), 14.

26. Yourcenar, *Mishima*, 13–14.

27. Donald Ritchie, *The Japan Journals, 1947–2004*, ed. Leza Lowitz (Berkeley: Stone Bridge Press, 2004), 47.

28. Mishima became obsessed with old age and what it does to us. He would say later, "Among my incurable convictions is the belief that the old are eternally ugly, the young eternally beautiful" (Scott-Stokes, *The Life and Death of Yukio Mishima*, 136).

29. Mishima, *Confessions of a Mask*, 21, 24, 28.

30. Mishima, *Confessions of a Mask*, 34, 35.

31. Mishima, *Confessions of a Mask*, 39.

32. Mishima, *Confessions of a Mask*, 39.

33. Mishima, *Confessions of a Mask*, 40.

34. Mishima, *Confessions of a Mask*, 41.

35. According to Henry Scott-Stokes, who knew him well, "Mishima's aim—his fundamental aim in life, it might be said—was to shock" (Scott-Stokes, *The Life and Death of Yukio Mishima*, 121).

36. Fyodor Dostoevsky, *Demons*, trans. Richard Pevear and Larissa Volokhonsky (New York: Vintage, 1995), 619.

37. Albert Camus, *The Myth of Sisyphus* (New York: Vintage, 2018), 3.

38. Schopenhauer, *Studies in Pessimism*, 50.

39. Quoted in Scott-Stokes, *The Life and Death of Yukio Mishima*, 88.

40. Nathan, *Mishima*, 123 (quoted in), 124.

41. Nathan, *Mishima*, 160.

42. Nathan, *Mishima*, 169.

43. Scott-Stokes, *The Life and Death of Yukio Mishima*, 127.

44. Quoted in Andrew Rankin, *Mishima, Aesthetic Terrorist: An Intellectual Portrait* (Honolulu: University of Hawaii Press, 2018), 22.

45. Naoki Inose and Hiroaki Sato, *Persona: A Biography of Yukio Mishima* (Berkeley: Stone Bridge Press, 2012), 601.

46. Jean Améry, *On Suicide: A Discourse on Voluntary Death*, trans. John D. Barlow (Bloomington: Indiana University Press, 1999), xxii.

47. Améry, *On Suicide*, 13 (italics in original).

48. Améry, *On Suicide*, 60.

49. Améry, *On Suicide*, 12, 130.

50. Améry, *On Suicide*, 78–79.

51. Améry, *On Suicide*, 27 (italics in original).

52. Phyllis I. Lyons, *The Saga of Dazai Osamu: A Critical Study with Translations* (Stanford, CA: Stanford University Press, 1985), 55.

53. Osamu Dazai, *Self-Portraits: Tales from the Life of Japan's Great Decadent Romantic*, trans. Ralph F. McCarthy (Tokyo: Kodansha 1991), 151–152.

54. Dazai, *Self-Portraits*, 156.

55. Dazai, *Self-Portraits*, 155.

56. Dazai, *Self-Portraits*, 160.

57. Dazai, *Self-Portraits*, 160.

58. Dazai, *Self-Portraits*, 161, 162.

59. Dazai, *Self-Portraits*, 164.

60. Dazai, *Self-Portraits*, 165.

61. Pierre Hadot, *Philosophy as a Way of Life: Spiritual Exercises from Socrates to Foucault*, ed. Arnold I. Davidson, trans. Michael Chase (Oxford: Blackwell, 1995), 82–83.

62. Lucius Annaeus Seneca, *Letters on Ethics*, trans. Margaret Graver and A. A. Long (Chicago: University of Chicago Press, 2015), 340.

63. Emily Wilson, *The Greatest Empire: A Life of Seneca* (Oxford: Oxford University Press, 2014), 191.

64. For more on this, see James Romm, *Dying Every Day: Seneca at the Court of Nero* (New York: Knopf, 2014).

65. Seneca, *Letters on Ethics*, 25.

66. Seneca, *Letters on Ethics*, 89.

67. Marin Heidegger, *Being and Time*, trans. John Macquarrie and Edward Robinson (Oxford: Blackwell, 1962), 289.

68. Seneca, *Letters on Ethics*, 414.

69. Mishima, observes Scott-Stokes, was "unnerved by the similarities between Dazai and himself, which were at that time personal, and not obviously literary. Both men were snobs; both desired to create a sensation and be heroes of the general public; and both were obsessed with suicide" (Scott-Stokes, *The Life and Death of Yukio Mishima*, 90).

70. Quoted in Inose and Sato, *Persona*, 162.

71. Quoted in Nathan, *Mishima*, 123, 92. Mishima could be more specific: "The disgust in which I hold Dazai Osamu's literature is in some way ferocious" (quoted in Inose and Sato, *Persona*, 163).

72. Quoted in Nathan, *Mishima*, 92–93.

73. John Nathan has a different interpretation. He writes: "What this [confession] suggests . . . is that Mishima was beginning to locate in himself the same self-destructive impulses he saw in Dazai and was converting the terror of this self-awakening to a hatred of the other man" (Nathan, *Mishima*, 93) .

74. Hadot, *Philosophy as a Way of Life*, 64.

75. Paul Veyne, *Seneca: The Life of a Stoic*, trans. David Sullivan (London: Routledge, 2003), ix.

76. Seneca, *Letters on Ethics*, 210.

77. Seneca, *Letters on Ethics*, 94.

78. Seneca, *Letters on Ethics*, 457.

79. Seneca, *Letters on Ethics*, 178.

80. Seneca, *Letters on Ethics*, 156.

81. Seneca, *Letters on Ethics*, 213.

82. Quoted in Inose and Sato, *Persona*, 506.

83. Quoted in Nathan, *Mishima*, 122.

84. Quoted in Rankin, *Mishima*, 42. Elsewhere he writes, "I never look at a beautiful boy without wanting to douse him in petrol and set him on fire" (in Rankin, *Mishima*, 42).

85. Quoted in Inose and Sato, *Persona*, 503.

86. "Notwithstanding the legend he created about himself," writes Nathan, Yukio Mishima "was not 'born a samurai.' In fact, his forebears on his father's side were peasants of so mean a cast they lacked even a surname until the early nineteenth century" (Nathan, *Mishima*, 3).

87. In 1967 Mishima wrote an ample commentary on *Hagakure* (*Hagakure Nyūmon*).

88. Yamamoto Tsunetomo, *Hagakure: The Secret Wisdom of the Samurai*, trans. Alexander Bennett (Tokyo: Tuttle, 2014), 42–43.

89. Quoted in Inose and Sato, *Persona*, 508.

90. Quoted in Wilson, *The Greatest Empire*, 121.

91. Yukio Mishima, *Sun and Steel*, trans. John Bester (Tokyo: Kodansha International Ltd., 1970), 14.

92. Mishima, *Sun and Steel*, 26–27.

93. Mishima, *Sun and Steel*, 27–28.

94. Mishima, *Sun and Steel*, 65.

95. Mishima, *Sun and Steel*, 65.

96. Mishima, *Sun and Steel*, 66.

97. Mishima, *Sun and Steel*, 67.

98. Mishima, *Sun and Steel*, 43.

99. Yourcenar, *Mishima*, 4. The "poem" quotation is cited in Scott-Stokes, *The Life and Death of Yukio Mishima*, 96, epigraph.

100. Ritchie, *The Japan Journals, 1947–2004*, 151. Apparently, he had decided to stop writing some time earlier. Toward the end of 1967 he said, "I've already given up on writing. I don't have a smidgen of interest in things like the Nobel Prize" (quoted in Inose and Sato, *Persona*, 544).

101. Wilson, *The Greatest Empire*, 127.

102. Veyne, *Seneca*, 10–11.

103. Mishima's political views "were a kind of madness, nonsense at best, at other times ugly and dangerous" (Nathan, *Mishima*, 247).

104. Quoted in Nathan, *Mishima*, 241.

105. For more on this, see Andrew Rankin's work on Mishima.

106. Quoted in Inose and Sato, *Persona*, 654.

107. Inose and Sato, *Persona*, 624.

108. Scott-Stokes, *The Life and Death of Yukio Mishima*, 162.

109. Tsunetomo, *Hagakure*, 97.

110. Inose and Sato, *Persona*, 698.

111. Mishima's suicide, writes Ritchie, "was a single, personal, creative act. It did not mean a resurgence of militarism, a reversion to wartime ideals, or anything of the sort because—and this Mishima must have known so well that the jeering of the soldiers he was addressing could not have surprised him—his suicide was entirely ritual" (Ritchie, *The Japan Journals*, 151).

112. Scott-Stokes, *The Life and Death of Yukio Mishima*, 104.

113. It is, Yourcenar writes, "natural for two beings who have decided to die together, and one at the hands of the other, to want to meet in bed at least once, and this is a notion to which the ancient samurai spirit would not have objected" (Yourcenar, *Mishima*, 142).

114. Tacitus, *The Annals*, trans. A. J. Woodman (Indianapolis, IN: Hackett Publishing Company, 2004), 335.

115. Seneca, *Letters on Ethics*, 55.

116. Tacitus, *The Annals*, 336.

117. Quoted in Scott-Stokes, *The Life and Death of Yukio Mishima*, 198.

118. *Patriotism*, writes Andrew Rankin, "puts the sexual symbolism of self-disembowelment on flagrant, almost pornographic display. Mishima depicts the lieutenant's seppuku as a mega-ejaculation in the course of which the lieutenant discharges every last drop of fluid in his body: sweat, saliva, tears, vomit, blood, and bile" (Rankin, *Mishima*, 111).

119. Quoted in Damian Flanagan, *Yukio Mishima* (London: Reaktion Books, 2014), 223.

120. Inose and Sato, *Persona*, 729.

121. Sophocles, *The Oedipus at Colonus of Sophocles*, ed. Richard Jebb (Cambridge: Cambridge University Press, 1889), line 1225, http://www.perseus.tufts.edu/hopper/text?doc=urn:cts:greekLit:tlg0011.tlg007.perseus-eng1:1225-1238.

122. E. M. Cioran, *The Trouble with Being Born*, trans. Richard Howard (New York: Seaver Books, 1976), 22 (italics in original).

123. Friedrich Nietzsche, *Basic Writings of Nietzsche*, trans. and ed. Walter Kaufmann (New York: Random House, 2000), 40 (italics in original).

124. Emmanuel Le Roy Ladurie, *Montaillou: The Promised Land of Error*, trans. Barbara Bray (New York: Vintage, 1979), 206–207.

125. André Comte-Sponville, *A Small Treatise on the Great Virtues: The Uses of Philosophy in Everyday Life*, trans. Catherine Temerson (London: Picador, 2002), 147.

126. John Williams, *Stoner* (New York: New York Review Books 2003), 179.

Epilogue

1. Gabriel Liiceanu, *Itinerariile unei vieți: E. M. Cioran; Apocalipsa după Cioran* (Bucharest: Humanitas, 2011), 94.

2. Richard Kearney, *On Stories* (London: Routledge, 2002), 3.

Acknowledgments

I was very fortunate to work with Joy de Menil at Harvard University Press. Thanks to her unfailing editorial instinct, sharp eyes, and uncommon dedication, this is a much better book than it would otherwise have been. I cannot thank Joy enough. Louise E. Robbins is the copyeditor of any writer's dreams. Her very careful work on the final draft of the manuscript improved it significantly and saved me many an embarrassment. Emeralde Jensen-Roberts was of great help throughout the process, and so were Joy Deng and Jeff Dean at earlier stages. Special thanks are due to John Kulka, who saw promise in this project when it was nothing more than an idea, and contracted the book. Two anonymous outside reviewers, as well as some Harvard faculty who serve as syndics for the Press, offered me important critical feedback, for which I am very grateful.

Nilanjan Bhowmick, Peter Catapano, Boris Dralyuk, Matthew Lamb, Ed Simon, Ajay Verma, and Stuart Walton read an early draft of the manuscript and made important suggestions. I cannot be grateful enough to these friends for their work and generosity. My dear friend Aurelian Craiutu stood by me as always and assisted with his encyclopedic knowledge (never ceasing to remind me that failure is something Romanians are particularly good at).

The book echoes conversations I had over the years with many colleagues and intellectual friends. For that reason, and others,

I'm particularly indebted to Susan Ang Wan-Ling, Mona Antohi, Sorin Antohi, Michelle Boulous-Walker, Malik Bozzo-Rey, Humberto Brito, Oliver Burkeman, Matthew Clemente, Francesco D'Isa, Pedro Duarte de Andrade, Irina Dumitrescu, Richard Eldridge, Olimpia Ellero, Markus Gabriel, Bruno Garcia, Marcelo Gleiser, Irving Goh, Robbie Goh, Jason Goroncy, Yugank Goyal, Jim Heisig, Pico Iyer, Pravesh Jung, Sarvchetan Katoch, Tom Lutz, Gordon Marino, Giuseppe Mazzotta, Wilfred McClay, Mohammad Memarian, James Miller, Bryan Mukandi, Robert Nixon, Antonio Pele, Joan Ramon Resina, Vlad Russo, Chetan Singh, Mario Solis, Susan Stanford-Friedman, Ngọc Hiếu Trần, Camil Ungureanu, Przemysław Urbańczyk, Wanwei Wu, Jason Wirth, and Robert Zaretsky.

Over the last several years, in the form of talks, lectures, conference addresses, and master classes, I presented parts of this book in different places around the world, from Australia and Taiwan to Chile and Brazil. I thank all of those—too many to name here—who attended these meetings and offered me their feedback.

While working on this book I received support, material and otherwise, from a number of institutions and funding bodies, to which I owe a debt of gratitude: Texas Tech University (Honors College, Office of the Vice-President for Research, Humanities Center); University of Wisconsin-Madison (Institute for Research in the Humanities); National Endowment for the Humanities (Public Scholar Award Program); Franco-American Commission for Educational Exchange (Fulbright Commission); Fulbright US Scholar Program; Lille Catholic University (Institute of Philosophy); Jawaharlal Nehru University (Jawaharlal Nehru Institute of Advanced Study); Indian Institute for Advanced Study Shimla; Polish Institute of Advanced Studies; Nanzan University (Nanzan Institute for Religion and Culture); and National University of Singapore (Faculty of Arts and Social Sciences).

"The Mud Cure" section of Chapter 1 includes text that first appeared in "Everyone Fails, but Only the Wise Find Humility," on August 18, 2016, in *Aeon*. Portions of the "Fragility of Democracy" section of Chapter 2 were first published on July 15, 2019, in the *New York Times* as "Democracy Is for the Gods." The section of this chapter titled "A Case of Misplaced Faith" builds on ideas first presented in "Always Narrating," published in the *Los Angeles Review of Books* on March 9, 2020. "The Problem with Revolutions" section includes text originally published in *Commonweal Magazine* on September 28, 2020, as "Sailing without Ballast." Much of the text of "Are We Doomed to Fail," published in *IAI News* by the Institute of Art and Ideas on January 12, 2018, and "The Philosopher of Failure," published on November 28, 2016, in the *Los Angeles Review of Books,* is reprinted in Chapter 3. Finally, Chapters 1 and 4 advance themes presented in a December 15, 2013, opinion piece in the *New York Times* titled "In Praise of Failure."

Index